Where
Is My
Doctor?

Where Is My Doctor?

L. DeWitt Wilcox M.D.
F.R.C.P.(C.) F.A.C.P.

Fitzhenry & Whiteside

Toronto   Montreal   Winnipeg   Vancouver

ISBN 0-88902-042-6

Canadian Cataloguing in Publication Data

Wilcox, Lewis DeWitt, 1905-
    Where is my doctor?

Includes index.
ISBN 0-88902-042-6

1. Physician and patient.   2. Medical care.
I. Title.

R727.3.W55   362.1   C77-001152-7

Fitzhenry & Whiteside Limited
150 Lesmill Road
Don Mills, Ontario

Printed in Canada

This book, which in so many ways reflects my life, I dedicate to my wife, Josephine, to my daughters, Jennifer and Mary Charlotte and to my son, Christopher. Their criticisms and encouragements, love and support have made this project worthwhile.

I also wish to thank Lilian Symons, Librarian at The University of Western Ontario Medical School; Betty Cromwell, my secretary; Ramsay Derry and Joseph Gies, my editors; Fitzhenry & Whiteside, my publisher; and the late Charles Vining of Toronto, who urged me to write, and who chose the title.

Contents

Introduction

The health of the people is really the foundation upon which all their happiness and their powers as a state depend.

BENJAMIN DISRAELI

A man in his sixties recently collapsed during a church service. The minister at once voiced the traditional plea, and three doctors responded. All three were well known and highly regarded in the community. One was a surgeon, another a nose-and-throat specialist, and the third an obstetrician. But none had a stethoscope in his pocket or in his car, and none even ventured to take the stricken man's pulse, because pulse-taking is not part of the routine of any of their three medical vocations. None had the experience or confidence that would allow him to place his ear on the exposed chest of the stricken one and pronounce him dead. The surgeon, the man of action of the group, ended their inactivity by directing the sexton to call an ambulance to take the patient to the hospital, where the judgment between the quick and the dead would be made by machines.

Thus a man was able to have a heart attack with three experienced doctors present, and none of them could do anything more for him than a lawyer or an engineer could have done.

There lies one aspect of the medical crisis of North America in our time. Another aspect is illustrated by three complaints heard during a week I spent in Toronto, examining medical students.

The first complaint was from a banker, head of a growing family: "I received a call this morning from my family doctor, a bright young fellow in his early thirties. He says he is closing his office — wants to go into research. I asked him if he had found a substitute to take over his practice, and he said no, not yet. Where does that leave my family?"

The second came from an advertising executive: "Our doctor has looked after my heart for fifteen years. For the last several years he has done part-time refereeing for an insurance company and now he tells me he is giving up his office work completely to devote himself to the insurance business. I haven't been able to find another doctor. What am I supposed to do?"

The third was from a justice of the Supreme Court of Ontario: "Our doctor has been a good friend who has cared for us for twenty-five years. He is apparently tired of working so hard and says he is retiring. He cannot recommend another man who will accept new patients. I shall have to sit down with the yellow pages and try my luck, or perhaps my wife's brother-in-law who is a specialist downtown can steer us to somebody."

I asked the justice whether lawyers and judges did not believe in retiring when they wanted to. His answer was revealing. "A good lawyer has clients who rely on him to such a degree that he keeps going to his office downtown for two or four or six hours a day after he has passed his seventieth or even his eightieth year. As for judges, they can no longer handle as large a workload in their advanced years, but the quality of their work is excellent; in fact, the knowledge and experience of some of our oldest members of the bench is simply irreplaceable, and, carrying fewer but more difficult cases, they richly deserve the full stipend."

Does it not seem that the knowledge and experience of a doctor past sixty-five would also be of value, even if he had to cut down on his work load? And what about the other two doctors — the young man who went into "research" and the doctor who found that it paid better or was more convenient to work for an insurance company?

These are by no means isolated examples. On the contrary, they represent powerful trends, all leading away from the old medical ideal of service to humanity and all leading to the impoverishment of the true medical profession.

Significantly, none of the three Toronto men whose stories I heard concerned public ward patients. Each represented what used to be called "good families", or "carriage trade", but which now includes all

Canadians with their medicare cards, most Americans with their private health-insurance contracts, and the U.K. population with its National Health Service.

The problem is the same in small towns as in large cities. In Wingham, a western Ontario town of 3,000 whose modern hospital was the focal point for the medical care of 15,000 people, two active doctors who together saw from 50 to 75 patients a day in their offices decided to give up their practices in order to specialize. One had decided on psychiatry and the other on anaesthesiology. Their justification was that they could not keep up the pace of their general practices without breaking down, and in self-defense they had to find easier work. But with another Wingham doctor recovering from his third coronary and a fourth doctor, the oldest, preparing to retire, Wingham's hospital was left with no local physician available for emergencies.

Looking at the picture throughout the United States and Canada, we find that more than 52 million people literally live and die without ever seeing a doctor. It becomes clear that the medical problem gets more acute daily. If the people are to receive adequate medical care, what is needed is not more half-trained doctors but a new generation of doctors who will practise good medicine. The sooner good medicine can be provided the better.

It does not seem sensible to look to government for the remedy, as everyone tends to do when a situation enters a critical phase. People generally expect that any social dislocation can be remedied by the wave of a magic governmental wand. In many areas, undoubtedly, this is true, but not in the matter of a doctor shortage. The doctors in government executive positions have all been removed from the active practice of medicine for many years. They work and live completely separated from the medical schools, from the live and urgent problems of practising doctors, and from patients.

There are medical associations for general practitioners, specialists, teachers, investigators, and administrators, and they have deliberated for years on the shortage of doctors. But there are so many of these associations, with such widely varying interests in patients and such unequal financial returns that their conclusions have always been contradictory and irrelevant, and, on careful examination, only stress the urgency of the question.

The medical educators have devoted endless committee meetings to the medical manpower shortage and the delivery of health services. But the number of medical faculty members who can examine a patient at home has been shrinking steadily, and so these exercises have become little more than games of musical chairs. The rarity of strong deans, their brief average tenures, their tendency to move from schools to foundations to government roles, all indicate a lack of commitment or purpose but, also, an abiding belief in the importance of providing better "health care" for this doctor-short society. This, in spite of the fact that "health care" cannot be defined.

A supply of good doctors should be better recognized as more important for human happiness than anything else the political or industrial forces of society could undertake to provide. If all of the available medical knowledge were wisely applied to the population, we would witness a substantial improvement in health for every member of society who is willing and intelligent enough to utilize it.

More medical know-how is available now than ever before in human history. And yet, for the reasons to be outlined in these chapters it is evidently not being used, as the scriptures decreed, "for the healing of the nations."

I do not believe that much lasting good can come from pruning the small branches of the medical tree such as fee schedules, the place of paramedical workers, and the evasion of responsibility to patients. My objective will be to get at the roots, the trunk, and the main branches of medicine's difficulties.

The usual explanation for the doctor shortage has been that we need more medical schools, more paramedical personnel, more extensive use of machines and computers, and more financial help from government. I think the problem is at once simpler and deeper. I think we have too many of the wrong kinds of doctors and too few of the right kind, and that the distortion in favour of the wrong kinds is increasing at an appalling rate.

I was moved to tackle the question posed by the title of this book because I had come to accept the probability that many wrongs exist in present-day medicine — otherwise there could not possibly be so much expressed public dissatisfaction.

Dr. John T. Edsall of Harvard University predicted in 1961 that "eventually the public will rise up in its wrath and display its lack of confidence in the doctors if adequate care is not provided". His prediction was unerringly correct fifteen years ago. In the 1972 nationwide survey conducted by the American Medical Association, 44 per cent of the Americans who were interviewed said they had had unfavourable experiences with doctors. The patient-doctor contacts, for one-third of those interviewed, had been so unsatisfactory that the patients said they would not by choice return to the same doctor if they got sick again. Most of those interviewed stressed the difficulties they had experienced in finding doctors who could communicate, who would take the time to explain the diagnosis and the treatment.

In Canada, the *Pickering Report,* commissioned by the Ontario Medical Association, revealed that more than three-quarters of the people surveyed had serious complaints about doctors, most of them about the service and human relations aspects of medical practice.

As a doctor I have to write from inside the complexities of the medical profession for people both healthy and sick on the outside. If the people get the message they will be able to discuss it with their government representatives and with their busy doctors. I hope that what I have to say may suggest to the medical student of tomorrow what kind of person he will have to be and some of the things he will have to learn if he is to be a good doctor the day after tomorrow.

The new generation of medical students, the seasoned teachers, and the best practising doctors all agree that medicine is in a sick state. From the teachers who influenced me and from my own observations, I know that there are many imperfections in medicine that need correction.

As a physician and teacher with more than forty years' experience, I feel an increasing urge to set out some of the problems and suggest some answers. I continue to be active in practice, teaching, and laboratory investigation. I participate in teaching sessions every week. I still see patients in their homes because I believe this is necessary in the practice of good medicine.

I believe that the element of personal healing power, meaning "to make whole or sound . . . to effect a cure," must be obvious for the patient to witness and to feel if the M.D. is to be a good doctor, whether he is a specialist or a general practitioner. As an example, the ear, nose, and throat specialist who, after checking the nose and sinuses, tells the patient there is nothing wrong and says or *implies* that his headache must be "nerves" or "in his head," does not accomplish as much for his patient as he could. If he takes just a few extra minutes and lets the patient tell him about some of the important things that bring on the headache he will be supporting and helping the patient instead of just examining him and charging a fee — a fee that could just as well go to an eye doctor, a dental surgeon, or a nerve doctor who does not listen. That E.N.T. specialist may be, and in today's rush for appointments often is the only doctor the patient ever gets to. When he does not behave like a doctor, the medical profession suffers because he has turned away another dissatisfied patient.

In the past, society viewed the doctor as someone quite different from any other member of the community. Even though his skills are in part technical like those of the electrician or carpenter, and he has well-established training standards like the accountant and lawyer, his work is not comparable to those trades and professions. The doctor has always been and should always be regarded as different from other human beings because he has dissected a cadaver, has worked with experimental animals, has assisted at and performed autopsies, has observed or taken part in operations, and has mastered the medical use of drugs. Above all, he is different because his work is directly concerned with the maintenance of human life, a responsibility that is regarded as sacred. Doctors today are damaging their unique historic status whenever they compare themselves, financially, and in terms of hours of work, with the trades and other professions.

I do not claim any originality for the ideas expressed here. They have all been assembled in the course of my lifetime in medicine. My views have been enlarged and modified by conversations with medical educators in Canada, the United States, the United Kingdom, continental Europe, and the West Indies, with teachers and practising doctors in large and small hospitals, with house officers and medical students, and always with patients.

I have no intention of criticizing any doctor for what he is doing now or for what he chose to do after finishing medical school. That is all past history.

This book would be milquetoast fare indeed if my statements were not occasionally contentious. My objective is to make every paragraph as constructive as possible. There will undoubtedly be some doctors with greater experience in practice, teaching, and investigation, who will challenge some of my views. Such challenges I must accept if the effort is to be worth while.

It has been said: "If the people understand what good doctoring means, they will expect better things of their doctors, and their doctors will respond." This I believe.

Addressing deans and medical educators at their annual meeting in Cincinnati in 1969, Doctor Roger O. Egeberg, Assistant Secretary for Health and Scientific Affairs, United States Department of Health, Education, and Welfare, remarked that to bring about the necessary changes in the education of good doctors would be "as difficult as moving a graveyard, but it is one graveyard which must be moved . . ." In conversation with Dr. Egeberg after his address, I sought his advice on chapter headings I was considering for this book. When he not only heartily approved but urged me to get on with the job, I set to work.

Admittedly I am strongly biased towards the benefits of sound medical practice. I do not want to be a party to the demise of the real doctor.

1.

What is your chief complaint?

Well my friend, how's the old complaint?

SIR JOHN A. MACDONALD

Canada's first Prime Minister, Sir John A. Macdonald, in his political travels had great difficulty in recalling names. When in difficulty, he would begin a conversation with this question and then by the process of associations of memory pathways the name would come to him. The experienced doctor who obtains the patient's chief complaint and identifies it further by experienced cross-questioning should likewise reach the right diagnosis quickly.

Anyone who gets sick and remains conscious develops some symptom that alarms him. This symptom is the chief complaint and it usually points to trouble in one part of the body and often to one body organ. It compels the patient or someone close to him to call a doctor.

Instead of setting down a long list of chief complaints I have chosen twenty-two of the common but important ones and I have added short case histories as examples of several complaints.

1. Insomnia

Many doctors oppose the use of sleeping medicines. They have a hang-up about the risk of addiction, which never occurs in the true meaning of this word. The fact that some acutely depressed people do take overdoses of sleeping pills is not because they are "addicted," but because it is less messy to swallow pills than to close up the garage tight and leave the motor running. Doctors who deny insomniacs life-giving sleep have not weighed the evidence the patient is giving or have not suffered the effects of loss of an important night's sleep themselves.

2. Blood in Urine

This startling complaint cannot be safely disregarded until a bladder tumor or an acute inflammation or a stone has been ruled out.

3. The Common Cold

A head cold with cough and laryngitis is regarded as a virus infection. There is no "flu" shot that will prevent the common cold. Treatment should be bed-rest for two or three days when possible, with an aspirin or an aspirin-codeine tablet every four hours. Lots of warm drinks, one of which may be spiked at bedtime if desired.

Should the doctor be called? Generally speaking, most colds clear up "in fourteen days or two weeks." If sinus pain in the forehead or cheeks or ears develops with fever above 101° F or 38° Celsius the doctor should be contacted. It may be an acute sinusitis or ear infection, and antibiotics — which have no value for the ordinary symptoms of a cold — will likely be needed. If the cough leads to fever above 100° F the bronchitis is likely becoming bronchial pneumonia and the doctor should see the patient. Repeated colds do not mean low resistance or lack of vitamins. Most of the repeat colds are caught from children with "virus cousins" to the one you began with.

4. Shingles

A woman of sixty-seven developed a pain over the right side of the abdomen. Her doctor called a surgeon and both agreed that the pain was caused by an acute gall bladder condition. They decided to operate and remove the gall bladder. At operation, the gall bladder looked so normal that it was not removed. The next day the rash characteristic of "shingles" appeared along the rib margin over the gall bladder location.

Shingles is a virus disease of the nervous system. "Shingle pain" may resemble gall bladder pain or appendix pain or heart pain or pleurisy pain. Of course, surgery never does the patient any good. It may do a lot of harm. One attack of shingles provides lifetime protection (immunity) against a second attack. It may take from two to four days for the rash around one side of the forehead or chest or abdomen to come out, while all the time the pain is hurting and puzzling the patient and the doctor. With shingles the white blood count is usually lower than normal but with acute appendicitis or an acute gall bladder inflammation it is higher than normal, so for want of a careful pain analysis and a blood count an unnecessary operation may be performed.

5. Phlebitis

This is inflammation of the veins of one leg that may occur for no known reason or may follow a leg injury. It is common after abdominal operations and heart attacks. It has two serious complications: a clot that breaks away from the inflamed vein and goes to the lung, or less frequently, chronic swelling of the leg.

6. Jaundice

It often comes on without pain and is noticed by the family rather than by the patient. The urine gets dark like tea and the stools are usually pale. It has many causes, but most patients have something wrong with the liver or gall bladder.

7. Broken Hip or Wrist or Elbow

The hip fracture must be suspected whenever anyone beyond middle age has a fall that results in pain in the hip or thigh region. Careful X-rays are mandatory to settle the question of a break, because surgery can correct such breaks quickly and effectively. The wrist and elbow are more frequently fractured than the hip. The reason for mentioning them is the desirability of a perfect setting to avoid a permanent handicap. When transportation is readily available, it is better if possible to send patients with such fractures to experts within twelve hours, so weeks and months of unnecessary travelling for physiotherapy after an incorrect reduction will be avoided.

8. Chills and Fever

A woman of fifty-eight was admitted to hospital with chills, a temperature of 104° F, and repeated vomiting to a point where she required continuous intravenous feedings. No cause for the fever and chills could be found in the first three days, but it was then noted that the thyroid gland was slightly swollen and very tender. The cause of the chills and fever was inflammation of the thyroid (acute thyroiditis).

One simple blood test, showing a very high sedimentation rate, settled the diagnosis at a cost of $5. Treatment consisted of four doses of deep X-ray and in a week the patient was much better. Cortisone usually cures as quickly as X-ray.

Repeated chills and fever mean a severe infection that may be as obvious as pneumonia or its complications. Most patients turn out to have deep infections that call for the most expert diagnostic skill. The cause could be meningitis, an abscess in or around a kidney, acute inflammation in veins, abscesses in the liver or pelvic organs, anywhere in the abdomen, or even in a bone. Occasionally, patients with malignancies come under attention because of chills and fever.

A doctor, to be able to ferret out the cause of chills and fever, has to be well trained and experienced. He cannot rely on the lab reports or on paramedical helpers. He will not find the cause and deal with it effectively, unless by accident, if he is a forty-hour-a-week man, because he will lack that essential possession — clinical experience.

9. Alcoholism

Every reader who drinks has his own ideas about what excessive imbibing means for him. Most drinkers use alcohol to reduce tension at the end of the day, at the executives' luncheon, or, in the critical stage, as a day-starter. The most-feared complication is liver cirrhosis. The most painful complication is pancreatitis. The most pitiful complication is permanent brain or nerve damage. Every complication, if recognized early, can be reversed if the poisonous libations are given up.

10. Shortness of Breath

The most common cause used to be heart trouble. Tobacco superceded heart by producing the bronchitis and emphysema that now account for the most disabling breathing difficulties. This is more than a hundred times as frequent as cancer of the lung. It is much worse because it lasts so long. The third common cause, which is reversible, is excess fat that produces overwork for the heart and lungs together.

11. Sudden Weight Loss

The most common causes are acute-onset diabetes, toxic goitre, cancer of the gullet, and cancer of the liver. Unfortunately from the standpoint of early diagnosis, marked weight loss is not a symptom of cancer of the brain or breast or bowel or kidney or womb.

> A bus-driver of forty had been losing strength and weight as his appetite and thirst increased. At the wheel he reached for a can of Coke every hour. At home he had a route of water-filled glasses and occasional Cokes on window ledges and side tables and window sills. Of course he had developed an acute case of diabetes and the doctor he consulted settled the diagnosis in a jiffy when he examined the urine. This patient was lucky — a short history, an early diagnosis long before any complications developed, careful treatment, and a normal outlook so long as he followed the rules.

Most persons who do not manufacture enough insulin to control the body's blood sugar can regain a normal balance for as much work as necessary since the discovery of insulin. The diabetic cannot take "natural foods" like honey or maple syrup and of course he cannot eat pie or cake without undoing what he may have achieved with a week of perfect dieting. It is not possible to take a bigger dose of insulin "to neutralize a slug of sweet".

The most successfully regulated diabetics I have seen in practice have all developed an attitude that makes them hate sugar in any form. They have learned that sweets for them are deadly, because they hasten the unnecessary complications of this disease.

12. Menière's Disease

This disturbance of the inner ear is still a mystery. It is characterized by a constant ringing "like a tea-kettle" in one ear. The attack is the terrifying part of this symptom complex. It comes on suddenly without relation to general health or activity or diet. The patient is always terribly dizzy and may sometimes be thrown out of his chair by the whirling effect. Vomiting occurs. The attacks may occur frequently or after long intervals. With the passage of time, and the persistent ringing, which may continue for months or years, deafness gradually becomes complete in the affected ear. By this time the attacks have ceased. Patients who are fortunate can control their attacks by taking a tablet of Gravol or Antivert after meals and at bed time. Others are not helped by any medication or by a salt-free diet. If the attacks interfere with work and living it is possible to have a surgical operation that permanently relieves the patient of the attacks.

13. Gonorrhoea

This is the most common venereal disease. It is only acquired by worshipping at the Shrine of Venus. Never from a toilet seat! The symptom is a morning drop of yellow pus before urinating and there may be increased frequency, especially in the female. An attack demands prompt attention. Although he or she is embarrassed, the advice of a doctor must be obtained for three reasons. First, to make sure that it is gonorrhoea. Second, to obtain the early treatment which fortunately cures quickly. Third, to get the quick cure that will prevent the serious complications of spread to the small tubes near the testicles or ovaries. If these tubes in either sex become inflamed there will be a strong probability of sterility.

14. Vomiting Blood

This alarming complaint comes usually without any warning feeling of sickness. Bleeding is a weakening experience, but it is painless. The blood comes from a ruptured vein in the lower part of the gullet or from an open artery in a stomach ulcer or a duodenal ulcer. The treatment is always complete bed-rest and relief from anxiety by hypos of morphine or demerol every four hours until enough blood has been transfused to make up for what has been lost. Occasionally, even with the best hospital care, the bleeding continues or stops and starts again. The physician and the surgeon share in the treatment of this complaint because a surgical operation is mandatory when the bleeding will not stop.

15. Pain in the Abdomen

This kind is defined as unpleasant steady pain that may begin on the right or left side above or below the level of the navel. It often spreads over the whole belly, and turning, or moving up and down, aggravates the pain. The belly is tender when the doctor makes his examination.

> A man aged 72 complained of a new stomach pain. He was known to be a heart case and his doctor concluded that this was the pain of a congested liver caused by the heart failure. Three days later the man died and at autopsy the pain was explained by generalized peritonitis caused by a rupture of diverticulitis. This man did not have to die. His heart was good for a long run when the pathologist did the autopsy. A simple operation would have saved him.
>
> He had been taking cortisone for his rheumatism. It is a well-recognized fact that patients with stomach ulcer or diverticulitis who are taking cortisone may get perforations and fatal peritonitis with pus all through the abdomen without the intense pain that the

normal patient complains of with peritonitis. Often the diagnosis is missed and the patient dies.

16. Chest Pain

This complaint may have several meanings but the one that is most feared originates in the heart with a coronary attack. The pain is in the middle, in the breast bone position, but it usually spreads across the chest to the right and left. This pain often spreads upwards to the right or left shoulder, along the cords of the neck, sometimes to the jaw like a toothache, and very often down the right arm or left arm, or both arms. The arms may feel awfully heavy. The patient is likely to be anxious, pale, and sweating. Sometimes he gets sick or is troubled with gas and this explains why doctors have mistaken coronary cases for acute indigestion.

Another common severe chest pain is the pleurisy caused by inflammation of the surface of a lung affected by pneumonia or by an embolus from a phlebitis leg. Pleurisy pain, unlike heart pain, is made worse by deep breathing or cough. It occurs on the right or left side but not in the middle.

17. Diarrhoea

This complaint most often comes with or after vomiting and it is caused by an acute viral or staphylococcal infection. It does not usually last more than twenty-four or forty-eight hours, but it makes the patient sick and puts him to bed. The over-the-counter remedies do not control this kind of diarrhoea, and when it continues after the vomiting has stopped it is comfortably controlled with codeine tablets or opium drops — especially in a foreign country where it may hang on for several days or weeks.

Loose bowel movements that occur as a new symptom before or after breakfast or during the night indicate trouble calling for a doctor's attention. The likely causes are colitis (there will usually be bleeding with the loose stools), small bowel diseases, diverticulitis, or sometimes a growth in the large bowel. Most of these causes of diarrhoea can be accurately diagnosed and successfully treated if attended to promptly.

18. Blackouts

These usually come so quickly and completely that anyone close to the patient puts in the distress call for the doctor or the ambulance. Often the patient develops a fit or convulsive spell and the doctor can sometimes make the diagnosis by questioning an intelligent observer.

> A man of seventy-nine sitting in church beside his niece, who had taken a first-aid course, slumped over in the pew. She noticed his colour fade from red to a deathly pallor and she could not feel his pulse. When the doctor came he listened patiently to the niece's evidence, obtained an electrocardiogram that showed typical changes, and made the diagnosis of temporary complete heart block to explain the slump in the pew, because no blood was pumped to the brain for the few seconds when the heart was not beating at all. He referred this man to a heart centre where a pacemaker was inserted as a protection against any future heart stoppage. Within four days he was living a life protected against the risk of attacks.

Most blackouts are caused by brain conditions and the attack should be diagnosed because of the risk of a serious fall and a fracture, because of risks at the wheel, and because the blackout may be the first symptom of a condition that can be corrected.

19. Crampy Abdominal Pains

> A very bright woman of seventy-four came to the hospital complaining of cramping pains in her abdomen. She was usually constipated but sometimes she had diarrhoea. She had lost forty pounds in four months and she appeared ill. She was X-rayed twice, stomach, small bowel, and colon. All the X-rays were normal. Two sigmoidoscopic examinations by good surgeons were found to be normal. A stomach-bowel specialist did the latest "colonoscopic" examination ($85.00) and this was normal! This patient was a graduate nurse and she was sure she had "a cancer that did not show in the X-rays". She had given up hope. Another doctor was called and after listening to her history and examining her abdomen he wrote his report: "In spite of all the X-rays and other examinations this patient

has intestinal obstruction and she should be operated on." Two days later the surgeon found bands of adhesions that obstructed the bowel at two levels. The pain had always come on after meals. A complete relief of the pain and diarrhoea followed surgery.

Intestinal obstruction is one of the most deadly abdominal conditions and the patient dies if a doctor does not suspect it and diagnose it. Unfortunately, adhesions never show up in X-rays. This diagnosis above all others requires an experience that can only be obtained from examining every kind of abdominal problem. Every time a case like this one turns up it emphasizes the need for doctors with broad experience.

20. Pain that Persists

A mother of thirty-four with three children went to a family medicine centre in June 1975 complaining of pain above the right shoulder blade. The doctor who saw her wrote down her complaint, listened to her chest, pronounced it neuritis, and prescribed a pain-killer. The woman continued to return to the centre regularly all summer and with doctors coming from and going on vacations she never saw the same one twice. She was given new pain-killers by different doctors but none of them relieved her suffering. In September a doctor added short-wave treatments, but they made no difference. By mid-December the pain was preventing sleep and she had lost weight. In the hope of getting some relief over the Christmas holidays she succeeded in getting an appointment with the first doctor whom she had seen in June. He was shocked by her appearance and admitted her to hospital immediately for blood studies, X-rays, and a surgical consultation. A biopsy (sampling) of a tumor four inches in diameter above the shoulder was done on December 22. The report came back the day before Christmas. It was cancer. The very radical and disfiguring operation was carried out by a surgical specialist early in 1976. It was hoped that the operation was not too late, but the final result will only be determined by time.

21. Headache

This is one of the most frequent complaints. Rarely does the cause turn out to be something serious like brain tumor or brain abscess or meningitis or encephalitis. Although headaches by the thousand are attributed to high blood pressure, this rarely explains headaches that do not begin when the patient first awakes from the night's sleep. Most headaches are due to nervous tension, life stress, or migraine. These are usually nuisance aches that are never fatal. The patient with headache needs more than an aspirin. He deserves the doctor's time for a careful history and examination because a headache may be caused by such unlikely conditions as over-exposure to carbon monoxide in a badly ventilated garage or to uremic poisoning.

A man of sixty went to his eye-doctor in October complaining of headache and slightly blurred vision. This doctor quickly recognized the signs of high pressure inside the skull that showed up in the eyes, and he referred the patient to a nerve specialist who agreed that the pressure inside the skull was high and that the diagnosis was a rapidly growing brain tumor. He referred the patient to the best brain surgeon in the state, who agreed and operated promptly. To the surgeon's great surprise he found a huge blood clot over the right half of the brain and was able to remove it easily. On going into the history more carefully after the man recovered, it turned out that the headache began on July 6 after a glancing blow on the man's forehead delivered in a friendly boxing match with his five-year-old grandson. Such clots sometimes follow trivial blows.

The diagnosis of a treatable cause of a severe headache not only relieves the patient but gives the doctor a great deal of satisfaction when the outcome is as happy as it was in that man's case.

22. Failing Vision

A woman of thirty-four went to her doctor with the complaint of loss of vision in her left eye. She was admitted to hospital for a general work-up, although he suspected that it was "just hysteria". The diagnosis had not advanced beyond "just hysteria" by the next day. One of the junior staff members, making his rounds in search of a patient to demonstrate at a student clinic, paused and took this young woman's history. He learned that her left eye was totally blind and that half of the vision in the right eye was gone. He made a diagnosis of a (pituitary) tumor at the base of the brain pressing on the nerves that carry visual impulses from the eyes to the areas in the brain where they are perceived. X-rays confirmed this diagnosis. A brain surgeon 120 miles away was telephoned. He made the diagnosis of a pituitary tumor over the telephone before the X-ray report was given. He operated as an emergency at eight o'clock the next morning. The tumor was successfully removed. The result was fortunate. The half loss of vision in the right eye returned within two days and within two weeks the vision in the blind left eye had returned. This patient was snatched from a life of blindness because the doctor was not only interested in "colds and sore throats and emotional upsets" but in every complaint a patient brought to him.

These examples of "chief complaints" illustrate the importance of obtaining a sensible, informed, and willing doctor to take command when the complaint strikes and a well person, in the twinkling of an eye, is changed to a patient.

Patients in the 1970's want to live, and they want the doctors to cure their physical illnesses with all the up-to-date treatments they expect them to know about. They do not stir up a fuss if a doctor mistakes a depression for an anxiety neurosis. The malpractice suits are set in motion when *organic* conditions are mismanaged. There is nothing unusual about the exhorbitant malpractice insurance premiums that continue to make the headlines. If doctors cannot and will not develop the *tactus eruditus* — the educated touch — and if they refuse to take enough time to listen to the patient's complaints, they are bound to make serious blunders. All the X-rays and laboratory tests and subspecialists' opinions in creation will never secure them against embarrassing litigation, because they are not practising sound medicine.

2.

What kind of doctor do you have?

When someone gets a severe pain or has a violent nosebleed or loses thirty pounds in sixty days or suddenly becomes impotent, he requires a doctor in a hurry. What kind of doctor does he want? What kind of doctor does he need? What kind of doctor does he get? All North American doctors have the M.D. degree. Doctors differ widely in personality, in training, in availability, and in the way they practise medicine or surgery.

A patient may be lucky enough to get into the care of a doctor who is the right one to treat his complaint of the moment. He may develop an immediate trust and confidence in this first contact with the medical profession. When this happens, his mind is at ease because he knows that "his doctor", whether he be specialist or generalist, will never see him stranded if something happens to him or his family. A great many patients do not get the right doctor on the first or the second or even the third call. They become panicky and unhappy with doctors in general, and with the ones they have called in particular. No matter who this first M.D. may be, he will belong in one of the following categories: general practitioner, physician-internist, medical subspecialist, general surgeon, obstetrician-gynecologist, surgical subspecialist, paediatrician, or family medicine doctor.

The General Practitioner (G.P.)

The G.P. is licensed to practise medicine, surgery, and midwifery. His education consists of at least:

- two years of university premedical studies, emphasizing the natural sciences and some arts subjects,
- four years at medical school that provide him with the basis of his medical education and give him his M.D. degree, and
- one year of general internship at a teaching or non-teaching hospital. (This is a poorly defined period of medical study, providing a range of experience that might be distributed as follows: three months of internal medicine, two months of surgery, two months of eye, ear, nose and throat, one month of obstetrics, two months of pediatrics, and two months of emergency room work.)

Years ago, most medical graduates in North America became G.P.s. In 1940 the figure was 60 per cent, but the proportion of students graduating as G.P.s declined steadily after that and in 1975 it was about 20 per cent.

The G.P. has traditionally been the most devoted and dedicated and the hardest working member of the profession. Without him, medicine would have had no identity, and despite the fact that he is disappearing his image is uppermost in the mind of the patient who calls for a doctor. It is uppermost in the response of the politician when the people insist on more doctors.

The amount and range of work done by the G.P.s varies with the individual. It depends on the man, his work territory (whether rural or urban), and his ability. He always does general medicine. Many G.P.s do a lot of obstetrics because they like doing their own cases. Others like surgery, and they perform operations for appendices, gall bladders, hernias, and the like. A large number remove tonsils and adenoids and give anaesthetics. I have known some who liked pinning fractured hips and who did this operation very well.

In many communities, the G.P. still practises medicine, surgery, and midwifery. For example, more than 20 per cent of all surgical operations and more than 80 per cent of deliveries of babies are still done by G.P.s in North America. However, surgery done by G.P.s is attended by inevitable risks. Hernias should be repaired by experts, because even after the best surgical repair a hernia may recur. An appendectomy is usually an easy operation but on occasion can become extremely difficult, even for the most experienced surgeon. The gall bladder operation is serious business that calls for great skill and anatomical knowledge. A tonsillectomy seems like a simple job, but in unskilled hands can result in bleeding and lung complications that should not occur. Good, busy G.P.s have told me that the most fearful experiences of their lives have occurred when obstetric cases have suddenly become complicated and they have found themselves in a crisis with no more help than a nurse or another G.P.

If a G.P. has an unhappy surgical or obstetrical experience, this can prove disturbing. It can shake the confidence of the patient and the family in the doctor.

Minor surgical procedures in the life of the busy G.P. may become major surgery with its attendant catastrophes, and the G.P. rarely has enough training from his one year of internship to be competent when tackling such potentially life-threatening situations. The patient's insistence that his own doctor fix his hemorrhoids or take out his wife's gall bladder is no excuse for a G.P's attempting work for which he is not fully qualified, especially in this day of quick and easy travel.

There is no doubt that, ideally, the G.P. should be the individual's regular doctor. He will go to see the patient in his home and make the initial big decision to treat at home or send the patient to the hospital, to call a surgeon for an operation, or to consult a specialist for an opinion.

Since such a large portion of the G.P.'s work today consists of emotional disturbances and minor ailments, it is being suggested that these maladies could be identified and dealt with by non-medical personnel under the supervision of G.P.s. Nothing could be further from the mark. Nothing could more certainly increase the death toll at the hands of the doctors. Any patient who is sick enough to consult a doctor may harbour a fatal disease. Only the well-qualified doctor can be trusted to differentiate between the near-sick and the really sick, because at best even the doctor's experience can prove fallacious.

To suggest that G.P.s should dispatch near-doctors (like the Russian feldschers) or specially trained nurses to settle the question, "Is this patient sick enough to see a doctor?" cannot be good enough in modern society. When a patient is sick, he is entitled to and deserves the service of a competent doctor.

Do you not think that your doctor should be able to diagnose and treat a sore tongue, enlarged neck glands, Parkinson's disease, a paralytic stroke, acute pleurisy, rapid heart action, low blood pressure, an attack of kidney colic, bronchial pneumonia, toxic goitre, a gouty joint, a swollen liver, or an attack of shingles? These are important everyday sicknesses that are not psychosomatic. Their diagnosis and proper management calls for a broad general knowledge which the doctor has and which is rarely found in non-medical personnel. Even the education of the average graduate M.D. in 1976, supplemented by what he learns during the internship year, rarely provides a solid foundation for handling these common disease situations.

The good G.P. may see upwards of fifty patients a day in his busy office schedule. The amount of time he can allow for each patient is therefore sharply limited. If he is called to see an obstetrical case, to set a fractured arm, to give an anaesthetic, or to make a hurried house call, the amount of time he can spend with patients in his office is even more limited.

Again and again, patients attending our medical out-patient clinics tell us that they feel too embarrassed to ask their G.P.s to do a complete history and physical examination when they enter their overcrowded waiting rooms.

Governments have become acutely aware of the G.P. shortage and in response to public pressure have been providing financial inducements to medical schools to turn out more G.P.s. Some medical schools have promised that they will graduate classes from which as many as 60 per cent will take up general practice. This implies that a school can direct its graduates into general practice. This has not happened in the U.S.S.R., let alone in the Western countries. It will never be possible to take the brightest young minds from college and, after four years in medical school plus one internship year, consign them to the exhausting work of general practice, *unless general practice changes*. The present life of the G.P. is too general to be satisfying, and too hard to persevere with. Statistics on the increasing popularity of general practice claimed by deans' offices are unreliable because so many of the students who express an intention to become G.P.s while in medical school or internship soon tire of it and decide to specialize.

The need for many more, better educated G.P.s is very real, and I do not intend to suggest that their day has passed. It cannot have passed. The big question is, what can be done to bring back this important and vital segment of the profession. The main thrust should be towards providing a medical education that will make general practise exciting and satisfying.

There always have been and I am sure there always will be G.P.s who opt for pure medical work rather than for venturing into tonsils, anaesthetics, deliveries, appendices, fractures, soft psychiatry, and the various other lines that many of them try to include in their repertoires. Doctors who are learners will continue while practising to read and travel, to attend medical meetings, and to keep up with what is going on in medicine. This is the constant opportunity that every intelligent, industrious doctor can always seize, if he will. In my experience, this kind of doctor is often much safer with and of much greater help to the very sick patient than most of those who become subspecialists.

Many doctors who began in an earlier day as G.P.s and who kept on growing have been numbered among my most highly regarded teachers. In Montreal, Dr. A. H. Gordon was the most admired clinical teacher when I was there. Years before, after he had graduated from McGill Medical School and while he was taking a year's internship at the Montreal General Hospital, he was told before an operation by Professor Francis Shepherd, who radiated the spirit of surgery: "A surgeon is born with that something extra that makes him confident. You just haven't got it, Gordon." We do not know how much this remark may have hurt, but Dr. Gordon spent the following year working as a mine doctor in British Columbia. During his spare time he studied, and a year later returned to Montreal and opened an office for general practice. He saw every patient who came along, sewed up their cuts, delivered the babies, and looked after all of the medical cases that came to him. After two years of general practice he began to devote all his spare time to study and gradually limited his practice entirely to medicine. No more surgery, no more deliveries, no more anaesthetics. He worked in the out-patient clinic of the Montreal General Hospital on Dorchester Street, to which thousands of patients came for diagnosis and treatment. There he developed a clinical acumen that was unmatched in Canada.

When Professor Henry Christian invited him to serve for a week as visiting professor at Harvard, the students and faculty realized that they had never before witnessed a doctor of his kind in action. He was supreme in diagnosis, a fascinating teacher, and a most humane doctor, who brought fresh hope to every patient he touched.

Dr. Gordon made no spectacular promises to his patients, and he taught that doctors often cannot actually cure a patient. But by his example he proved to confreres and students alike that every patient can be helped and that medicine is the profession above all others, even if it turned out that only one patient in a hundred could be cured.

With the foundation of a sound medical education and one year of general internship, Dr. Gordon proved that if a doctor is concerned about his patients and committed to self-learning, and if he refers the energy-sapping work of minor surgery, obstetrics, and anaesthetics to doctors who are experts in those fields, he can enjoy the high satisfaction of the physician's life. He proved this by example in the days before medicine had many tools to work with. During the last two decades of his active practice, he delighted in applying new discoveries, such as the use of liver extract for pernicious anemia, the uses of sulfas and penicillin, and the beginnings of surgery of the lungs and heart. He lived to see the day when he was able to say that medicine was a wonderful profession even if only thirty patients out of 100 could be cured. Perhaps, with the low scores that the doctors still make in treating strokes, heart diseases, and cancer, and the constantly increasing population of geriatric patients, we may wonder whether Dr. Gordon did not see medicine go about as far as it was likely to go. Doctors will always excel if they follow his teaching that every patient can be helped.

The need for more good general practitioners has never been greater than it is today, for despite the introduction of the concept of family medicine, the general practitioner who constantly enlarges his experience with sick patients will remain the foundation stone of good medical care.

The Physician-Internist and Medical Subspecialist

I do not know anyone, doctor or lay person, who likes the term "internist." The doctor's parents have trouble differentiating it from "intern," which they associate with the time when their son or daughter was getting the M.D. and beginning hospital work. Patients all have trouble grasping the meaning of the word when the G.P.s tell them about referral to this kind of specialist. The other professionals in society and university faculty members at large rarely grasp the true significance of the term. Editors of publishing houses as a group admit that the word baffles them, and I have only encountered one editor who could define "internist". He had been treated by one through a long illness that had a happy ending!

The physician-internist is a specialist in general medicine. Like the surgeon, who has four or five years of specialized surgical training after completing medical school, the physician-internist has four or more years of post-graduate medical training with the object of giving him a firm understanding of the interworking of all the vital organs in the human body.

His hospital training might include six months in heart; six months in liver, stomach, and bowel; six months in brain and spinal cord; six months in diabetes and glandular diseases; 12 months in general medicine; six months in lung; six months in kidney; and possibly 12 months in another hospital clinic to round out his studies. In his day-to-day practice, he must have a growing knowledge of the brain and the spinal cord, and the nerves; the organs of special sense; the glands; the heart and arteries and veins; the bones and joints; the lungs; the stomach, liver, pancreas, and bowel; the kidneys and bladder; the male and female genital organs; the blood, spleen, and lymph glands; and the skin.

The physician-internist is often confused with the G.P., but his practice is very different. One busy G.P. told me in 1974 that during his 23 years of practice he had seen five cases of meningitis. All five had been sent to internists for diagnosis and treatment. The internist whose work is consulting may work with forty or fifty G.P.s in his community. On the law of averages, taking meningitis as an example, he might see more than 200 cases of meningitis in 23 years. The internist therefore experiences the different satisfaction of diagnosing and treating with precision. He does not have as many patients, but they are the sicker ones. Through his experience with sicker patients he is able to teach, to publish in medical journals, and to speak at medical meetings. With his longer training and experience, the internist is better equipped to handle the many details and complications of disease. This is why he is known as a specialist in diagnosis — a diagnostician.

The physician-internist is therefore quite different from other subspecialists, whose most intensive training usually focuses on one organ. As one example, the respirologist will usually devote more than 95 per cent of his practice to diseases of the lungs. The antibiotics have eliminated most of the fatal pneumonias of youth. This leaves the lung man with the incurable degenerative diseases like bronchitis, emphysema, the elderly patient's pneumonia, and, of course, lung cancer. On the law of averages, this subspecialist, if he is successful and busy, will not have 5 per cent of his time and thinking to devote to the rest of the patient's body machinery. Even though the heart lies between the two lungs, it is considered out of bounds for the lung man.

A senior executive, 74, was having difficult breathing, with a cough and expectoration of large quantities of sputum. Rejecting his general physician, he chose his own lung man who had ordered dozens of X-rays and hundreds and hundreds of sputum checks and blood tests over a period of four years on his patient.

The advice given to the patient after all of the tests was "exercise" to keep the lungs working, although most of their elastic structure had been destroyed as the emphysema had advanced. The patient was required to walk up hill and down dale on his farm — at least two miles every day. This always left him completely exhausted, but he was game and he persevered. One night, he got a chest pain and, fearing a heart seizure, insisted that a certain heart specialist be called to the emergency room where he had been taken. He had a coronary attack and had developed complete heart block. The heart man put in a pacemaker and buried the mercury battery, about the size of a large watch, under the left collarbone. With this gadget, the patient was discharged in good shape with his heart ticking along at seventy-two per minute. He returned to business as usual.

Later, the patient suffered a severe attack of bronchitis. His lung man ordered him to hospital for another complete review of tests with special attention to the blood gases. This subspecialist made breezy visits every day accompanied by his retinue of students and interns. They all listened to the back of the patient's chest, because that was where they found the congestion. The patient was given antibiotics, and he got better. A physiotherapist was then called in and ordered him to start walking as fast as possible four times a day up and down the long hospital corridors. The patient was shocked one day when an old friend passed him during his walking exercise and did not recognize him. The friend said he looked "old and worn and grey". Quite by accident, the patient's regular physician happened by during the exercise period, and he recognized the patient only by his old red velvet dressing gown! On inquiring, his physician learned that the chest expert had never completely examined the man in this bronchitis attack but had relied completely on the tests in directing his treatment of the bronchitis. The lung doctor, without realizing that the man's heart was paced at seventy-two beats per minute and could not speed up with exercise to maintain the normal blood flow to the head or body, kept pushing him to exercise. No wonder the executive looked grey when he was ordered to walk quickly. His blood was going to his muscles but not to his head. The wonder was that he had not dropped dead while following his lung man's orders!

Young doctors have preferred to subspecialize for various reasons: it is easier to learn about a small field; they often imagine themselves doing something original or even making a discovery; subspecialist skills can be more easily mastered and controlled with the new advances as they come along; the hours are shorter; and (sad to relate) also because the vacations are longer and there is no one to recall the doctor but his banker.

Most new physicians have subspecialized in one of the following:

- Allergy — sensitivity to foreign materials resulting in conditions like asthma
- Cardiology — heart, blood pressure, arteries, veins
- Computer medicine
- Dermatology — diseases of the skin
- Diabetes
- Gastro-enterology — the gullet, stomach, small and large bowel, liver, pancreas
- Glandular diseases — thyroid, ovaries, adrenal, pituitary
- Hematology — blood, lymph glands, spleen
- Infectious diseases — resulting from bacteria or viruses or fungi
- Laboratory medicine — blood chemistry, isotopes
- Neurology — brain, spinal cord, nerves
- Oncology — diseases characterized by cancer of organs or systems
- Renology — diseases of the kidneys
- Respirology — diseases of the lungs
- Rheumatology — diseases of joints, muscles, bones

But while there has been more pay for the more marketable skills in the subspecialties, the life of a subspecialist can be monotonous. When asked what he had found most interesting in a heavy morning's clinic through which more than forty patients had passed, a rheumatologist, surrounded by his cohort of younger associates, recently admitted to me that "it was all run-of-the-mill stuff".

On the other hand, one day in the life of an internist may engage his clinical ability for resolving such problems as:

- Myxedema (lack of thyroid)
- Pernicious anemia
- Tension headache in a patient worried about the possibility of a brain tumor
- A patient with chills and high fever and sweats and delirium
- Coronary thrombosis complicated by phlebitis and pulmonary embolism

- Convulsions
- Abdominal pain with vomiting
- A patient with dropsy and albumen in the urine
- Stroke

The current prediction for all medical graduates after 1976 is that more than 90 per cent of them will subspecialize within five years of finishing medical school. At first glance this suggests progress. Actually it has become quite the reverse. The steady rise of the "doctor-made-you-sick", or iatrogenic diseases points up the fallacy of the subspecialization landslide, because so many doctors now know so much about so little.

Despite the current trend, I expect that the subspecializing in medicine of the last twenty-five years will slow down and that with the next generation of doctors we shall see a return of the more broadly based physician-internists. The good students today are disillusioned about their prospects in the one-organ branches of medicine. They want to be doctors who can bring the best of medicine to the greatest number of people. Real doctors can be born again if the teaching programs are modified appropriately in our medical schools and hospitals. A new generation of consecrated students will stimulate the production of that long-lost commodity — good teachers.

The following account of a patient's experience brings out some of the disadvantages and risks that come with too many subspecialties:

In April 1974 an insurance executive was vacationing in the south. After a game of golf he had a shaking chill and vomited. He felt hot. His wife called a doctor under the direction of their motel office. The doctor told him to go to the hospital emergency. There he was met by nurses and two junior interns. His temperature was 103°. He told them he had been coughing up blood but when they had examined him they said he must have *thought* it was blood because it couldn't have been. They told him that they had both lost money on their bets on his blood pressure because they were sure it would be high. "We thought you were a high-tension kind of guy." It was just 110/80. Blood tests were ordered and an X-ray was taken.

Then a more senior resident, who seemed about thirty came along. He was a nice sort of chap and he examined the chest. All three doctors pronounced it "bronchitis", but just to be double sure he was ordered off for another X-ray.

In half an hour the three doctors and a visiting staff doctor came on the run with the second X-ray. They all said: "You've got pneumonia.'' Then they put their stethoscopes on the spot they showed him in his lung X-ray. In unison, they chimed: "He's really got it . . . we can hear rales just where the X-ray shows the trouble.'' The patient was instructed to take eight antibiotic capsules every day for ten days.

They did not have time to look at his abdomen. He was just getting over a gastrectomy and vagotomy operation for a complicated duodenal ulcer. He was still having the diarrhoea which is common after this operation. The drug, the double dose, the long 10 day course they insisted on his taking carried the high risk of incapacitating diarrhoea because many intestinal bacteria can be destroyed by this antibiotic. He was discharged to his motel. The next morning he jetted home.

The professor in that hospital was a kidney expert — highly regarded and the author of a book on Bright's disease. His disciples had a reputation for ordering more kidney tests than any other group of interns on the continent! But they could not tell the difference between bronchitis and pneumonia. Blood pressure does go up with kidney trouble, so they were keen about estimating "hyper" patients on sight just the way their professor did. But their guessing was bad. Pneumonia is fifty times as common as Bright's disease. Pneumonia can be diagnosed and cured. Unfortunately, such is not usually the case with Bright's disease. That hospital would be a much safer place for sick people if the man at the top was a broadly-based physician-internist. The patient in question summed it up well: "I was afraid of those fellows . . . I was afraid I would die.''

The insurance executive's experience exemplies unscientific medicine:

● The telephone history taken by the motel doctor was shoddy — it should have prompted him to make a house call.
● The man had indeed spat blood although the doctors said "he *couldn't* have''. The patient is so often right — he deserves to be heard.
● Tense people usually do not have high blood pressure.
● Chills and high fever do not mean bronchitis.
● An X-ray should follow, not precede, a doctor's careful examination.
● The routine laying on of hands would have disclosed the recent gastrectomy and vagotomy and diarrhoea.
● The treatment prescribed involved twice the average dose of antibiotic and it was ordered for twice as long as is necessary for the average case

of pneumonia. The more antibiotic given, the more likely diarrhoea will complicate the treatment.

● No note about the sputum culture was sent to the home doctor.

● This patient in a kidney man's hospital was mishandled diagnostically and then over-treated for a straightforward case of pneumonia. Going to the emergency room sick with one curable malady, he was nearly sent home with another serious and incapacitating diarrhoea that could have prevented a return to work for weeks after the pneumonia had vanished.

One power group of four policy-molders of post-graduate medical education in 1973 concluded a two-day retreat with this amazing statement: "It is recognized that we have no conclusive evidence that the presence of physician-internists in any practice setting substantially improves the health care of the population served." This communique is utterly incomprehensible at first glance. However, on second glance it becomes quite understandable. The chairman was a heart expert, the second man was a blood subspecialist, the third a subspecialist in infectious diseases, and the fourth was a cholesterol-triglycerides authority.

These men, like Aaron worshipping the golden calf, were planning how to make way for the ever-rising wave of subspecialists in their own images. They were not versed in medical history or even in contemporary medicine or they would have called some of the following great internist-physicians to mind:

Arthur Bloomfield	*Stanford*
Paul Beeson	*Yale*
Henry Bockus	*Philadelphia*
Ray Farquharson	*Toronto*
Louis Hamman	*Johns Hopkins*
Tinsley Harrison	*Birmingham*
Chester Keefer	*Boston University*
Jonathan Meakins	*McGill*
Walter Palmer	*Chicago*
Wilder Penfield	*McGill*
Sir George Pickering	*Oxford*
Eugene Stead	*Duke*
George Thorn	*Harvard.*

These giants of medicine of this century are not and never will be outdated. Had they not done their work so well, the profession would enjoy a less honourable position.

The young deliberators on subspecialist teaching trends should have appreciated that the excitement of working with the new technical and laboratory toys that came with the specializing of medicine after 1945 has been waning. They should have been asking themselves whether bright, personable doctors are likely to continue to be satisfied with lifetimes spent as kidney dialysers, joints men, blood men, glands men, or heart men — with the broad life of the physician-internist beckoning — were it not for the high fees collected by the subspecialists.

They should have known that patients do not bring their lungs or glands or kidneys or spleens to their doctors. They bring themselves. It is true that they may worry, for example about their prostates, but once these are reamed out and they are voiding clear, sparkling urine again without hesitancy their interests revert to their whole body machines and their workings. The physician-internist is the only doctor who can make all of the organs work in the harmony of good physical and mental health.

In the aftermath of so much subspecializing, the population of physician-internists has decreased critically. The students have become fearful of ever trying to emulate the internists. Those who are sure that internal medicine is their life work are being told that they must spend all the time they can scrounge from the care of their sick patients "to learn psychosomatic medicine and the behavioural sciences". I have known the occasional internist who was impersonal and disinterested in his patients' personal and family and environmental worries. But most real doctors as they mature during their years in practice realize that psychosomatics and behavioural sciences are better learned by experience than by lectures and discussions. Every good teacher emphasizes the importance of these factors at the bedside, after he and the students are sure that the patient has no body cause for the illness. It is safer for the doctor (and the patient) to think in terms of somato-psychic medicine, a sound mind in a body that is known to be in good working order.

Surgeons, and Surgical Subspecialists

> *No one can be a good physician who has no idea of surgical operations, and a surgeon is nothing if ignorant of medicine.*
>
> HARVEY CUSHING

The surgeon is a doctor who actively treats the patient with the scalpel. Most of the patients who consult him have already accepted this probability. The general surgeon is concerned with surgical diseases of the thyroid and other related glands, surgical removal of all kinds of tumors, internal and external injuries, breast diseases, surgical shock, gangrene, infections requiring drainage, surgical diseases of the liver, spleen, stomach, bowel, gall bladder, gall ducts, and pancreas — to pay out only a short line.

The surgeon, like the physician, should possess intellect, compassion, and "the touch". Unlike the physician, he wants a quick cure. More than the physician, he has to have physical energy and resilience as he moves from one operation to another through a long day with no certainty that his night will not be interrupted. He is the consultant on whose words the patient waits with the keenest anticipation. To operate or not? What will be the chances of cure? What is the life risk?

The general surgeon should have the longest and broadest training. I note that many recent graduates reject general surgery because it is too demanding. What a pity! No work can be more engaging or varied or satisfying.

I constantly admire our surgeons who, after heavy days attending their regular patients, begin emergency work resulting from the use of alcohol and drugs and from highway carnage that takes them through a whole night of meticulous operating — without fees attached — to save a hand or a leg or a face or a life.

In no other professional field does such a calibre of skill show up so selflessly, working on human wreckage that might often be called useless if every fact and every life hope for the patient were known. The facts are never known and the surgeons in their finest hours always play the game to win. Often they do succeed brilliantly against terrific odds and in doing so risk their own lives as evidenced by the exhaustion written indelibly on their faces when they take off their masks and gloves and gowns and head homewards after 5 a.m. for an hour's sleep before starting the regular work of the day.

To the patient, the skilled surgeon is the great man. The patient knows the operation will hurt, and it does, but he recovers. The surgeon's greatness comes with his skill and compassion.

> Dr. Roscoe Graham, one of the great surgeons of his day, going around his ward at the Toronto General Hospital, stopped at the bed of a teen-ager on whom he was to operate the next day. She was sobbing. Instead of passing the buck and telling her that her medical

man would come in and order a sedative to settle her troubled nerves, he sat down unhurriedly on her bed and with his arm around her shoulders said, "Don't worry, my dear, I'll build a fence around your trouble." The operation went well.

The men who do not choose to do general surgery or are not chosen for general surgery, but who want some part of surgery, get into one of the following special areas:

Ophthalmology — *diseases of the eye*
Otolaryngology — *ear, nose, throat, and sinuses*
Neuro-surgery — *brain, spinal cord, and nerves*
Obstetrics, Gynecology — *obstetrics and female pelvis surgery*
Plastic surgery — *corrective and reparative*
Orthopedic surgery — *of bones, joints, tendons, and muscles*
Urology — *kidneys, bladder, and extensions*
Cardiovascular surgery — *heart, arteries, and veins*
Pulmonary surgery — *lungs and all other chest contents except the heart*
Oncology — *the surgery of cancer*
Paediatric surgery — *limited to children*

The surgeon must, of course, know anatomy. He must know pathology. In the experimental laboratory he must learn physiology — how the organs work. Every surgeon should do experimental surgery in the dog.

It seems unbelievable that a century after Lord Lister — the man who made surgery safe and who opposed Queen Victoria in her anti-vivisectionist attitudes as he insisted on the need for the surgeon to use the experimental method humanely on animals — so many surgeons begin and end their surgery on human patients. Thousands of doctors still operate with only the foundation of one year of general internship, during which they have done a few tonsils, a few appendices, a rare hernia, and perhaps never so much as a gall bladder. They get into busy general practices and without adequate supervision begin learning surgery by operating on the innocent human freight that comes their way.

Why should animals get the good surgical care resulting from the experimental training of veterinarians when humans who happen to fall sick away from centres of accredited surgical skill have to face high risks at the hands of inadequately trained surgeons?

The number of sound surgical operations has increased unbelievably since Lord Lister made it safe for the surgeon to look into a bone, a joint, the abdomen, the chest, and the head, a century ago. Hardly a month passes without some valuable new operation being described.

It is impossible to mention the quite miraculous exploits in all of the eleven subspecialties of surgery — orthopedics, for example. In 1929, when I graduated, a person who fell and broke a hip was usually confined to bed for six months. If he was fortunate he was able to limp around again. Most of the hip fracture patients died of bronchial pneumonia. Now a woman of eighty-two with high blood pressure and diabetes who breaks her hip at 5 p.m. can see an orthopedic surgeon who will replace the broken neck and head of the thigh bone with a metal substitute and have her up in a chair the next day and walking unassisted in two weeks. Patients with crippling, painful hip joints can have them completely replaced and can walk out of the hospital in three weeks.

While interning at the Johns Hopkins Hospital in 1932 I was assigned to a retired but dynamic army general who was treated for sciatica, quite unsuccessfully for many weeks, in a hammock arrangement. He had the best physician, the best neurologist, the best neurosurgeon, and the best orthopedic surgeon. The diagnosis was sciatica — probably explained by a mild form of diabetes, because there was a slight increase in his blood sugar. All the king's horses and all the king's men failed to help this man, and he was sent home unchanged. Anyone who has suffered from a bad back will recognize that this man had a ruptured disc. Today he would be diagnosed before he got to the hospital. Operation and complete release from pain would take less than two weeks. In 1932 the story of ruptured disc had not been told. W. J. Mixter and J. S. Barr described it in 1934.

Motor vehicle, skiing, and occupational accidents and miraculous new operations have compounded the workload of orthopedic surgery hundreds of times. Most of the other surgical subspecialists can claim comparable advances.

Unfortunately, with today's system of choosing candidates for medical school, the chances of getting enough potentially great general surgeons are less than they should be. No yardstick for measuring stamina, the steady hand under stress, and the ability to make the important decisions quickly and correctly that characterize the master surgeon is available to admissions committees. These attributes do not parallel high marks and they almost never occur in women, who are the high-mark-gatherers. It can be stated that the more women candidates who enter medical school the smaller the number of master surgeons there will be. This is bad because master surgeons are always in short supply.

The Obstetrician-gynecologist

This is a doctor who specializes in childbirth and the diseases of the womb, ovaries, and vagina. He takes five years of post-graduate training where he is taught and where he teaches on hundreds of normal confinements, and on abnormal and complicated cases. A large part of his training is surgical and it includes Caesarian sections, therapeutic abortions, abortions on demand, and all of the operations on the female pelvic organs. It was customary for the obstetrician to deliver babies in his early years of practice and then to move gradually into female surgery (gynecology) which consists largely of the diagnosis and repair of the parts that have suffered with the stresses of childbearing, and in which tumors may develop.

It is now routine for every medical student before graduation to deliver at least ten babies in what are expected to be normal confinements. Few skills of practical obstetrics can be acquired in this brief experience. The problems of the new-born infant are hardly touched. When the student becomes an intern he is too rushed to spend enough time with the mother before or after delivery. In his twenty-four hour hospital routine he finds that obstetrics is a crisis-oriented subject inserted into his already crowded program. He must cope with forceps, tears, epesiotomies, stitches, shock, bleeding, infant injuries, prematurity, and even fetal death, as well as explanations to an anxious family. It is a job for which he rarely has much enthusiasm.

In North America about 80 per cent of all obstetric deliveries are still done by G.P.s with this inadequate background. Most deliveries are done in community hospitals. The troublesome complicated cases may be referred to the obstetric specialists in the teaching centres if time and distance permit.

The expectation that the average G.P. will be skilled in obstetrics is unlikely to be fulfilled. Once in practice, if he ''gets a name for obstetrics'', he may do fifty or even 100 cases in a year. When a busy doctor does this many deliveries, he will have too many days and nights broken up by hurried and often prolonged tension-packed visits to the hospital, which may be a mile or thirty miles from his office. Such activity places a severe physical and nervous strain on him and he gets back to his office tired out. Patients are waiting to see him and he is interrupted by telephone calls from the obstetric ward nurse about the mother or the infant he has just delivered. The volume of his office practice is swollen by pre- and post-delivery examinations, which more than 95 per cent of the time are perfectly normal.

The handling of so many obstetric cases by family physicians makes these doctors more and more "general". They cannot continue to learn and practise better medicine if they sap their energies by night and by day doing normal obstetrics. Their vacations have to be dovetailed into their patients' delivery schedules. Money can determine their interest in obstetrics.

Obstetrical cases, both normal and abnormal, are handled by specialists rather than by G.P.s because many patients insist on obstetric specialists if they can have them. Yet midwives can be of great value, and they are fundamental to the medical services of most European countries. In the United Kingdom the Central Midwives Board holds that "the midwife must . . . always form an essential foundation of any good maternity service". Every mother having a baby in the U.K. can have a midwife during pregnancy, at her confinement, and in the first weeks of the post-natal period. By any standard, this implies sensible service. In 1974 there were 20,909 practising midwives in Britain and there were 646,004 births. The midwife always collaborates with the obstetrical specialist when she is in doubt, before or during or after confinement. The midwives work with hospital specialists but they do not compete with them. While they are not qualified to practice "medicine, surgery, and midwifery" as is the G.P., they do become very proficient in delivering babies.

The new mother, no matter how well briefed, entertains fear and apprehension of the unknown. Help is expensive if it is available. She cannot rest. After giving birth, she is home in four days. She needs the care, the understanding, the patience, and the attention of a trained person. Her obstetrician is too busy. For the mother's problems, the midwife provides an immediate solution and she imparts confidence to young mothers who need it badly. She provides excellent obstetric care for the normal confinements. Of most importance is the fact that, by performing the routine obstetrics, she makes it easier for the G.P. to attend to the rest of his practice.

Training programs for midwives in North America are developing. Since so many deliveries are normal, it was no surprise that the Johns Hopkins department of obstetrics developed a pilot program for training midwives in order to correct the doctor shortage in a constructive way. Sad to relate, the G.P.s were the main objectors to this idea. But Yale has its program flourishing and the advantages for the patient and the profession of medicine at large are being recognized slowly but steadily.

General practitioners have told me that some of their most terrifying experiences have occurred when obstetric cases unexpectedly become complicated and the life of the mother or infant or both is threatened. At least four out of five deliveries are normal but it is the abnormal one in five that calls for the closest attention. This close attention is not possible if the responsible G.P. is over-busy with the numerous commitments of a heavy general practice. I am always distressed as I watch generation after generation of G.P.s burn themselves out prematurely because they cling so tenaciously to obstetrics. They could be spending those long hours of waiting in the labour room more effectively without risking their own health unnecessarily. The nurse who has taken the advanced training to qualify as a midwife and whose profession is delivering babies is on the job before and during and after delivery. She can call for special help in plenty of time if it is needed. Working in a hospital where obstetric-gynecology specialists are always within reach, the mother and the infant get much better total care.

Of course, such a reorganization of obstetrics in America will take some time, but it will pay high dividends. The patients will be better cared for. The specialty of obstetrics-gynecology will become much stronger. It will attract more trainees, who will all take the five years after the M.D. to become not only competent obstetricians but skilled gynecologic surgeons. Of equal importance, these experts will have the responsibility of teaching medical students and interns how to examine the female pelvis skilfully and competently, not only for purposes of diagnosis but also for non-surgical treatments. They will teach them how to deal with the common irregularities of menstruation, so that when they get into practice they will not have to refer so many thousands of women with this symptom to specialists. The obstetrician-gynecologists would teach them more if the curriculum committees in the medical schools gave this specialty its proper emphasis.

The Paediatrician

The paediatrician devotes his life to the care of infants and children. Like other specialists, his training comprises one year of general internship after medical school and four years in the study of diseases of the new-born and of children up to the age of fourteen.

The number of paediatricians has been decreasing for the last twenty years. The sulfas, penicillin, and the other antibiotics discovered after 1934 have nearly eliminated the infections that accounted for so much paediatrics. After 1949, penicillin when combined with cortisone obliterated the ravages of rheumatic fever. Poliomyelitis vaccine after 1954 brought another reduction in the work of the paediatrician. Cystic fibrosis and the other "new" childhood diseases are not common and unfortunately do not respond well to paediatric care of any kind.

In Toronto the biggest children's hospital in the world has had to increase the age-range of its patients (originally from birth to fourteen) to from birth to twenty-one. Paediatrics is no longer a steadily growing area of specialization in medicine.

The not-yet-born and the new-born infants present the greatest challenges to today's paediatricians. To deal effectively with this rapidly-growing interest, the new infant specialist must be attached to a large obstetrical service with the most modern laboratory and nursing techniques. This kind of specialist will extend his skills from the time of the infant's conception over the first two years of life, where most of the modern modifiable paediatrics occurs. After the age of two, the G.P. or the physician-internist will tend to take over the care of the growing child and the teen-ager. The public health nurses will give children their inoculations against the infectious diseases.

Family Medicine

A comparatively new medical specialty is the field known as family medicine. Whether it can truly be called a specialty and whether it is a genuine advance in medical care for patients who are really sick is still open to question.

As subspecializing in medicine and surgery increased after 1950, a number of concerned general practitioners in North America decided almost simultaneously that, since subspecialists were being supplied with patients by the G.P.s, something should be done to make the G.P. a more intelligent receiver of the patients after the subspecialists had finished with them. Early in the ensuing discussions it was realized that there would always be a wide gulf between specialists and G.P.s but that the quality of medicine could be improved if the G.P.s realized that they were serving a specialized and important function. These G.P.s believed that they should come together in order to maintain their self-respect and to try to better themselves so that they would be more generally appreciated by the patients as well as by the subspecialists.

They founded the College of General Practice. The originators were concerned doctors who had practised well and were respected by their peers as good G.P.s who had been in practice for a number of years. The College of General Practice was a dedicated but unwieldy group. In order to belong to it, a doctor must agree to attend a minimum number of medical meetings, approved as learning experiences by the college executive. In order to continue as a member of the college in good standing, a doctor is expected to attend the equivalent of one hour a week at meetings that are approved for credit. This establishes a new method for improving the G.P.s' knowledge, for it had been found through surveys that the study-time of the average busy general practitioner amounted to something less than one hour a month during his working career.

Once the College of General Practice was established it was necessary to accept the fact that certain G.P.s would have to be teachers. This need introduced the first stumbling block because at no time in the history of the medical schools of the Western world had practising G.P.s ever been approved as teachers. Many G.P.s had regularly attended teaching hospital out-patient clinics on one or two half-days a week, where they worked under the direction of senior teachers. Their attendance at these clinics was regarded as an honour, and, by working close to senior consultants, they improved as doctors. Some of them through their own interest in clinical work and their own study habits became consultants.

By 1960 the increasing ratio of subspecialists to G.P.s required the G.P.s to find an exciting new term to replace the old horse-and-buggy concept and the newer Model-T concept of the G.P. which was still uppermost in the minds of the students, the academics in the medical schools, the public at large, and the politicians who are responsible for health care.

The term chosen was "family medicine". This term was thought to have a more respectable and specialized dignity than the dreary and banal "general practitioner". The new term could not be defined and was used with a sort of awesome reverence. There was a change in the attitude of students who, previously, when asked by friends or teachers about their post-graduate objectives, had almost hung their heads in shame as they replied, "Oh, I'm just going to be a G.P." With the new specialty, students who were asked this question could face up and state proudly that they were going into family medicine.

This new branch of medicine needed a new look, with additional subject material to separate it from the old G.P. image. Its early leaders had stated that their protégés would be trained in the "art and science of medicine". This was not sufficiently different from the Hippocratic tradition and so new subjects had to be added and they had to be emphasized. These included research, anthropology, psychology, psychosomatic medicine or soft psychiatry, economics, behavioural sciences, disease control, health maintenance, the education of doctors' assistants, thanatology, and sociology. When old-fashioned general practice was garnished with these intangibles, the mystique of family medicine seemed assured.

The time was ripe for the change. For years many students had been disenchanted by so much teaching by subspecialists who were very enthusiastic about the minutiae of their own subjects but were quite incapable of dealing with the whole patient. The students had entered medicine to learn how to practise, and a great many were dissatisfied when after the four years of medical school and the one year of internship they were not even equipped for the life of a good G.P. Many could not for personal or financial reasons take the extra four years after internship in order to qualify as subspecialists. For this growing group of students, family medicine, with one or one and a half years in hospital internship plus a year or more in family practice clinics away from the teaching hospital environment, provided a middle course that seemed next best to subspecialization.

It must be pointed out that, with the creation of family medicine, a great weight was lifted from the shoulders of the deans and the specialty teachers who had failed to satisfy their students. Indeed the programs of family medicine came into existence because the subspecialist teachers had abdicated their responsibilities as teachers of medicine. The family medicine movement was simply the filling of a vacuum that had been building up for more than two decades. The medical faculties eagerly welcomed this new and all-embracing subspecialty.

Most traditional medical schools in North America have not given serious attention to the question of family medicine, and, organized as they are, it is unlikely that they will ever be able to face the task effectively. They cannot in all honesty add family practitioners to their faculties on an equal footing with the other members of the academic community, all of whom will have had from five to eight years of postgraduate training before ever being considered as teachers and who may gain the rank of associate professor only after several additional years of teaching and research.

Family medicine begins with several serious disadvantages. It is an area that cannot be defined. All of its members have about the same amount of training and this averages one year of general internship and occasionally a second year. Good teachers are not to be found within the group. Those who pose as teachers are more like exemplars to their apprentices, going around with them to see patients but unable to do any teaching in the true academic sense of this term.

The special training for family medicine is highly informal, and has a surprising similarity to the old apprentice system that existed in medicine until the end of the nineteenth century. The family medicine man completes his regular medical education and one year of internship like all other doctors, both G.P.s and specialists. He then joins a family practice group for a one- or two-year period, and is well paid while learning from those already practising. During this period he attends seminars in a variety of subjects, chiefly the non-medical subjects listed on page 34. These are taught by the family medicine doctors or the trainees themselves. At the end of this period, some of the lucky trainees may get another three-month period of hospital training, with perhaps six weeks in Internal Medicine, three weeks in Cardiology, and three weeks in Diabetes. It is never quite adequate.

Of some importance to the candidate who is contemplating this program is the fact that the two years he spends training in a family medicine centre have no academic credit. If he should decide that he wants to become a physician-internist (or surgeon or subspecialist), he must start from square one and begin the regular formal four years of accredited training.

The content of family medicine has never been defined. No two medical schools with family medicine programs have similar courses of study. The diploma of family medicine cannot be conferred by a university. It is granted by the College of Family Medicine (of the College of General Practice, which is a name still used).

No state or provincial college of physicians and surgeons responsible for granting licences to practise can recognize family medicine men as any different from regular G.P.s who are equally entitled to practise medicine, surgery, and midwifery. The diploma of the College of General Practice or Family Medicine does not entitle a doctor to charge his patients any more for their services than the regular G.P. charges.

As in any experiment, difficulties presented themselves, and even in 1976 the leaders of the family medicine movement had not been able to make it stand firmly on its own feet because the G.P. influence was still all-powerful. If a doctor is not first of all a G.P., he simply cannot be a doctor of family medicine. There is still complete uncertainty as to whether the long list of extra subjects advised for family medicine has any true importance in the flesh-and-blood practice of medicine. Anthropology and economics and sociology and thanatology ring pretty hollow if the diploma-holder in family medicine cannot distinguish a serious heart murmur from an insignificant one, cannot decide whether a spleen is enlarged or not, cannot form an opinion about a breast lump, or fails to differentiate between a bad migraine attack and a sub-arachnoid hemorrhage.

Sometimes the study of these non-medical subjects can lead to false confidence in a student. For example, a young intern, having taken a course in thanatology (care of the dying patient and his family), may not have a total grasp of this sensitive and intuitive subject.

Certainly, today's threadbare medical education in anatomy, physiology, pathology, and pharmacology produces doctors who can be much less capable of caring for the sick patients than their resourceful forebearers of the 1920s were. They lack the foundation.

> A twenty-two-year-old housewife had a stroke that injured the important area in the left side of her brain concerned with understanding and speech formation. Thorough investigation indicated beyond any reasonable doubt that she had a small-artery disease called disseminated lupus that was affecting her brain. After all the evidence had been submitted, this difficult problem in diagnosis and treatment was thoroughly discussed by the students, regular interns, assistant residents, clinical professors, and the physician-in-chief.
>
> At this juncture, the visiting intern in family medicine, fresh from heavy indoctrination in thanatology, got to his feet and somewhat vehemently addressed the group: "From the vantage point of family

medicine I find all the investigations that have been done on this woman simply appalling. Instead of informing her that she is about to die and helping her in her need to make peace with her Creator, you are only giving her cortisone. You have not informed the poor husband of his wife's impending death and he is therefore totally unprepared for the awful grief reaction that will soon engulf him."

The chief physician, who was an authority on disseminated lupus and who had taken a very special interest in the young woman, quietly replied: "You could be quite right. Perhaps we should have applied the modern teachings of thanatology to this woman and her husband but we are very glad we did not. She is responding quite dramatically to cortisone and this morning, before she was brought over to the clinic, she had good understanding and her speech was returning. I have seen other patients like this who have carried on in surprisingly good health for more than five years with the treatment she is receiving. If you had assured her and her husband that she was about to die, how would you extricate yourself from the dilemma caused by her improvement? Do you not think that the observance of a splendid silence, when a doctor cannot be absolutely certain, is safer and better medicine for the patient and the family, and better for the doctor's own credibility?"

A third-year student who had taken a thorough history from the family and the husband added this lighter touch to the thanatology pall: "I learned from the family that the husband had a girl friend. If he had been given the death warning and his wife had then begun to improve he could have been bitterly disappointed!"

The spirit of thanatology, if it is ever understood, comes late in the career of the best physician. He knows that, although his speech may be silver, with life's constant uncertainties his silence is usually golden. Thanatology is not something that can be pasted onto the new wall of family medicine by occasional seminars organized by youthful and enthusiastic instructors who have read a book or two in preparation. It comes with years of trying experiences at close range with the dying and with their families. The forty-hour-week doctor can never learn about it at first hand. An announcement on a hospital bulletin board saying, "Thanatology Seminar at 8 a.m. Friday" does not make much of an impression when you realize that not one of those who will be attending have ever helped with an autopsy. The aims of family medicine are sincere but they are too vague. They begin with medicine and obstetrics and minor surgery, but they must always borrow heavily from ear, nose, and throat, orthopedics, eye, office gynecology, dermatology, office proctology, soft psychiatry, laboratory tests for office use, and psychosomatic medicine. The questionable relationships with behavioural sciences and all of the other new subjects prove confusing.

I am not at all sure that this scattering effect is good or safe for the patient. My view is strengthened as I observe the family medicine clinics springing up with tenuous ties to medical schools or community hospitals in many parts of the U.S. and Canada.

Family medicine stresses family. This carries the disadvantage of tying the doctor to a social unit which may not actually exist and which may not be the best basis on which to select a doctor. For example, those who live in communes or convents have just as much right to this kind of doctor as families do. A couple on the verge of divorce or a young person with difficulty communicating with his parents may find sharing a doctor with other family members well nigh impossible.

The learning experiences for students exposed to these family medicine groups remind me of a doctor picking up useful tips for dealing with patients who are not usually very sick. With hoards of patients going through these centres, the whole operation presents an assembly-line aspect that patients are quick to discern.

One of the weakest features of the program rests in the fact that where from three to six family doctors work together they work and charge as equals. They spell one another off on Wednesday afternoons and Saturdays and Sundays and assure the patients that they will get equally good care regardless of which doctor happens to be on duty. No matter how well this plan operates for the convenience of the doctors involved, it does not always work out well for the patient.

A thirteen-year-old boy developed a painful throat and cough one week before his family was to leave for holidays in July 1974. He was taken to a group centre and examined by a doctor who looked down his throat and told his mother that it was a streptococcus throat with swollen glands and he would take the penicillin ordered until he got better. At the weekend, just before the family was to leave, the boy's throat was worse. On Friday afternoon, they visited the family medicine building once more.

The doctor who had first seen the boy had left for a long weekend. The doctor whom the mother finally spoke to (after a long wait) asked the secretary for the boy's card. On it, the first doctor had scribbled "strep throat — gave him penicillin." His doctor substitute looked at the card and without looking at the boy scribbled out another prescription for penicillin and told the mother to carry on with the same dose for another week. By the end of the second week the family was up in northern Ontario in their motor-trailer. The boy was coughing so much at night that the family's sleep was disturbed. Their supply of penicillin was exhausted. Having been told to keep giving the boy penicillin until the throat was better, they went to the next town and found a doctor in his office on a Saturday morning in the hope that he would give them a new prescription.

This doctor asked to see the boy before giving him anything. He was not impressed with the throat but the face was swollen and enlarged glands were found along each side of the neck. The boy was gasping for breath and coughing. An immediate chest X-ray showed a large tumor mass above the heart which was blocking the veins carrying the blood from the head and neck to the heart. The boy was admitted to hospital and on Monday morning a small gland was removed for examination. This proved the condition to be Hodgkin's disease, a malignant (cancer-like) disease of the lymph glands, usually appearing first in the neck. The disease is not uncommon in younger people. Fortunately, when it is recognized early, the outlook is better than with other malignancies. In comparison, a "strep" throat can be completely cured within seventy-two hours when properly treated with penicillin.

This case provides examples of the deficiencies that show up in family practice groups, some of which are:

- The quick and incomplete examination directed at the sore throat without any careful examination of the neck.
- The ordering of far too much antibiotic without taking a culture of the throat to see whether the bug responsible for the throat infection would be killed by the antibiotic prescribed. This was an error of omission.
- The second visit to the group building, with cursory attention by another member of the group who relied entirely on the assumption that the other doctor who examined the boy had been correct in his diagnosis and his treatment.
- The second doctor's failure to recognize that, if the streptococcus diagnosis had been correct in the first place, the antibiotic would have cured it within four days and there would have been no need for the second visit.
- The re-ordering of penicillin was a mark of ignorance. This carried the risks that always attend the administration of too much antibiotic of any kind.

The comparison between the performance of the group and that of the doctor working alone in a small town and practising medicine in the traditional way reflected badly on the group method. Did it suggest that group practice is for the good of the patient or for the convenience of the members of the group? One could fairly conclude that, when the letter from the cancer clinic arrived at the family practice office, it would have less than a one-in-six chance of being read by the doctor concerned. Would anyone profit from this tragic case? These groups are dreadfully busy. They are busy doing unnecessary tests and ordering unnecessary drugs because their members do not appear to take the time to work over a case carefully before ordering medicine.

Since it is being widely discussed and advocated, family medicine is becoming a way out for students who are unable to make up their minds about what kind of doctors they want to be. In some places the word has been passed around, with no basis in fact, that unless the graduate qualifies at least in family medicine he will be denied the privilege of admitting his own patients to hospital when he gets into practice. This does not hold true in the U.S. or in Canada. Those who have spread this rumour have assumed that the North American system will follow the pattern of medicine in the U.K., where hospital privileges are rarely granted to ordinary G.P.s. There is no basis for the suspicion that the American system will eventually follow the pattern of the National Health Service of the U.K.

It is to be hoped that, as general practice improves on this continent, those who practise it will be better educated and better trained during their medical school years and their hospital internship. The profession will have to have more doctors who do not have to depend on attendance at refresher courses to keep up to date but who know how to go through the journals with a critical eye and choose the articles that apply to the work they are doing.

Unfortunately, the family medicine doctors do not want to learn anything but the bread-and-butter items of everyday practice. We see this in the students in medical school who are aiming at family medicine as a career. They avoid the clinics at which seriously ill patients are discussed, "because we will refer all our tough cases to specialists," they say. Surely this approach to medicine will lead to a very dull professional career.

The family doctor must learn how to choose specialists. He must know how to work with them and this usually means knowing them personally and knowing something about the quality of their work, and whether they are up to date — if his patients are going to be well looked after.

At a session on the modern treatment of cancer staged by the cancer group for a group of doctors in family medicine at a teaching centre in the midwest, a question about brain tumors was asked by one of the doctors in the audience. The panel chairman, who was the leader of family medicine in the district, ruled the question out of order because, as he explained it, "You fellows in family medicine won't see one brain tumor case in ten years, so don't worrry about such things."

His answer illustrates the weakest link in the family medicine chain. Certainly, with the never-will-see attitude, these doctors may not encounter one patient with a brain tumor in ten years. The vitally important point is that every busy doctor in every family medicine group will see at least one patient a week who *fears* that he may have a brain tumor. If the thoroughness of the doctor's history and physical examination does not convince the patient that there is no tumor, the level of that doctor's reputation suffers severely, with his patients and in terms of his own self-esteem. He will never enjoy his work as he should.

The family medicine doctor is unlikely to face serious disease in any patient that he can deal with adequately himself, and he is therefore forced to use his psychosomatic knowledge instead of the best techniques of diagnosis and treatment. If the patient is really sick, this is not a very safe substitute, because we see scores of patients whose physical disease has been overlooked because the family medicine doctor stressed the psychosomatic angle while he neglected the organic factor. Careful studies have shown that not 17 per cent of family medicine doctors are competent to deal with simple psychosomatic problems, because even these can only be handled if the doctor is first well trained in medicine.

In discussing their programs in family medicine with three authorities in January 1975, I was interested in their comments:

● A professor of medicine said that his school did not know where family medicine was going because it had no teachers with sound clinical experience. His faculty had not succeeded in defining family medicine.

● A senior resident in medicine to whose service the trainees in family medicine came to get their three months of internal medicine observed that these trainees, fresh from family medicine clinics, acted more like social workers than doctors.

● Another professor of family medicine in a medical school where this subject has been very heavily stressed regretted that their trainees were all lacking in paediatrics and internal medicine — the two subjects they should know best.

Without a unified organization and a regular curriculum taught by qualified teachers (that is, by teachers with at least five years of training in teaching hospitals like all the other medical teachers), this nebulous field will have increasing difficulties in establishing itself.

3.

Perhaps your doctor never got to medical school

The big problem today is to get the right kind of candidate into medical school and to give him the right kind of training.

DR. CHARLES MAYO

Every year our medical schools announce that their registrars have received thousands of applications for entrance and that only one hundred or so candidates can be admitted to the first year classes.

In the face of this dilemma the deans and their committees on admission, entrusted with screening applicants, and in effect determining the character of the profession, might seem to face a task of insurmountable proportions. On the contrary, however, their work is usually reduced to one of simplicity itself. The great majority of the more than 14,000 seats available each year in the medical schools of North America are still allotted to the students who in their last year in college, or in the two-year pre-medical course, obtained the highest standings in the mathematics and science part of the Medical College Aptitude Tests (MCAT). Cut-off points are arbitrarily imposed at the 80- or 82- or 85-per-cent level on the test scores, and those candidates who fall below this are summarily excluded. At one faculty meeting in 1970, the chairman of the entrance committee cheerfully confided that his secretary had gone through his 2,170 letters of application and picked out those with the top 200 MCAT scores. He did not even glance at the other 1,970 letters.

43

The result of this overpowering emphasis on the mathematics and sciences standing is that prospective pre-medical students must strive to excel through high school and college in mathematics, physics, chemistry, and biology. Their reading, talking, thinking, and cramming must be constantly slanted towards these subjects. Even the best students dare not risk their only chance of entering medical school by giving more than a minimum nod to language, literature, history, geography, and social science. Their intense concentration gives them a narrow viewpoint on life even before they plunge into the most narrowing and most expensive of all university curricula, that of the medical school.

From my personal observations of students in and from medical schools, I have concluded that the distinctly mathematical brain does not excel in clinical performance and that as a rule it even falls short of the mark. Albert Einstein's comment in this regard is pertinent: "Biological procedures cannot be expressed in mathematical formulas . . . living matter and clarity are opposites — they run away from one another." The great and inventive surgeon Dr. J. M. T. Finney said when he was preparing for the study of medicine: "I could without difficulty keep up with my work and make good grades in every subject except one, mathematics, which, no matter how hard I try to understand, has always remained to me an undiscovered country." Dr. Finney added, "I have heard Sir William Osler remark that he only knew enough mathematics to convince him that there was 'something rotten in it' but he could never learn enough to find out just what it was."

Personal qualifications, once an important consideration in medical school admissions are more and more giving way to the impersonal math-science proficiency. The tendency is being reinforced still further at many schools because of the new stress on computer technology, laboratory gadgetry, and bio-engineering.

There can be no doubt that the student with a high math-science score can make it through the present medical course if his nerves stay steady and his health holds out. It is made doubly difficult for the high-scoring student to fail because every failure in this very expensive curriculum reflects on the competence of the admissions committee and the dean.

They are insisting (and their selected students are in full accord) that such intelligent candidates for medicine will have to be supported by paramedical aides like the Russian "feldschers" or near-doctors, and by nurses, who will do the pedestrian work. So convinced are the deans and their faculties that their high-scoring applicants will be exceptional doctors that they insist that these superior intellects cannot be expected to look after colds, emotional upsets, and other everyday ailments, or make house calls.

Surprisingly, despite the honours standing demanded for admission to medical school, the candidates who are chosen do not graduate as first-class doctors. I base this judgment on more than twenty years of examining final-year students, on my own experience in observing the attainments of several generations of medical graduates, and on the corroborating views of colleagues in other medical schools. The fact that not more than one in ten of the bright candidates taken into medicine graduates from medical school with honours standing calls for some sharp analysing.

This disappointing drop in achievement between college education and medical education probably means at least one of three things: the gifted students are not being challenged, or the teaching methods are failing, or the selection standards were wrong in the first place. That the third is the chief fault in the system can hardly be doubted. The Medical College Aptitude Test does not measure motivation, sincerity, ability to read critically, self-discipline, or intellectual honesty. These are all hallmarks of the real doctor and they must be determined in other ways.

Many thousands of high-school and college students who have it in their natures to be doctors shrink from trying for medical school because they refuse to submit to the narrow, soul-constricting courses that will monopolize their thinking, and that, if mastered with maximum concentration, cannot guarantee their entry to medical school anyway.

Most of the medical schools freely admit that they have not found a fair and rational way of screening applicants. Some of the largest schools have seriously considered using a lottery system.

Many administrators are advocating the rating of honours graduates in the Humanities equally or above those with high math-science scores. They argue convincingly that bright hard-working students with a broad general knowledge can acquire the indispensable science background in the first year of medical school. Other administrators believe that candidates for medicine should not be "professionalized too soon" by being required to get a science degree first. They have observed that such candidates often develop symptoms of academic fatigue that may prove critical during the four hard years in medical school and the still more demanding five years of post-graduate training.

Modern schools like Boston University, Johns Hopkins, and Northwestern are finding that two years of good college work is an adequate preparation for medicine. Their younger students do as well or better than those who have taken three or four years to obtain science degrees before beginning medicine. These students will not have squandered so much of that most vital asset, their youth.

Back in the days before computers and test scores, a well-to-do woman who was a regular passenger on a Baltimore street-car line happened to notice a young conductor who was unfailingly courteous in his ticket-taking and who seemed to have other noteworthy personal qualities. One day she asked him if he had any amibtion beyond his present job. He replied that he had always wanted to be a doctor but he could not afford the fees. The woman told him that she believed in his ability and that if he was serious she would finance his education at Johns Hopkins. The young conductor not only graduated from Johns Hopkins but went on to make a name as the school's chief of orthopedic surgery.

It was a rare, fortuitous encounter, and proved an unusually shrewd estimate on the part of the woman passenger. What we need today is a test that measures the values she perceived in the young conductor.

The Medical College Aptitude Tests somehow seem to screen out precisely those candidates who would measure highest on a humanistic or patient-oriented scale — in other words, the candidates who would make the best doctors. Oddly enough, though the present system has flooded the medical schools for forty years with math-science geniuses, those chosen have rarely attained scientific distinction. Indeed the slowing down of the age of medical discovery that flourished in the 1920s, 1930s and 1940s seems to raise the question of whether the preoccupation with science is even good for science. On the economic side, all of the available studies tell us that the present system is dreadfully expensive and that it does not deliver enough real doctors for living patients.

While it is known that the percentage of the best college graduates who apply for medicine tends to rise and fall from decade to decade, many educators believe that an increasing number of potentially excellent doctors with a deep desire to study medicine do not apply. Of those who do, it will admittedly always be difficult to choose the one best candidate out of ten applicants. But to say that there is no better way than to go on relying so heavily on the one-sided, wrong-headed, misleading math-science score is an irresponsible excuse.

First, and most basic of all the changes needed, we must utilize the careful, time-consuming, face-to-face interview. Of course, interviews alone cannot solve the problem, but they can be of great help. In many medical schools there is no informed interview of applicants at all. In others it is too hasty and too cursory to form a rational basis for accepting or rejecting. To be meaningful the interview must be thorough, and it must be integrated with all of the other information submitted to the committee on admissions. The interview along with the integration of information should be done by general physicians and surgeons who practise and teach. The subspecialists are rarely equipped for this task because they are narrow in outlook and they are usually very busy people.

"Little solid evidence about personal interviewing is available, and today's consensus suggests that it has slight if any value in predicting. It does provide an opportunity for senior faculty members to meet the applicant and to spot any glaring personality defect or any signs of emotional instability. If any such features are discerned, the applicant may be required to subject himself or herself to a complete psychiatric interview." This suggests inadequacy in the interviewer, and it certainly stresses too heavily the power of psychiatry.

The psychological impact on the applicant of a thoroughgoing interview cannot fail to be beneficial. When he has been accepted, he must have a deep sense of being headed in the right direction. He has been accepted by a real doctor who knows what medicine is all about and who has no interest in setting his signature to an application, beyond the sense of responsibility for the future of this exacting profession.

Even for those rejected, the thorough interview proves invaluable. Whatever his disappointment at being turned aside from medicine, the rejected candidate will be saved much painful experience later and will profit from being pointed towards a more suitable goal. Such cannot be the sentiment of the young person who feels a true vocation in medicine and who is blocked from it solely by his failure to get into the upper fifth segment of applicants on an esoteric and largely irrelevant test score without the chance of an interview with someone who is experienced as an active physician. The following is an example of good non-medical counselling.

On a June morning in 1973, I picked up a man waiting at a bus stop and dropped him off in the city on his way to the hospital. He was one of the night orderlies in our hospital, and he told me that he had just retired after thirty-six years and would be living with his older maiden sister who had also retired. I asked him if he had always held the one job and he told me he had. A withdrawn sort of man who had never been jovial about the hospital, he had intrigued me because I had never felt that I had succeeded in "getting through to him". His expression softened and for the first time I saw a smile cross his face.

This man had graduated in arts from the university I had attended, several years after me. He revealed his year by naming two of his classmates, whom I knew well. One of them had become general manager of one of America's largest insurance companies. The other had gone into medicine and had long been a prominent physician in the city. Why had this man, a graduate in the same class and at a time of expanding opportunity, taken a different life course and ended up at such a different social level, but with no sign of discontent?

It turned out that he had counted on a teaching career. About graduation time, one of his professors, whom he had always admired, called him into his office and congratulated him on his standing. He mentioned the possibility of a teaching career and then, to the surprise and relief of this man, he said: "I am confident that with your ability you will be capable. The one thing that worries me is what I perceive as a lack of calm when you go to express yourself and I wonder if you would not be more contented doing something that did not put you under the steady tension of the life of the teacher. Think it over. Life satisfaction is sometimes not the same as the thing we refer to as career success."

"Was the professor right?" I asked.

"Yes, indeed he was. Even my work in the hospital has often seemed almost too much for me."

What a wise professor! He had counselled well. His counsel was heeded because this man believed in his interest and sincerity.

If a wise professor in an arts college could give such helpful counsel to a graduate in arts why can we not expect the most careful estimating of personality in the interviewing of candidates who are considering the most stressful of all professional careers?

Many medical schools today assign M.A.s or Ph.D.s in non-clinical departments, such as anatomy, physiology or pharmacology, to the job of interviewing. Even more frequently, they borrow from the psychology, sociology, or psychiatry sections Ph.D. interviewers who regard the job as a research opportunity, believing as they record their findings that in ten years their material, thoroughly computerized, will define the exact ingredients for the ideal candidate for medicine.

That petty dream reflects the growing tendency to concede that this most important of human choices will in the end be left to the faceless computer. That will be the ultimate tragedy. Bits and pieces of information assembled on cards by hundreds of different questioners who are not doctors and are ignorant of the work that doctors must do can have no value before they are fed into the computer. The non-M.D. interviewers are not competent to evaluate bright youngsters eager for the chance to become doctors of medicine. The interviewers are under the further handicap that they, as well as the applicants, are aware that they themselves could not make it into medicine. Applicants who succeed in passing interviews with such people feel that they have outsmarted them, or have simply been lucky.

It should be possible for any high-school student who is seriously considering medicine to have an opportunity of an exploratory interview by his seventeenth or eighteenth year. This would be made possible by committees of reputable doctors in every state and province on this continent. The aim would be to identify candidates with the inborn desire to doctor. Character traits rather than the amount of stored information would be the qualities that would be looked for. Students who manifested such traits at that stage would be encouraged and appropriately advised about the college work to take in preparation for the second interview, which would take place by age nineteen or twenty, when they were ready to try for admission to the medical school of their choice.

This kind of personal interviewing has been done on a small scale by some American schools for a long time. Students living in the east who were considering Chicago could apply for a personal interview with a doctor in Boston or New York who had been a faculty member in Chicago. One of my mentors, who did some of this interviewing, told me about useful estimates he was able to form in chatting unhurriedly and informally with students, without reference to subjects and marks.

From observing medical students who are still floundering in search of their destinies by the final year in medicine and who are showing signs of fatigue, I am sure that careful searching for "the keen spirits with eternal fire" should begin years before it usually does in today's system. The searching out of all the students for the schools of North America, with its 250 million people, should have top priority with the deans and the committees who are responsible for this fundamentally important task. Instead of worrying so much about top marks, blood cholesterol, unstable blood pressures, and the erratic scores of psychological tests of prospective candidates, they might utilize the accumulated wisdom of the ages in filling first-year classes of medicine.

Doctors with experience in practice and teaching are most likely to be able to counsel hopeful candidates wisely. My colleague, Dr. David MacKenzie, does not believe that the interview can tell everything but that it does allow the experienced doctor "to pick the lemons from the grapefruit and the oranges".

Dr. James Means of Harvard said: "The doctor must love medicine." No one would be so naïve as to encourage a student who had trouble with the sciences to enter the field of medicine. But the science-math index is no measure of the intellect, much less of the compassion, or of the hand that tells the physician or surgeon what is wrong. I am convinced that there are more than enough students with the intellect, the compassion, and the touch to deliver the doctoral care that will be worthy of the profession of medicine, the doctoral care that the people deserve. It is a matter of searching them out.

4.

Should your doctor be a doctor?

Blessed is he who carries within himself a god, and an ideal, and who obeys it — an ideal of art, of science, or gospel virtues. Therein lie the springs of great thoughts and great actions.

LOUIS PASTEUR

It is ironical, as has been noted in the press and elsewhere, that at a time when the tools of medicine are improving dramatically the medical profession comes under sharply increased criticism. If the tools are better, how can it be that the doctors are worse?

Today's doctors seem to lack the mental and physical energy that the good doctor must have — an energy that is transmitted to the patient as a contagious spirit of optimism. There is no place among doctors for the slow-thinking, the heavy-footed, or the sour puss, because there will always be patients, hundreds of patients, to see, think about, and help. The doctor has to impart an air of calm whenever a difficult decision must be made, whether on the hospital ward, in the emergency room, in the office, in the operating room, or in the patient's home. All too often doctors appear to lack the concern, the compassion, and the decorum that have always been hallmarks of their profession.

While I was visiting a sick doctor and his family in Chicago, the conversation moved to the changing attitudes of people towards doctors. One of the sons suggested that part of the trouble was the too obviously well-stuffed wallet of the doctor and what it stood for. The wife settled the

51

discussion positively. "I have always observed that all people, by nature, turn to their doctors with respect and admiration. Perhaps not all of today's doctors deserve the sort of respect and admiration they have for my husband and other good doctors I know. It may well be that too many of the wrong people are being admitted to medical school."

Self-examination by the prospective medical student is the important first step when a life in medicine is contemplated. I will mention some of the personality or character traits that impressed me, in retrospect, as poor omens for such a life. My attention has been drawn to the following types who should hesitate to choose medicine and who should be dissuaded by medical counsellors from trying for the unusually exacting life of the doctor.

The Student Who Begins by Putting Research Ahead of Medicine

In this time of medical and surgical breakthroughs, it is common to find that a candidate wants the M.D. degree only as an entree to a life in research. I have known many a parent who in discussing a son's or a daughter's plans for medicine has assured friends that the family contribution to the profession is not going to be an *ordinary* doctor but that he (or she) is going "into research". Such candidates are discouraged by seasoned interviewers, who know that this goal is rarely attained and that it is wise to direct such candidates into Ph.D. courses in sciences.

The students with high research potential, as estimated by admitting committees, do not fulfil the expectations of the policy-makers in medical education. For many students, research in medicine is becoming one of the bad words. Early in 1974, while discussing with two unusually bright senior medical students the kind of practice they were aiming for, I learned something that was new to me about the impact of the research emphasis. One of the students had been approved for medical school when he was twenty-three because he had a degree in biochemistry. He was told that with this degree and the M.D. he would be fitted for a career in laboratory medicine or research. By the time he had reached his third medical year he was completely fed up with lab work. He realized suddenly that he would be twenty-seven by the time he graduated, and that he would still have to do his internship before he could even be a G.P. It embarrassed him when he was reminded that the tax-payers had paid $75,000 for his Ph.D. as a "first instalment", before adding the $250,000 for his M.D.

The other student's marks in mathematics and sciences in the first college year had been so high that he was placed in a special group with thirty-four other smart students. They were all assured that if their marks remained high in second year they could enter medicine directly and get the M.D. six years after high school instead of the usual seven or sometimes eight years. The reason for this special consideration was that the committee studying the second student's science standing had predicted that he would become a "research doctor". The student spent the next two summer vacation periods in the lab with rats. He had to sacrifice them, cut their organs up, and do special fat fraction examinations of them. In his graduating year he had to decide about his future. What would he go into: Research? Teaching? A Specialty? Or would he just be a horse-and-buggy doctor? "I chose family medicine (G.P.) work, because I wanted to get as far away from research as I could. Every time a teacher mentioned the word, I thought of all those rats and I got nauseated."

The Candidate with an M.A. or Ph.D.

With so many good students applying for medical school and with a fixed list for the first class, the dean has to say no to some whose marks are simply not quite high enough. Some of the rejected students are very intent on getting the M.D. and they insist on making another try. A dean may take the path of least resistance and suggest to some of the disappointed students that they should go back to college, get an advanced degree, and then reapply. Quite a few deans do, later, give the nod to graduates with degrees in engineering, physiology, pharmacology, biochemistry, and even business administration.

When artificial hearts and kidneys and joints are the fashion, it is natural to anticipate unusual ability in a candidate who has a degree in engineering. Deans hoping for original discoveries have frequently been wooed successfully by Ph.D.s with physiology or biochemistry degrees. The deans justify their actions by stating that such candidates, after they get the M.D., can at least adorn the faculty calendars even if they do not make original discoveries. The "societal aspects of medicine" is a new cliché, and, by the third of fourth year, we are finding more and more student misfits in the clinic whose entrance to medicine has been eased by a degree in sociology.

The accomplishments of the students who enter medical school with degrees in science are usually superseded by those of bright, dynamic students who enter with two (or three) years of appropriate pre-medical education and who possess the instinctive desire to be doctors. When we follow what happens to them in the ten years after graduation, this truth becomes increasingly obvious. Not all, but most of the students with advanced degrees should be dissuaded from becoming doctors of medicine. Although often extremely bright and long-suffering, they burn out prematurely when dealing with the complaining human being who is the patient.

> One evening in 1967 a junior intern with a Ph.D. and an M.D., working in a 300-bed hospital, was called by a staff doctor and told that a private patient with a very unusual combination of heart murmurs was being admitted and that he should take a few minutes to get this patient's history and to examine his heart. The patient was being admitted to the floor below the one he was on at the time. The intern was polite, thanked the staff doctor, and said that although he was pretty busy he would try to see the heart patient if he had time.
>
> While this graduate had attained honours standing in science and then in medicine he had not gained a broad experience with patients during his four years in medical school. Without this foundation, he lacked the necessary confidence to slip down to the other ward, glance at the chart, introduce himself to the patient, check the heart, and in ten minutes be back on his own ward. To have tried might have taken two hours of his time, and even after that he would have been painfully unsure of what he had observed.
>
> The findings in the heart patient were unusual and their understanding only required logical thinking. With this exercise mastered, the next twenty heart patients would have been easy for the intern, and from that vantage point the mastery of many everyday problems would have been downhill running. The physician had never found these particular physical signs in a heart patient before, but his experience made it easier for him to put them together and he wanted to share the knowledge with the budding doctor. The budding doctor, weary from the long run for the Ph.D. and then the M.D., did not have the sustained drive he needed to salt down successive patients' histories by the dozen, the score, and the hundred, as he would have to do if he were ever to match his Ph.D. with an effective clinical experience.
>
> Having to face the second-degree hurdle saps too much of the

student's best power in those golden seven or eight years for the Ph.D. and then the M.D. degree, before he ever assumes personal responsibility for sick patients at the start of his first year of hospital internship. It is only the very rare "Ph.D., M.D." doctor who attains to a high position in medicine or surgery and holds it.

The *avant-garde* medical schools are doing everything possible to whittle down the number of years the good student has to spend between high school graduation and the M.D. degree. With the post-graduate hospital work that must always be done after that, a man should not work so hard and so long that he almost seems ready for his first heart attack by the time he opens his own office. Everyone has seen these older house officers develop coronaries before they completed the long training programs. Often they were too old and too degree-laden before they started. The most intensive part of the doctor's education occurs in the hospital years, and ultimate success depends on what the M.D. does in this post-graduate period. He must not be burned out before he gets into it. There is too much exciting and demanding work ahead.

The Student Who Chooses Medicine by Exclusion

The student who does not know what he wants to do and who decides on medicine after *excluding* other career possibilities should settle for one of the others. Just as the good nurse has known from childhood that she wanted only to nurse, so the likeliest doctor will have nurtured an instinctive feeling for living things from early life. I do not mean to imply for a moment that these feelings by themselves will ever justify a student setting his heart on medicine. He must, of course, possess many other capabilities in addition to these instinctive feelings.

The Student with Cash Interests

Dr. William Osler long ago noted that the doctor whose carriage stopped before his broker's office on the way to the hospital would rarely be an example of professional worth. The temptation for the specialists, with their high earnings of the 1970s, to confer too frequently with their stockbrokers seems inevitable. As this occurs, their best contributions to their profession decline. The doctor who lacks a sense of high purpose will tend to substitute the acquisition of goods for the nobler aims of medicine. He often does this, sometimes without realizing it, by rendering services and doing operations that are not essential. Such candidates would be well advised to tackle some other line of work. Money does not make the man in medicine or surgery or obstetrics. As Dr. Joseph Aub of Harvard said, "Some doctors have minds like cash registers."

One busy medical practitioner, a leader in the business section of his local medical society, devoted much of his spare time to outlining the subject of medical economics to his fellow members. One day he stopped one of his less money-minded colleagues and told him that he had just experienced a great surprise. A patient to whom he had rendered an account for $37.00 had sent him a cheque for $40.00, and a scribbled "thanks". By his own admission, the "thank you" appeared to be quite unique for a doctor who drove a yellow Cadillac and had been in practice for twenty-seven years!

In comparison, another doctor was approached by an elderly couple each of whom had a heart condition. Their own doctor had cut down his practice and they needed medical attention. The doctor agreed to take them on and began by giving them physical examinations. Following her examination, the woman gave the physician's secretary her medicare number and a small parcel for the doctor. The parcel contained a string-tied hot-plate mat she had made herself. The card said, "Thanks for taking care of us." The doctor, in telling me this story, said that the medicare number counted for far less in his estimation than this hand-crafted expression of gratitude.

One of our best general practitioners was asked to look after a woman whose many complaints had never been taken seriously by her doctors. She admitted to being known as a "pest". This doctor listened with tolerance that was seriously tried by the woman's seemingly exaggerated but not unreal complaints. He examined her in his thorough, reassuring way, and gave her his opinion. A month later, just before Christmas, his wife received a huge poinsettia from the "pest". Who can ever estimate how much a doctor can help a patient, even if the patient may seem quite unreasonable?

A junior intern was required to catheterize a crusty old man before and after his surgeon operated on the prostate gland. It was a job of work the intern had to do whenever the man was in pain by day or by night. On the day the old man was ready to leave the hospital, his bladder now working well, he called for the intern, thanked him for his attentive service, and handed him a gold piece. Not the value of the five-dollar gold coin but the sense of gratitude it expressed taught this young intern what having a faithful doctor means to the patient.

Dr. William Mayo was called into consultation one afternoon on the case of a boy just out of high school. When he decided the lad needed an operation, the boy exclaimed, "But I haven't any money to pay for an operation." Dr. Will looked at him soberly. "Do you think you could earn some after you get well?" The boy was sure he could. "All right, you see if you can send me ten dollars a month till you've paid a hundred dollars." Two five-dollar bills came to his desk regularly each month, and when the tenth pair arrived he sent the boy a cheque for a hundred dollars plus generous interest, with a note, "You've shown yourself and me you could do it. Now you can put this in the bank and make it grow."

The Mayos early decided to rest their case with the honesty and conscience of men, believing, as Dr. Will once expressed it, that "if a man can pay, he will. The variations from fundamental decency and honor are too rare to be taken into calculation." If Dr. Will's spirit pervaded the profession today the doctors would not have to mount campaigns for better public relations. Ralph Nader would not be observing that the public relations campaigns and emotive slogans have lost their old impact. Good medical or surgical practice is a self-selling product. The patient does not have to be convinced of its worth.

The Impersonal Student

Students who by nature are withdrawn rather than outgoing had better avoid medicine. If they have brains they will likely get through medical school, but their joyless, uninspired rounds will leave unhappy and alarmed patients in their wake. Such students use their modicum of medical knowledge in an entirely humourless and unsympathetic way, and they never leave their patients contented. No matter how critical a patient may be, he looks forward to the visit from his doctor and expects to feel better following it — and he should feel better, regardless of his illness.

The Student Who Is a Non-Reader

The medical student must be able to read quickly and critically and retentively. Otherwise he will find at the end of each day that he has fallen farther behind, and he will develop the deep inferiority complex that destroys many enthusiastic students and graduates. Reading as a habit of life keeps the doctor informed and confident so that he can face any consultant who comes out to see a patient with him. It permits him to visit foreign medical clinics and to learn easily from the masters. Some of my most admired mentors have been doctors in towns of from 5,000 to 50,000 who always kept active, kept keen. A visit with Dr. Howard Alexander of Tillsonburg, in his seventies, is always stimulating because of his incisive comments. It was the same with Dr. David Smith in Stratford when he was ninety. Reading is the thread in the real doctor's life that does not break while he remains active. I was dismayed one summer when I asked a medical resident where his chief was. The resident said his chief was on holidays and (implying that his chief was a bit wacky) had departed with a whole stack of books. How else could a chief hold the lead over his residents if he did not keep in touch! The study habit may not appear to be the accepted norm these days, but without it the professional roots can never go down far enough. The book-plate in our library carries this line: "To study the phenomenon of disease without books is to sail an uncharted sea". There is no substitute for self-education and the doctor has to get it by himself in his library.

The Student Whose Main Strength is Mathematics

There is great emphasis on mathematics in medicine these days, but I observe that students may understand calculus when they cannot use a tape-measure on a patient with a swollen belly or a swollen limb or emphysema.

A certain student was the state scholar of his year in mathematics. He thought he would follow in the footsteps of his father and become an engineer. However, the high-school principal, on looking over his record, observed better-than-average marks in mathematics and science and suggested that while engineering was interesting there was never any monotony about medicine and the earnings were usually better. The boy's father had wanted to be a doctor when he was a lad and, with this nudge from the boy's principal, he followed through financially. The student got his M.D. When he interned in the teaching hospital he was cold and scientific with the patients. They did not like him and he soon came to see that he did not like them. He "escaped" into one of the more lucrative and impersonal subspecialties. This man would have been much better in engineering, and many hundreds of patients would have escaped his cold, impersonal attention.

The One Who Lacks an Inquiring Mind

The student must be inquisitive; he must be restless till he has made a correct diagnosis. Dr. Samuel Levine of Harvard wrote that he worried about patients who were not "solved cases". A man had been referred to him as a heart case with unusual pain. After examining the man, Dr. Levine did not feel happy about the heart explanation. As he was driving home from his consulting room he wondered if it could be pressure on the man's spinal cord and nerve roots that was producing pain over the heart. He re-examined the man. He left the heart and explored the nervous system, had X-rays made, diagnosed a tumor pressing on the left side of the spinal cord, had it operated on successfully — and the man was cured.

Thomas Irving Hoen, the New York brain surgeon, when a resident on Dr. Wilder Penfield's service in Montreal, had to examine a man with headache and evidence of pressure on the brain but with no signs pointing to the position of the suspected tumor. He worried as he retired after a hectic day. He awoke at 3 a.m., got dressed, and went over to the ward to re-examine the man. He found a malignant mole on his back — the kind of mole he had been taught to look for whenever such a brain-tumor situation arose. Inquisitive restlessness led to the diagnosis, and it saved an unnecessary operation, because the spread to the brain of this particularly malignant tumor created a hopeless situation that was beyond the skill of any brain surgeon.

A doctor's son was wondering what he would do after high school. The father took the boy on a round of house visits one winter's night. As they were driving along the road they saw a rabbit struggling in the snow and they stopped. A quick examination revealed that the animal had been struck by a car and had sustained a bad fracture of a hind leg. Splinting was impossible, and it was obvious that the only means of saving the rabbit's life was amputation. They went to the hospital and got a surgical tray and a bottle of ether, and within half an hour they had the rabbit anaesthetized in the surgery. They proceeded to carry out an amputation through the upper part of the thigh. The operation seemed a success. The rabbit was put in a warm basket, and the two operators went to bed. The son did not have any difficulty in falling to sleep. He did not get up in the middle of the night to see how "the patient" was. After breakfast the father and son went into the recovery room and found that the rabbit had died during the night — some hours before, because its body was cold. It had not died of bleeding but of shock. Quietly, the son said, "Medicine is not for me, Dad."

It was fortunate for this high-school student that the experience came when it did. He might very easily have been counselled to try for medicine. He might have made it, because he was intelligent and had an engaging personality. But he would have been an unhappy doctor.

The Student Who Lacks Innate Kindness

No student should be considered for medicine who lacks an innate kindness in his nature, and who does not have the reassuring gaze and warm handshake that prove to the patient that his doctor is to be trusted and is anxious to help him. Those who recoil from the prospect of examining and treating the broken body when the spirit may be hostile and unreasonable, and the body (washed or unwashed) calling for personal care, should not consider medicine.

The Student Who Is Profane or Smutty

Without exception, my experience with generations of medical students has convinced me that the foul-mouthed candidate will become a less than excellent doctor. The most common outbursts of profanity are heard in the operating room. I have observed and assisted at operations of almost every kind, done by every kind of surgeon. When the surgeon swears at his assistant or at the nurses, he is putting the blame unfairly on the wrong shoulders and he is not in cool command of the situation for which he is responsible. Such a man belongs in the abattoir, not in the sacred precinct of the operating theatre, where the surgeon should exemplify the golden calm in time of crisis.

Profanity and vulgarity are common cloaks for ignorance and insecurity. The coarse-mouthed doctor can usually explain things very clearly to the patient if the patient wants to hear it that way. However, the patient is concerned and is likely afraid. His bowel, his bladder, his genitals, his heart are actually giving him cause for grave concern and there must be a building of confidence in and a flow of genuine respect for the doctor who is going to help him. This may not happen when a doctor resorts to foul or crude language in his explanation. It is better when reference to anatomy is clear but delicate. These opinions I hold because as a consultant I have listened to so many patients — themselves both coarse and refined in speech — who have assured me that such is their reaction to the doctor with the dirty mouth.

The Celebrator

Long before the days of the new psychology, it was well known that sometimes even in public school and certainly in high school, there was no difficulty in picking out students who had a deep-rooted need to celebrate little life successes in self-indulgence. Day-to-day successes are taken in stride by the balanced students. The celebrators usually kick up the dust without good cause. Most of them do it just after finishing an examination or test, but not because the results of the examination have been unusually good. In medical school, in post-graduate work, and in practice, the compulsive urge to celebrate is not only a handicap. It is a serious fault.

When this kind of doctor does an unusual operation faultlessly or makes a remarkable diagnosis, he has the compulsive urge to go out on the town. In the course of celebrating, he boasts of his exploit to those around him. His night's sleep is lost. The drying out process burns up the next day. When the average citizen celebrates, nobody suffers very much, but the doctor does not belong in the average citizen group. His patients do not always behave, and they rely on him whenever they fall sick. Post-operative complications may mar the most brilliant surgical feats and difficult medical cases saved from one catastrophe have a habit of developing even worse troubles. A doctor must keep his wits about him in case of an unexpected complication. If he is in a scotch mist he may not always give the right orders over the phone. If during the mist he has left his calls and responsibilities with someone who is pinch-hitting for him and a critical situation develops, the pinch-hitting doctor may encounter something serious in the patient that he must recognize and treat at once. The patient and the family quickly forget the miracle the first doctor performed. They are only concerned because father is bleeding *now* and the doctor who saves the patient last usually gets first credit. Next time somebody in that family connection gets sick the call goes out to the second dependable doctor and the brilliant first doctor is passed over. This makes him re-celebrate to bury his loss of self-esteem, and before he knows it he is embarked on a humiliating downhill course.

The real golfer does not celebrate because he can not risk the steady co-ordination needed for tomorrow's round. No doctor can do his work with the self-promise of celebrating his victories without getting caught out.

Miscellaneous Misfits

Applicants who exhibit unmistakable evidence of gluttony with its resulting ponderosity often possess the steady brain power that seems to make medicine come naturally to them. After many years of observing such candidates, I have found that ponderosity is rarely compatible with health to age fifty. This is explained by the intense activity of the successful doctor's life; obese doctors are usually tired doctors when they are working hard. They burn out too early.

Others who are over-reliant on tobacco or who show clear evidence of great nervous tension should hesitate about trying for medicine. The doctor who uses tobacco is a tense person, and he does not set a good example to those who would avoid bronchitis, emphysema, mouth, throat, and lung cancers, and the arterial change to which nicotine predisposes a man.

High nervous tension shows up in smokers and non-smokers. Its presence is usually apparent to the student as well as to his advisors. The H.N.T. individual does not have the equanimity that stamps the good doctor. Unfortunately, there is little he can do to correct this so as to be capable of stiff medical practice without the risk of nervous breakdown.

A 1974 survey of nervous breakdowns leading to suicide pointed out that more than 100 doctors destroy their own lives every year in North America, and that the percentage of suicides is much higher among the female doctor population than in the male sector. These high nervous tension doctors were that way as students.

With the degrading references in the media to "sexicare" by far too many doctors, the inborn tendency to licentiousness needs to be considered dispassionately. Some men are cast in the libertine mould, just as some women are nymphomaniacs by nature. The lascivious individual by nature is selfish and always indulges his self-interest first; this trait is incompatible with being a good doctor. No apology need be made for counselling such candidates to side-step medicine, because the ubiquity of temptation is not confined to the psychiatrist's couch. Members of admissions committees who advise misfits against studying medicine render an important personal service to them. Moreover, by excluding them they provide the other candidates with a better environment in which to study.

The Bright Neurotic

An advanced standing pre-medical candidate of twenty-four developed chest pain and went to a doctor. He had come up the hard way and had managed to negotiate college and the two pre-medical years. He had just been interviewed by one of the professors and had been given the green light to begin medical school.

The doctor listened to his story, examined him carefully and reassured him that all was well. Still not satisfied, he insisted on being referred to a heart specialist for an electrocardiogram. In taking the history, the cardiologist quickly learned about several things that had relevance to the chest pain. The student's parents had been separated by death when his mother suicided at thirty-six. One sister was a very tense girl. He had married a girl four years his senior. She had a serious heart condition and a complexion that was always blue. They had two children who had been delivered by Caesarian section. He was a compulsive eater and while standing only 5'6", weighed 200 pounds. He had had pain over his heart two years before and an electrocardiogram then had been reported normal. He was in debt and was dependent on small emergency hand-outs from his in-laws and on over-generous government grants based on his high marks. He usually tried to study for three hours every night "if the kids were quiet and if the wife's heart wasn't out of control".

This student *may* have merited a place in the class of 100 when 2200 applicants were besieging the dean's office. He had made 92 in math and it was this high mark that had boosted his average to the level that entitled him to compete successfully for medicine.

The following factors, considered separately and together, prompted the cardiologist to drop the dean a personal note about this candidate:

- His unstable family history.
- His indebtedness before he began the medical course.
- His compulsive eating and his obesity.
- His neuroticism and ignorance. He was having pain over his heart too frequently, and he had demanded two E.C.G.s in two years. Even at

twenty-four, as a candidate for medicine he should have known that an electrocardiogram rarely explains pain *over the heart*.

● His two little children whose care was his responsibility when his wife was ailing.

● His age. A doctor should be graduating at twenty-four, not starting medicine with nine years ahead of him before he begins to practise.

● His immature judgment and lack of self-discipline in marrying a girl four years his senior.

Yet another student came with high personal recommendations, a good appearance, and marks that satisfied the committee. During his early course in pre-medicine he smoked forty cigarettes a day. Preparing for examinations was always a strain, and he was never at ease in his work and never sure of any of his subjects. After graduation he went into anaesthesia. He had to learn about the modern types of anaesthesia, but found his foundation was insecure. He lost a patient through incompetence and his hospital privileges had to be taken away. More careful exploration of the eight years between his time of graduation and the time of this tragedy disclosed the sad evidence that he had been seriously involved with demerol and morphine and alcohol, and had been in and out of mental hospitals prior to this incident. In this man's case, it would have been a great kindness had a discerning admissions consultant sat down with him early, estimated his personality strengths and weaknesses, and counselled him to go into some other, less strenuous field than medicine.

The careful counselling of neurotic candidates by experienced committee members is sound practice, when the annual permanent loss from the doctor force in the United States exceeds 300 because of incurable demerol addiction alone.

Students with Domestic Responsibilities

The growing tendency, particularly in the last three decades with world turmoil and the rising costs of college and medical education, has been for medical students to marry earlier. Students sometimes marry to get moral support during the long medical course. Admitting the ubiquity of romance, it is still the shrewd student who keeps the emotions on ice until at least a modest store of clinical and life experience has been accumulated.

Doctor interviewers with experience know that, in a young family living in cramped quarters, it is difficult for the father to study *Gray's Anatomy* and *Immunological Theory* intensively enough to get honours standing during the hard medical school course and the four or five hospital years that follow. Some students marry for romance and financial assistance, while others marry for financial assistance and romance.

One student I know of, before beginning his first year, married a girl who worked in a bank and was earning $250.00 a month. With this and his government grant they were able to rent an apartment, get a car, pay his fees, and start living. Another student married a school teacher and followed the same line. Interviewed at the end of the second year, when students begin deciding what they will do after graduating, each told me he would have to choose a profitable specialty. The one was going into ear, nose and throat and the other into heart surgery. They believed that they were obligated to reimburse their wives for their help and their own fathers for the sacrifices made to get them through medicine!

No one can deny medical students the right to marry and begin a family while training. However a young doctor who begins his career with a heavy debt to a spouse or an especially needy parent can be deflected from his sense of service which should be at the heart of doctoring. Mounting indebtedness will unquestionably influence a doctor's choice of career.

The medical person who chooses for a spouse a patient with an obvious organic or psychic illness acts unwisely. On general grounds, such a choice carries the challenge of curing the sick one, and of course this is what doctors are supposed to do, although not within their own families. Unfortunately, in medicine, cure does not always follow the doctor's best efforts and it is often relative rather than complete. A student, intern, or doctor who knowingly chooses a mate who is obviously unhealthy courts the possibility of life-long difficulties.

The Student Doctor without Healing in His Wings

The American Medical Association survey 1972 found that many doctors with good knowledge lacked those personal assets that convince and satisfy a patient. Of all the patients interviewed in this survey, having placed themselves under the care of their doctors for some sickness from which they recovered, 37 per cent decided that, if sickness ever struck again, they would never call the same doctor again. Here are two cases involving doctors without and with the healing touch.

A marketing manager of fifty-four took sick in an American city in November 1972. He could not swallow. He was seen by a young nerve specialist who was able to make the diagnosis easily and accurately. This doctor told him that he had a progressive paralytic condition for which there was no cure. The highly intelligent manager struggled on at his work with increasing weakness for another two months. Utterly nonplussed by weakness, which was then interfering with his voice and swallowing, and urged by his business friends to seek another medical opinion, he phoned the first specialist and explained his worsening condition and the pressures that were put on him by his friends to get other advice. A new appointment was made. The second specialist took an hour to thoroughly examine him and to discuss the pattern that this disease of his might follow. He assured the patient that the diagnosis made by the first specialist was right and said he would send that doctor a complete outline of his own findings and suggestions. At this point the patient balked. He said in his thinned, weak voice: "I will die before I will ever go back to that doctor. He told me I had a hopeless disease but he did nothing for me — he offered no help for my weak voice, my difficulty with swallowing, my hand weakness, or my choking attacks." The second specialist, realizing that the patient was adamant, made other more kindly medical arrangements for his care through what he knew would be a difficult illness, requiring resourcefulness, skill, and compassion. He chose a physician who lived in the patient's neighbourhood who was not averse to making house calls, and who had the resourcefulness every doctor must have in treating progressive illness.

A young woman began to develop early symptoms of nervous disease in 1927. She was a trusted employee in a bank and her superiors were so concerned that they arranged for her to consult the then most highly regarded authority on multiple sclerosis in London, England. He was very certain in his verdict: "Your doctors back in Canada are right: you will run a painless but steady downhill course and you will be confined to a wheelchair within the next couple of years. There is no medicine you need to bother with." The young woman wrote her bank manager that she had seen the famous specialist and that he was brusque, brutal, and expensive. She came home to Canada resigned to her sad fate. She later came under the care of a younger neurologist who had been taught that patients with *most* kinds of nervous diseases do not suffer, do not become totally helpless, do not go mental, and do, with resourceful attention to their changing symptoms, often enjoy life at least in a modest way for an indefinite period. This patient is now seventy-two and she continues to work as a typist. She uses a tri-pod cane for getting about.

The doctor-specialist who can quickly and decisively attach a diagnostic label to a patient's complaints has always been regarded with awe by students and by the non-specialized doctors who wait for the great man's word. Today, the best doctors, in the eyes of students, other doctors, *and the patients,* are the ones who do not make the hopeless diagnosis but are willing to see a patient with a difficult disease at sensible intervals when the referring doctor does not feel that he can take total responsibility for the patient's care.

This kind of continued interest is greatly appreciated in the specialist who continues to be concerned about Mrs. Jones with ulcerative colitis. The anticipation of seeing the consultant every six months or every twelve months has the highest therapeutic importance for a sufferer with a slow though not fatal malady. This is harder treatment to administer than the quick appendectomy. It requires a different kind of doctor and it means more to the patient. It also means a great deal more to the patient's own doctor, who does not feel that he has just referred another interesting case to a specialist.

I believe that candidates should conscientiously consider these self-limiting character traits before heading into medicine. If a candidate has the intellect and stick-to-it-iveness to do a good cadaver dissection, assist at post-mortems and record his findings, work through hot and cold nights on all classes of society's wounded ones in the hospital emergency wards, hold the retractors or take the scalpel under the eye of good surgeons, visit the pitiful lunatics on the back wards of mental hospitals, and become proficient in the examinations of difficult patient problems on good hospital wards, without losing the respect of his teachers and fellow students, I would not hesitate in congratulating him on his graduation.

Long before a prospective medical student arrives at the gates of a university, there are opportunities for him to assess his own suitability for the field.

By the time a boy or girl is sixteen or seventeen or eighteen and is thinking of medicine, a sense of wanting to help sick people should be germinating. This desire will take root if the youth spends two summers as an orderly or a nursing assistant in a community or chronic hospital. In this environment there will be opportunities for seeing and helping patients with strokes and fractures and heart failure and chronic kidney disease and amputations and colostomies and congenital defects and the anxieties that accompany every disease. They will see doctors at work.

If the brain is going to absorb in this environment, the concern and interest will grow through reading. In developing a feeling for textbooks as they relate to patients, the student will gain opportunities that will guarantee a better start than most of today's first-year medical students have. They will have lost that fear of the unknown that seizes most medical students during their first two years in medical school.

If the prospective candidate for medicine does not like being close to real sickness, I would simply say: "You are very lucky, because the world of medicine is simply not going to be your oyster. Get on with something else!"

The candidate who has ministered to patients, waited to see medications relieve pain, observed the suffering that follows surgery, befriended relatives and seen patients die, will not feel insecure when he later meets with the committee members on admission to medical school. Instead of cringing when they ask the all-embracing stock question: "Why do you want to study medicine?" the student who has helped patients will be able to nail them! Those clean fellows in research and psychology and psychiatry who have never given an enema or held the head of a vomiting patient or watched a patient die in pain, would be caught up by this candidate.

> In 1875, the Professor of Surgery in Middlesex Hospital, London, England, was struggling with a group of students at the bed-side of a patient in a teaching ward. They seemed very slow as they parried question after question with the weakest clinical answers. After a final try, the professor, in desperation and disgust, berated the last of eight students by muttering, "even Sutton, that orderly across the ward, could answer that one". He called Sutton over to the patient's bed and posed the same question to him. The students waited. Sutton gave the correct answer. After the clinic had dispersed, the professor drew Sutton aside and, having recognized his ability, offered to pay his tuition through medical school. Sutton grasped the chance, qualified, and trained in surgery. He became the most renowned surgeon at The Middlesex. He was a pioneer and author in the surgery of cancer. Sir John Bland Sutton became one of the greatest names in British surgery.

A high school or college student will be capable of making a better judgment about settling for medicine if he has spent one or two summers among sick people and doctors. He will be working for the good of the sick for life if he later succeeds in getting into medicine.

There is a story of a student who had always wanted to be a doctor. For years his parents and grandparents had talked about John going straight through high school and college with one goal — medicine. At a time when the number of applicants numbered four times those accepted, John and his family were delighted when he was interviewed by a member of the admissions committee and the report was favourable.

But John never entered medicine. A sudden realization that he was not meant to look after the sick came when he went home one evening to change his clothes for a date. He found his mother waiting in the library for news from the family doctor who was attending his grandmother upstairs. The latter had had a sudden collapse and the ambulance was on its way. John was impatient and reprimanded his mother for just sitting when he needed clean jeans. When she explained that his grandmother was very ill, and was leaving for the hospital John found himself saying that he didn't care — he had a date and he was on his way out. Later that night his attitude got to him and he realized he was about to start something he could not finish. Lucky for him — he might have been a miserable doctor.

After a performance in the Shakespearean Festival Theatre in Stratford, Ontario, one Saturday afternoon in July 1970, a white-haired woman had a heart attack on the outside stairway. A gynecologist in the crowd moved through the commotion towards her, kneeled down, examined her, and asked one of the onlookers to call an ambulance. A few steps behind, a cardiologist glimpsed the scene and veered away. He was heard to mutter to his wife, "Let's make ourselves scarce." Which of these doctors was more fitted for the M.D. degree?

A neurologist was asked to see a woman, eighty-four, in November 1974 because of weight loss, and difficulty with chewing and swallowing. It did not take him very long to find that she had high blood pressure, a keen mind, and progressive weakness of her tongue muscles that made mastication even of finely ground filet very difficult.

The neurologist made the diagnosis of bulbar paralysis and then called the patient's daughter into his consulting room while he explained the condition to them both. But he did not hustle them out and take the next patient. He asked about their Christmas plans. He suggested to the daughter that she and her sister prepare a delicious soft meal for everybody, so their mother would not feel conspicuous. He did not say it but he knew it would likely be the mother's last Christmas.

The family doctor's note to the neurologist pleased him so much that he has permitted me to include this part of it: "I want to thank you for your letter re. Mrs. G. I have tried to convey to Amy and her sister, Mary, what the symptoms mean. It is very reassuring to the girls to know that their mother has been to see you. There is good understanding because of your clinical acumen as applied to 'the patient as a real person'. I did really ask myself, who else but you — would have taken the time and interest to spell out the degree of 'participation' for Mrs. G. over the festive season. And do you know what? The message came at just the right time and the girls are co-operating wonderfully."

Although tens of thousands of high-school and college students annually in the United States want to be doctors, fewer than 14,000 seats are available. So much damaging evidence has accumulated since 1927 when the math-science emphasis became "the way, the truth, and the light" for choosing medical students, that other approaches must in my opinion be considered. Reliance on the computer is not only wrong but immoral, because it cannot estimate integrity, and, in this very important choice, integrity is the word.

5.

Does your doctor know enough?

Your most important business is to learn disease and how to treat it.

PETER MERE LATHAM

So said Peter Mere Latham, one of the great English physicians of the 18th century to his medical students. Dr. Latham's succinct view is as sound today as it ever was, yet in today's medical schools too large a part of every student's time goes for non-medical or over-specialized subjects.

During the four years in the medical-school-and-hospital period, the student has to learn how the foundation subjects apply to medicine and obstetrics and surgery. If he is to become the real doctor he continues to enlarge his experience day by the day during the post-graduate period and throughout his professional career. During the four medical-school years the teachers carry a heavy responsibility because, as they teach and by the personal examples they set, the competence of the graduate is determined.

While there may be a plethora of good teaching in most medical schools, there are too many important topics that escape the attention that I believe they require. Large blocks of time that could be employed more effectively in the tough traditional ways are spent unprofitably. These are some of the important topics that are neglected:

- *Cancer*
- *Circulation*

● *Nervous diseases*
  (a) The most feared of the organic nervous diseases are stroke, brain tumor, meningitis, neuritis, disseminated sclerosis, and paralysis of the legs or bowel or bladder.
  (b) The most serious kinds of deviation of the mind are mental defectiveness, schizophrenia, the manic-depressive states, and the pre-senile ablations of normal thinking.
  Then there are:
  (c) The common, if less critical, neurotic illnesses
● *Diseases of the abdomen*
● *Pathology*
● *Drug reactions*
● *Diseases of the eye*
● *Diseases of the pelvis*
● *Anatomy*

Cancer

More than fifty million North Americans now living will die of cancer and a hundred million will have some kind of cancer in addition to the disease that causes death when they die. Yet in some medical schools the time spent by a student in the cancer clinic may be as little as two weeks out of four years. Very few medical students at graduation are capable of doing a thorough examination of the breast and of recognizing changes in other organs if breast cancer spreads to them. Breast cancer is the most common cancer in women. A woman with a bad heart can accept that emotionally, but if she gets a breast lump she is terrified. Woe betide the cardiologist who neglects to examine the breasts while using his stethoscope on the heart between the breasts.

I suspect that most students dislike the subject of cancer because they are not required to examine and treat enough cancer patients to develop the interest and confidence they need for its diagnosis and general management. In some medical schools cancer is an "elective", which means that the students can "elect" not to have anything to do with cancer patients at all.

For generations cancer was presented to medical students as a hopeless disease, and most students disliked it. Their dislike was perhaps rooted in the shortage of effective treatment but subconsciously it may have originated in a personal distaste for carefully examining a cancer patient. The fear of getting cancer by touch is completely unfounded. No one ever develops cancer from handling it in any form with or without gloves. The possibilities of curing cancer are steadily increasing. Much more important is the fact that every cancer patient can be helped! This is just the same as with heart patients, who are rarely cured but who can always be helped by a good doctor.

Dr. Francis Moore, Harvard's well-known professor of surgery who has contributed so much to the subject of cancer, observed in the July 5, 1973, issue of *The New England Journal of Medicine:* "The discovery of signs of cancer on routine physical examination often results in prompt and effective treatment. This points up a startling fact. Many cancers run their course from being early operable, easily removable, and highly curable, to advanced, inoperable, and incurable, in the course of less than twelve months. The cancer may have been there for years, but the change from being operable to inoperable usually takes place in less than twelve months. Therefore, the doctor's failure to check the cancer areas whenever he examines a patient may carry deadly end results. Despite the improbability of having worthwhile examinations done more often with cancer in mind, and despite the trend of the medical curriculum away from the everyday simple realities of medical practice, the message for the teaching of the physical examination is clear.

"Every patient who sees a physician deserves a complete physical examination with particular attention to the mouth and throat, the neck, the lymph node areas, the breasts, the abdomen, the female pelvis, the rectum, and the prostate. It is from this routine approach (now taught about early in the second year of medical school but soon forgotten during the third and fourth years) that much early cancer is detected."

Doctors are understandably so intent on making the diagnosis that they may forget that the patient really comes for treatment that begins after the diagnosis has been settled. This is especially true of cancer. Every kind of specimen examination (biopsy) is routine nowadays, as are gastroscopic (stomach) and bronchoscopic (bronchial tubes) and peritoneoscopic (abdomen) inspections. However, after the pathologist has reported that cancer cells are present, the relatives have been told the whole truth, and the treatment (which may be palliative rather than curative) has been given, there are usually months or years that the patient must spend under the cloud of cancer. It is the quality of treatment in this period that determines whether the patient's life will be one of hope or despair, comfort or pain, and whether the doctor is great or less than great.

A patient seen in my office in August 1973 told me that her brother, a farmer, had developed cancer of the rectum in 1971. It was removed but he had to have a colostomy. Two years later the cancer recurred, he began to lose strength and weight, and he experienced sharp pain over his liver. None of his symptoms were dramatic enough to require hospitalization. A practical nurse was obtained and the patient stayed at home.

The encouraging part of the account of this patient's terminal cancer illness, for me, was the fact that his doctor, who lived eight miles away, came to see him once a week throughout his long illness. The doctor told the nurse what diet to offer, how to manage the bowel, and what hypos to give for pain. He answered this intelligent farmer's questions and after every visit the man felt encouraged instead of despairing. In the later stages he was given intravenous fluids to control the sickness and thirst, not to prolong life unmercifully. By every standard this doctor represents the best the profession can provide. He compares favourably indeed with the "team members" in hospitals and cancer clinics who are often too busy to pause and inquire and encourage patients suffering from this disease — patients in whom they don't find enough to kindle their research interest.

Circulation

The skill of estimating the circulation in the feet is very important to the patient, because many people fear that their circulation is poor. This may be because so many have cold feet or have known relatives or friends who got gangrene of a toe or a foot that required amputation. Only very few doctors can give a firm opinion about the condition of the arteries in the legs and feet. And yet I do not know any words of reassurance that gladden the heart of a patient over forty so much as when he or she is told that "the circulation in your feet is good". Students almost never come to graduation with confidence that they can demonstrate the arterial pulses in the feet. Quite as worrisome is the condition of the leg veins, particularly in women who have borne children, and in everyone who gets phlebitis. Giving a sound opinion on the vein circulation calls for a tremendous amount of experience and reading and thinking, because the answers for correct diagnosis and treatment are not all in yet, in spite of the many advances that have been made and of the thousands of articles that have been written about phlebitis and its complications. Again, from lack of clinical exposure, most students are not competent to assess this very common malady.

More important than the arteries and the veins is the motor of the circulatory system, the heart. A student should know how to assess the enlarged heart; he must learn as much as he possibly can about heart murmurs, the circulation of the heart muscle (the coronary arteries), and inflammation of the heart covering (pericarditis). This all takes a great deal of lecture time by good teachers and it calls for as much clinical experience developed around heart patients with these diseases as the timetable will permit. Rare indeed is the student who comes to graduation feeling that he knows as much as he would like to know about these common heart conditions.

Nervous Diseases

Rarely does a medical student learn enough about nervous diseases to feel confident when examining a patient with brain or nerve trouble. Because one out of every four human beings will some day suffer from functional non-organic or psychiatric disorders, or from organic disease of the brain or the spinal cord or nerves, it is impossible to overstress the importance of knowledge of the nervous system. Is it not reasonable to expect that every graduate, whether he is going into surgery or medicine or psychiatry, will have a sound working knowledge of nervous diseases? The patient with the most common nervous disease — stroke — is always an emergency; he is terribly worried if he is conscious, and his family and his employer need to have the best answer about the future probabilities. Will he regain the power of the paralysed side? Will his speech return? Will he always be emotionally unstable? The exact diagnosis in large medical centres is almost automatically left to the nerve specialist. Yet not 1 per cent of all patients in the world who suffer strokes will ever be examined and treated by nerve specialists. It is important for every doctor to know as much as possible about strokes, because so many stroke patients can be helped.

Today the nervous system diseases are diagnosed more exactly with the use of the brain scan, X-rays of the brain arteries, filling of the brain cavities (ventricles) with air, and computerized axial tomography, "C.A.T." In spite of all these advances, the following conditions require the examination of the spinal fluid which bathes the brain and the spinal cord. This fluid is altered whenever the patient suffers from meningitis, a brain hemorrhage, or inflammation of the brain. It is obtained for examination by doing a lumbar (spinal) puncture. This can be carried out by any doctor who has learned the technique, at home or in the hospital, and it settles the diagnosis.

A 32-year-old woman, mother of four children, and an accountant, was admitted to a teaching hospital because of intense headaches and difficulty in doing the calculating that her job demanded. She was given the usual battery of routine tests along with such exotic extras as a brain scan, an echogram, head X-rays, and X-rays of the arteries of her brain. An eye specialist's opinion was obtained. At the end of seven days, during which she was under the care of final-year student clerks, interns, assistant residents, the chief medical resident, and the visiting doctor on the ward, the diagnosis remained unsettled. At this point the senior physician made ward rounds. He was surprised to find that three important possibilities — small blood vessel disease, a slow-growing tumor, and inflammation — had not yet been ruled out, because no lumbar puncture had been done. A lumbar puncture consists of the removal of a small sample of fluid through a fine needle delicately inserted in the lower part of the back. It is one of the most revealing and least expensive of examinations. Despite many excuses, it was found that the lumbar puncture had not been done in this patient for the reason that nobody on the duty staff had the skill and assurance to perform it. Instead of doing it, they did every other conceivable test. When the puncture was performed it showed normal pressure in the patient's head, and no evidence of inflammation, stroke, or tumor. The patient went home reassured and well. It was only a tension headache.

This hospital staff was not unique, nor even unusual. Today's medical students and doctors rarely master this important and constantly available technique as emphasized in *The New England Journal* editorial of January 24, 1974. So few doctors today can do this examination skilfully and painlessly that when it is suggested it often conveys to the patient a frightening sense of some sort of ultimate probing, "the final puncture", instead of something as routine as a blood test. Yet a doctor examining a patient with a stroke, a severe headache, a ruptured aneurysm, meningitis, or polyneuritis cannot form a sound opinion without it. The lumbar puncture is an essential diagnostic procedure but it requires skill and practice; done ineptly it can be painful and it can give inaccurate information.

A graduate nurse and mother, aged thirty-four, was referred to our hospital in April 1973 because of a bursting headache of two days' duration. A careful general examination and a complete neurological examination did not give the diagnosis. The headache still persisted after the blood tests and skull X-rays, and a specialist's opinion had fallen short of a diagnosis. The woman's physician then told her that a sub-arachnoid hemorrhage over the surface of the brain seemed the likeliest diagnosis and that only a careful lumbar puncture would settle the question. The patient demurred at first, but then agreed. The puncture was carried out painlessly. It showed no hemorrhage and no evidence of pressure on the brain. The woman then told the physician that she had never experienced such an awful headache before and that she was sure she had something very serious. She had resisted her husband's efforts to bring her to the hospital because she knew the examination would include a lumbar puncture. As a nurse in training, she had seen so many unskilled doctors attempt lumbar punctures and fail that long before her headache started she had decided she would die before ever having a lumbar puncture herself!

Students can master the technique of doing a lumbar puncture on dummy models, on cadavers in the autopsy room, or in the morgue. They can always be where the action is during their hospital training and become increasingly proficient in this life-determining examination by doing it under good supervision. Patients with certain brain diseases or meningitis or encephalitis may die unless the diagnosis is firmly established by this one examination. A patient who gets syphilis cannot be accurately treated unless the doctor checks the spinal fluid as well as the blood. The doctor must know if the brain has been affected, because, if it has, the treatment must be modified accordingly.

Every doctor, whether he be a specialist or a general practitioner will encounter patients *with brain tumors or with deep rooted fears that they have tumors*. Just as it makes good sense for the medical student to follow his losses to the post-mortem table, so the student who is concerned with the diagnosis of brain tumors and brain clots and brain abscesses in his patients should go to the operating room to find out what the real cause of the headache or the convulsion is — when the skull is opened.

In a third-year clinic one morning we had a man of sixty-three who had low back pain, impotence, and weak legs. The history and the examination led the students to conclude that the best explanation was a low spinal cord tumor. At the conclusion of the clinic the man was wheeled to the operating room. The neurosurgeon made the students welcome at their first experience in the neurosurgical theatre. They did not worry about lunch until they saw the tumor removed at three o'clock.

The next case of spinal cord tumor will be easier for those students to diagnose because they personally examined the man, studied his X-rays with the neurosurgeon, and watched the removal of the tumor. There is no substitute for seeing and touching and following through to the final answer in organic nervous diseases.

Diseases of the Abdomen

A sixty-year-old woman developed severe abdominal pain late one Satuday night. Alone in her apartment, she was unable to get to the telephone because of the pain, and it was not until Sunday morning that a neighbour called her physician. He examined her and told her that he was calling an ambulance at once because she had generalized peritonitis caused by a perforated ulcer.

The resident in surgery who examined the woman in the emergency room, after ordering routine blood examinations and an X-ray of the abdomen, called the senior surgeon. The senior surgeon, arriving at the hospital at 2:30 p.m., looked at the X-rays, concluded that they were negative, and decided that the trouble was an inflamed gall bladder that could be safely operated on next day. The surgeon phoned the physician and gave his opinion. The physician, who was convinced that no instrument is as perceptive as the human hand, asked that another X-ray be taken immediately with the patient positioned differently. At 2:45, the surgeon called back to say that the first X-ray (and the negative blood tests) had led him astray, that the second X-ray showed evidence of stomach perforation, and that an emergency operation would be started at 3:30 p.m. Operation did show the stomach perforation, and it was carefully closed. The post-operative course in the intensive care unit was stormy, and although everything possible was done the outlook continued to worsen. The patient died.

Every hour that passes between the first pain of an acute abdominal emergency that will require surgery and its diagnosis invites death. A third-year medical student, with a history of the onset, distribution, and severity of this patient's pain, should be able to make a correct diagnosis with one touch, one tap, and one listen over the abdomen.

Skill in examining the abdomen enables the doctor to save more lives than his examination of any body region. Abdominal catastrophies are numerous, many are killers, and many occur before the age of forty. But because no two abdomens are the same, a doctor must examine many normal and abnormal ones every week to develop and maintain the touch that tells so much. The number of doctors who never develop this touch, and who must depend on consultants' help, laboratory tests, and X-rays by the dozen is frightening. Those who do develop the touch experience some of the greatest rewards in medicine. When doctors are greeted by a congratulatory nod from the radiologist as they enter the X-ray room, or from the surgeon when they follow their patients to the operating room, or from the pathologist if the patient has succumbed and the autopsy shows that the diagnosis in life was correct, their satisfaction curve in medicine keeps rising. They are practising the art and science of medicine effectively.

Pathology

Whenever a difficult patient dies, the conscientious doctor must try to obtain the family's consent for an autopsy so that he can learn a lesson that may save another life. The better he is, the more often he experiences a sense of relief that comes when a pathologist reveals that his treatment could not have been improved on.

The morgue is often called "the palace of truth". When the pathologist does the post-mortem examination, the courageous and honest doctor will be there to see whether he has been right or wrong. Confirmation at post-mortem is the only way of accurately checking success in diagnosis and failure in treatment. Regular attendance at the autopsy table both keeps the doctor humble and increases his confidence as he practises. In requesting consent for the final examination after losing a hard battle to cure the patient, he proves to the family of the deceased and to the hospital staff that he is trustworthy.

In every hospital where I trained, the request for autopsy on the cases we lost was routine. Attendance at the autopsy and later at the weekly autopsy conference was a very important part of the learning experience at the Royal Victoria Hospital in Montreal, and at the Johns Hopkins Hospital and the City Hospital in Baltimore. At the weekly autopsy conferences all of the cases of interest were presented, with the histories and findings in life. The organs and the mircoscopic sections of the organs were discussed and the picture completed in every case.

After beginning practice in London, Ontario, with colleagues who had trained in Boston, Montreal, Edinburgh, Chicago, and the Mayo Clinic, we followed the same routine. Having been associated with the clinical and autopsy services of three London hospitals with a total bed capacity of 2,600 patients, I can look back over some thousands of these exercises.

From this experience I have formed the impression that the accuracy of diagnosis by the doctors after the takeover by so much laboratory and specialist-oriented medicine has decreased drastically. I have matched this impression with professors of pathology in Toronto, Boston, Edinburgh, and in our own centre. While it is not possible to be exact, the consensus points to a post-mortem diagnostic accuracy in most hospitals of less than 50 per cent of what it was before 1950.

There is no mystery about this startling failure to determine why patients die. The broadly based doctors who alone can develop *the complete diagnosis* in complicated cases have almost vanished with the increase of specialists. Even the good pathologists are vanishing. The current tendency is to appoint professors of pathology with narrow interests, so that their research in their small fields will be of high quality. Such pathologists, when called to give an opinion on why the patient died to the expectant physician and his interns and students who have cared for the patient and who come to the autopsy to get the answer, are inadequate. Even pathology has become ultra-specialized. If the liver is diseased, the professor (whose interest may be primarily in genetics or immunology) will send an urgent call for the liver man. If several diseases of several organs turn up, then several experts may need to be summoned. Needless to say, these specialists are never all on duty at the same time and the case is unsettled then and usually for good so far as the doctors who looked after the patient in life are concerned.

A seventy-seven-year-old man was sent to a teaching hospital because of increasing jaundice. The physician who first examined him diagnosed cancer of the pancreas. In every case of persisting jaundice a surgical opinion is requested, and for this man the chief surgeon advised an operation. Since the chief surgeon was about to leave for a meeting in San Francisco, he left his two associate surgeons with instructions to watch the patient in his absence and to operate when the time was ripe. In the next two weeks the two associate surgeons pushed hard for operation. The physician questioned the wisdom of operating despite the condition of the pancreas. In view of the patient's bad heart, bad brain, and bad kidneys, he was opposed to an operation because he did not think it would do any lasting good. The surgeons amazed him by their argument for operating. They said they did not like to see a man die of jaundice. This, in spite of the fact that jaundice leads to a painless death.

The patient himself could not be consulted because he was too drowsy and mentally disorganised. All of the laboratory tests failed to give a definite "yes" or "no" to the question of operating. The decision had to be based on what is called clinical or bedside judgment. In the end the physician's advice was followed and the patient subsequently died. All of the doctors attended the autopsy. The heart was found to be so seriously diseased that if the man had survived the operation he could never have lived usefully. There was, as predicted, a large cancer of the pancreas that would have continued to grow and cause pain. The kidneys were damaged by chronic Bright's disease, and the liver of course showed the effects of long-standing jaundice. The brain arteries were all hopelessly diseased. The man had died quietly.

An operation would only have changed the date of the funeral and caused much suffering. The importance of "masterly inactivity" in surgery was well demonstrated in the management of this elderly man.

A man of sixty-two, an accountant with a history of high blood pressure in the 210/130 range and three major attacks of coronary thrombosis, came to hospital with increasing pain in his chest and hips and thighs. X-rays of the bones had not explained the pain. A third-year clinic group of six students examined the man in his room on a Saturday morning. The student who had done the history and the physical examination reported that the patient had been a heavy smoker until his first coronary attack nine years before. He found signs that indicated enlargement of the heart, with a blood pressure of only 150/90. His examination suggested that the evidence for a tumor at the root of the right lung was pretty strong even though the X-ray had not been reported. One hour before the clinic, the patient had a convulsion followed by paralysis of the right side with total loss of understanding and speech.

Considering all the evidence the clinic group's diagnosis was: "Diastolic high blood pressure with heart enlargement. Coronary arterial blockages corresponding with the three coronary attacks. Probable cancer of the right lung with spread to the bones to explain the pains which brought him to the hospital, to both adrenal glands to explain the recent fall in blood pressure, and to the left side of the brain to account for the convulsion and paralysis and speechlessness. Terminal broncho-pneumonia."

Early Sunday morning the patient's temperature went to 104 and he died. Consent for a post mortem was obtained and at noon the clinic group assembled in the morgue to witness the autopsy.

The pathologist's diagnosis was: broncho-pneumonia; bronchogenic cancer right lung; secondary cancer in left brain, liver, adrenal glands, and bones; gross enlargement of heart; and obstructed coronary arteries wtih scars through the heart muscle.

That clinic group learned that correctly diagnosing a curable or incurable disease affords the doctor a most rewarding satisfaction. The patient had developed lung cancer from smoking cigarettes. The pattern of spread of lung cancer has to be understood by the doctor, because it may be that convulsions, or bone pain, or an unexplained fall in blood pressure makes the patient seek medical attention long before lung symptoms appear. The students also learned that very high blood pressure does not always kill and that bad coronary attacks are not necessarily fatal.

In many of today's medical schools, students can graduate without ever having followed one of their patients to autopsy. Only rarely do the students participate personally in post-mortem examinations. Yet without such participation the medical graduate will go on treating his patients to death without ever finding out why he failed.

At the time of writing, I learned that students in one of America's greatest medical schools can *elect* to attend autopsies! Particularly in cases like the two cited above, it is the doctors' job to decide not merely what they can do *with* the patient, but what it is best for them to do *for* him. The post mortem is a vital balancing experience. My teacher, Professor George Hale, always stressed the folly of inhumanely striving to prolong a life that had been spent. Too often, today's doctors do not know when to let the patient die in dignity because they have not learned pathology.

Drugs

For many years the medical schools have regarded pharmacology, the study of drugs, as a hopeless subject to even try to teach because of the multiplicity of new drugs and the complex medico-legal aspects. Yet the truth is that the most important drugs used in everyday medical and surgical practice do not exceed twenty-four. Is it too much to require that at least this many should be thoroughly understood by every graduate in medicine?

A great many hospitalized patients have drug reactions and their time in hospital may be doubled or tripled as a result. In addition, as many as one in twenty of all hospital patients are there because of reactions to drugs. The economic consequences are staggering. One-seventh of all hospital time is now devoted to the care of drug toxicity, at an estimated yearly cost of more than $3 billion in the United States alone.

There is no useful drug that does not have toxic or poisonous effects in certain patients, which is reason enough to exercise informed restraint in prescribing drugs. Digitalis is the most-used heart drug. Its improper use now produces more cases of digitalis poisoning than at any time in the history of medicine. The use of many drugs at the same time is likely to be dangerous, and is in any case contrary to common sense. How often does a patient have five sicknesses at once? Can five drugs that are almost bound to work at least in part against one another help him? We often see patients who are taking seventeen pills a day. Their chances of serious drug reactions multiply while their purses become depleted.

The drug culture that afflicts so much of American society provides another reason why doctors should be knowledgeable about drugs and their effects. The drug problem has always been present in society but it has increased critically with the enlargement of the affluent middle class. Many of the drugs are new, but they are all used for the same escape-life purpose as the daddy of them all, heroin.

I believe that medical students should know from experimentation on laboratory animals how these drugs affect the circulation, the digestion, and the brain. Their laboratory experience should be carried on simultaneously with their participation in the management of acute drug crises in patients. They should assist in the treatment of addicts in jails and large hospital emergency departments, where the experience can teach them something realistic about social consciousness.

One of our most public-spirited citizens had managed his insurance business effectively until he retired at eighty-five. When he was eighty-seven he developed a cancer that spread to all parts of his skeleton and caused so much pain that he finally had to be admitted to a general (teaching) hospital. One Sunday afternoon his family, including his daughter who was an active nurse, visited him and was so upset by his suffering that she telephoned the doctor who had referred him to the hospital. This doctor was not a staff member of this particular hospital but he went out after 10 p.m. to see his patient. He immediately noted that the patient could not be moved because of pain in his left shoulder. Apart from the pain, he was fighting for breath and sweating, and was pale. A quick examination of the chest told the doctor that along with his shoulder pain this mentally alert man had embarrassed breathing because of fluid in his chest. He got the intern on the phone, gave him his impression, and asked him if he would order some demerol to relieve the suffering. The intern vehemently refused to order demerol, "because that guy might get to like it". The doctor, having promised the family that he would do all he could for the patient's relief, then called the chief medical resident and repeated his plea to him. The resident was shocked at the suggestion of giving a standard dose of 100 mgms. of demerol, but after much arguing agreed to ordering 30 mgms. at once (this dose would have been conservative for a ten-year-old in the same distress). The 30 mgms. was given. Two hours later this man died with his pain and breathlessness. The doctor obtained the family's consent for a post-mortem examination, which showed that the skeleton was riddled with cancer and that the left shoulder pain was explained by a fracture through a part of the bone that was softened by cancer. The hard breathing was explained by the presence of one and one-half quarts of fluid compressing not only the right lung but also the left lung.

What chance will either of these post-graduate doctors have of becoming real doctors when their ignorance about treating a very sick patient is so abysmal at such a late stage in their hospital training period? The doctor who from lack of experience has no diagnostic ability, who lacks compassion, and who is ignorant as well, is a medical catastrophe.

Diseases of the Eye

The ophthalmoscope is the instrument used for examining the small one-square-inch area at the back of the eye that is the only spot in the body where it is possible to see magnified an artery, a vein, and a nerve (the nerve for sight). Many blood diseases, kidney diseases, blood pressure conditions, brain diseases (especially tumors), and diabetes show up in this part of the physical examination and nowhere else. Cataracts can be diagnosed with this instrument.

Every medical student buys an ophthalmoscope at a cost of about $120. Yet few graduates from medical school and following hospital internship possess skill and confidence in using this instrument. Not more than 10 per cent of all physicians and surgeons *ever* develop an authoritive ability in using it, although no patient with a severe headache can safety be advised unless the doctor has properly done an ophthalmoscopic examination.

> An ambassador's wife, aged sixty-nine, came to our clinic for a general examination in 1973 before leaving Canada. A year earlier she had asked to be referred to an eye specialist because she thought her glasses needed changing. In giving us her history in 1973, she said her eyes were fine. She then added that the eye specialist in 1972 had told her quickly that she was getting cataracts and to see him every six months and he would operate "when the cataracts were ripe". He had asked if she or any of her relatives were diabetic. Then he had sent her to the hospital for a special glaucoma screening test. Two weeks later he had phoned to tell her that she had a bit of glaucoma in her left eye but not to worry about it.
>
> In the following six months she developed all kinds of troublesome anxieties about cataracts, diabetes, glaucoma, and operations. In our clinic she was reassured that her vision was still 20/20 and that she would not need to think of cataract surgery for a long time if ever. She was reassured that she did not have glaucoma or diabetes. At this point she posed the question: "Wouldn't you expect that an eye man with a doctor's degree would be more exact in his diagnosis, less interested in six-monthly examinations, and less inclined to set such disturbing and alarming complexes in motion?"

There are evidently some ophthalmologists who do not spend enough time teaching medical students how to use ophthalmoscopes. There are some others with the M.D. degree who do not practise like good doctors. A much less expensive eye instrument than the ophthalmoscope is the tonometer. It is used to measure the tension in the eyeball; when the tension is increased the patient may have glaucoma. There is no reason why the well educated student-doctor cannot use the tonometer in his general examination, but only the very rare student at graduation has the competence and confidence to use this instrument.

There is nothing about the eye examination that cannot be mastered by an interested medical student who is humble enough to ask for help from members of the eye department when he is uncertain. A final-year student heading for internal medicine told me that he had a field day every day working in the eye clinic and afterwards just because he had resolved to learn as much as he could. By comparison, a very successful family physician after fifteen years in practice recently confided that he had never found anything significant with his ophthalmoscope in the thousands of patients he examined every year. With the same opportunity as the student, he had never taken advantage of it. It was disheartening to note that this man examined every patient thoroughly but he always marked the ophthalmoscopic part of his examination "normal". He had never swallowed his pride and learned how to use his ophthalmoscope.

A woman of sixty-nine was transferred from a mental hospital where she had been incarcerated for three months with a diagnosis of arteriosclerosis of the brain. Quite by chance her family doctor came to visit her, and, doubting the correctness of this diagnosis, asked that she be transferred to the community hospital where he worked in order that any possibility of organic disease of some other kind might be excluded before she was relegated to the psychiatric hospital for life. She was first examined by an ophthalmologist, who merely said that she needed her glasses changed and wrote out a prescription for the change.

The next day a physician came along with two medical students to take her history and to examine her. The heart was normal, and the blood pressure was normal. The lungs were clear. There were no findings in her abdomen. The power and reflexes were equal on both sides and mentally she did not seem to be very abnormal. They concluded their examination by using their ophthalmoscopes and they were surprised that the nerve to the right eye was wasted (atrophied) and in the left eye they found two unusual hemorrhages. On these findings they advised the family doctor to transfer her to a neurologist at one of the university hospitals. His findings were exactly the same but because of the eye findings he asked for the opinion of one of his associates in ophthalmology. This expert, on the basis of what he saw in her eyes, made a diagnosis of inflammation of the arteries in her head and suggested that the same condition probably existed in her brain. He advised the removal of a small sample of artery from her left temple for pathological examination. The diagnosis was inflammation of the artery, and the patient was placed on cortisone. Six weeks later in her home she was managing very well and behaving in a perfectly normal way.

There can be no way of telling why the first eye expert overlooked the important findings and prescribed glasses so quickly. Perhaps the students who volunteered the answer, "It was mainly because of the money," were right; he wanted to get on to the next patient.

Everyone knows that even in the largest cities there are few eye surgeons who have a name for doing cataracts especially well. Eye surgery has been subdivided in the last twenty years and we have watched the emergence of surgical experts for corneal transplants, glaucoma, retinal detachments, and cataracts. Once such specialists become secure in their engrossing surgical practices they slough off the tedious work of refractions. Shouldn't this fact give us a message? It would certainly reduce the drain on new medical graduates if the work of refracting was placed in the hands of well-trained optometrists as it is in Britain. Everyone knows that vision is never destroyed by a refraction that is not perfect. Lots of people must do a lot of shopping around among the M.D. ophthalmologists without being satisfied with the glasses made up from the doctor's own prescriptions by the most reputable optical firms. The woman in the case above certainly got no satisfaction from her new glasses prescription.

After years of reassuring healthy people whose ophthalmologists have questioned them about diabetes or frightened them about high blood pressure or arterial disease during their eye examinations, I am convinced that, before making such alarming statements, the eye men should examine the patient's urine for sugar and take the blood pressure. The eye specialist may be the only doctor a well person will see in a lifetime. It is bad medicine when a specialist creates a patient out of a person.

Diseases of the Pelvis

Cystitis, piles, impotence, ulcers, abscesses, tumors, venereal diseases, and many other disorders are associated with the pelvic region. Studies have revealed that not one doctor in five doing regular examinations of all kinds ever makes a rectal examination or a female pelvic examination. Many doctors have an unprofessional abhorrence of these examinations and prefer instead to send the patients for a $35 colon X-ray to start with. Medical students must gain the confidence that only comes with experience in this region. This is where V.D. shows up. Many other infections in these parts can be diagnosed and cured. Curable cancers here can be seen and felt early. Instead of emphasizing and re-emphasizing this part of the examination, teachers push students into expensive cancer-research projects when few of them before or after graduating ever learn how to detect a tumor that is already present and growing.

A seventy-year-old bachelor on a Caribbean cruise lost his voice, and was examined by the ship's doctor and a throat specialist in Miami. A biopsy was done. The pathologist reported cancer and the man was sent home to Toronto. There his physician had the biopsy slides examined by the hospital pathologist, who reported no cancer, only inflammation. Another throat expert was consulted, and he also found only inflammation. A physician was then asked to give the man a thorough examination. This showed normal head, neck, mouth, throat, chest, heart, blood pressure, abdomen and rectum, reflexes, spine, and joints. The prostate was abnormally small and both testicles were withered. These parts of the examination explained his bachelorhood and the exceptionally thin voice, which he had overstrained on the cruise while playing bridge and talking. No test could have made the correct diagnosis here. It required a thorough physical examination.

Not 10 per cent of graduating students I have examined have displayed any confidence or skill in examining testicles or the pelvic organs of their female patients. Perhaps they have not all had an abhorrence of the body, but they have abhorred the not unimportant sex organs of their patients. Soap and water and towels exist wherever patients need to be examined. There should be no such thing as ''Doctor Clean'' in medical practice. Lacking the routine washing habit, the student will never be at clinical ease and he will make some awful blunders which will be embarrassing to him and to his patients.

Anatomy

From the beginning of medicine, anatomy has been its foundation. One of my younger U.S.-trained neurologist colleagues told me that he built his medical education on anatomy. At his medical school the course in anatomy consumed more than 500 hours. He made more than 2,000 pages of anatomy notes. Our own professor, Paul McKibbon, who came from Johns Hopkins, always maintained that knowledge of anatomy taught the student three essentials: anatomy, the basic vocabulary of medicine, and discipline.

In the "new curriculum" of many up-front medical schools anatomy is regarded as old hat. If an occasional student later decides to do surgery, he can easily take a year off to learn anatomy. The medical people and the specialists and especially the behavioural scientists and the psychiatrists do not want it. It is always hard to stop the downhill run away from a subject that involves discipline. In one first-year class beginning anatomy in 1973, the 100 students were asked how many wished to dissect a cadaver. Out of the 100 only twenty signed up for dissection. The other eighty listened to the instructors who demonstrated the different muscles and joints and arteries and veins in the arms or legs which they had dissected for the students who evidently abhorred the flesh and would not touch it.

At a gynecology clinic, the professor asked one of the women students to describe the uterus (the womb). To his utter amazement, she replied: "I'm awfully sorry, I had 'flu' the day our anatomy instructor took up the pelvis."

Could the reader be confident in a doctor who had received only a smattering of anatomy? Would it make much difference to such a doctor if the patient's liver or heart or spine or muscle or lung was causing his pain? Not really. A doctor who has never learned anatomy the right way will always be unsure of his diagnosing and uncertain in his prescribing. He will not be capable of distinguishing with authority between a pain in the lower left chest caused by pleurisy and a pain originating in the heart, the spine, the spleen, or the stomach.

These nine areas of clinical knowledge should be familiar to every doctor but they are not. Why? One reason is the increasing proportion of curriculum time in medical schools given over to "electives" or "selectives". The principle of electives is not in itself bad. Since the beginning of modern medical education, gifted and interested students have done more than take the prescribed lectures and the laboratory and clinical work of the four-year course. For example, at Harvard, after the Medical Grand Rounds on Saturdays, the keen students looked forward to the experimental laboratory in the afternoon to work with Dr. Sydney Burwell. Similar opportunities for the eager students have always been available in every good medical school, but during the last twenty-five years medical school administrators have decided that research or elective time must be made available for every student.

This idea at first seems attractive. Many students do work in plastic surgery, or neurophysiology, or nose and throat, or chest, or skin, and they do get closer to the subject of their choice. Some students move from one specialty to another in their electives during their four years. Others stay with one specialty and end up devoting their lives to it. However, electives are threatening to destroy the entire curriculum. At present in every medical school 25 to 40 per cent of the net time is devoted to electives. These blocks of time are used as the student chooses, and they often result in the student avoiding the major clinical areas I have mentioned.

A great many students do not do anything with these large blocks of elective time. The lazy students just grow lazier. Others elect to take a major subject like medicine or surgery or obstetrics for ten weeks in a foreign school. When average students leave their home schools to take a major subject at some renowned school, they learn very little. They have not made a mark at home, and they are likely to be parasites when they go abroad. It is not a sound idea. While there is a great advantage in taking part or all of one's post-graduate education in a different teaching hospital, shuttling about for short periods as an undergraduate rarely pays the student, his home school, or the host school any substantial dividends.

Electives taken properly under individualized tutelage require the tutor to keep ahead of his bright students. To do this the tutor must spend at least one-half day a week with two students. This entails effort, sacrifice, and interest. When possible, such experience is very meaningful and profitable for students and tutor. But to provide electives under these conditions for a class of 100 students calls for teachers of uncommon power and devotion. In some schools where electives are talked about, not ten out of 100 students obtain this kind of superior individualized training. It is usually an abdication of teaching responsibility by a tired faculty. Most of the students do not get enough from their elective sessions to justify them. Unreasonable as it may seem, one medical school calendar for 1975 announced that during the first two years while its students are learning anatomy, physiology, biochemistry, pharmacology, and pathology — the very backbone of the medical course — 40 per cent of these critical two years will be elective time.

A faculty, in yielding 30 per cent of the whole four years for students to spend in any way they wish, although the students lack the background for deciding how to spend it to the greatest possible advantage, is really giving the immature student *carte blanche* for more than $50,000, which is a quarter of the cost of his medical education. The result is that some choose a lucrative specialty and stay with it, others go skiing in Switzerland, or skin-diving in the Caribbean. After watching this waste of precious time in chasing the elective myths, I think the net results need to be checked. This is taxpayer's money that is being spent. It should be invested effectively, not spent wantonly.

As recently as the November 1973 meetings of the Association of American Medical Colleges, in the general sessions and panel discussions, it became clear that in many of the best U.S. and Canadian medical schools it is possible for students to graduate with the M.D. degree without having:

- Assisted at or conducted or even seen the delivery of a baby.
- Attended and actively helped in saving a patient who was hemorrhaging critically.
- Dissected a cadaver.
- Scrubbed up with a surgeon and assisted at a major operation.
- Removed a foreign body from an eye.
- Performed or assisted at or even witnessed an autopsy.
- Dis-impacted a badly constipated patient with serious brain or heart or lung disease. The straining at stool in any of these may be harmful or lethal.

Do the doctors who dodge these essential experiences have weak stomachs? Will today's highly sophisticated patients, who still possess the eternal built-in visceral feelings about the doctorly image, become suspicious of doctors who refuse to make house or apartment calls? Will patients ask if these modern doctors lack the experience and skill that are necessary for examining and treating critically ill patients who do not happen to be in hospitals?

Dr. Edward MacMahon, one of the most illustrious teachers of pathology, wrote: "It is the responsibility of the teacher to teach what the medical student has a birthright to know and not what might be the personal whim of the instructor at the moment."

6.

Did your doctor disappear into research?

Research pays too well, it has become too respectable, and its output is too scant.

SIR GEORGE PICKERING

In one medical school there are more than 200 workers in the department of virology. In another, the department of immunology has forty on its payroll. Neither of these subjects, which utilize hundreds of doctors in their expensive laboratories, has practical importance in diagnosis and life-giving treatment of the patient populations in our hospitals and offices. Granted, they are interesting, but do they deserve so much emphasis in dollars and doctors when so many patients must go uncared for?

Clinical skill and teaching effectiveness are allowed some recognition for advancement within the faculties of medicine, but the whole balance between the science and the art has been seriously disturbed by the emphasis on research. With this change in emphasis, the practice of medicine and its teaching have become second-class ratings for advancement in the medical schools. Again, Dr. MacMahon has observed that the appraisal of success in the academic world is directly proportional to the sum total of one's research grants and one's acreage of floor space.

Modern medicine is going to have to find a better balance between research and the professional education of doctors. All of the teaching cannot be left to George when George is a white-coated pseudo-scientist.

During the past twenty-five years these members of medical faculties who do not and cannot carry full responsibility for patients have been basking too respectably in the halo-glow that surrounds university hospitals and research institutes. They have fashioned and carried this research torch of flaming straw that is burning away the very body of medicine.

After 1910, medical education moved steadily towards research and science. After the introduction of insulin, penicillin, and the other antibiotics, the blood thinners, heart surgery, and the cortisone series, the "medical science priesthood" developed not on a foundation of its own making but on the false assumption that, with more and newer discoveries, sickness and even death would eventually be no more. This high hope has not been realized and in the last three decades the mortality statistics have not decreased significantly. Dr. Charles Mayo, deeply concerned with this trend, said: "I am not opposed to research but I resist the tendency of my profession to value it above care of patients."

With all the medical miracles, the people and their governments have become convinced that research points to the longer and better life. Medicine is no longer a profession but a science. It is not the sick patient of 1975 but the sick patient of 2075 who gets prime consideration. Coronary disease we are still stuck with, but should our resources not be marshalled to protect future generations from this scourge? It seeems that a similar attitude should pertain towards cancer and stroke. We seem quite willing to write off today's patients because it is obvious that after a bad stroke nature will take its own course; physiotherapy, the low fat diet, salt restriction, and all the blood-thinners notwithstanding. Likewise the bad cancers defy our best medical efforts.

In the light of this modern if disappointing attitude of resignation but high hope, with money and space and scientific doctors, it is only human to be pushing on to fresh discovery in the three lunar orbits of heart, stroke, and cancer. Just what might be done *then* with the inevitability of geriatrics lurking in the shadows has not yet been considered. The indomitable spirits dream that by then it will be possible to modify the genes in order to bring a superior race onto the stage.

Research is a word overused by those who go back to medical schools to teach. In most of the medical and surgical departments I have visited since 1950 the workers might better have been engaged in "read-search". One man went through more than a million dollars of grant money producing coronary attacks in dogs without discovering anything fundamentally new. Sir Thomas Lewis had done this originally in 1909. In the thirties, Dr.

Charles Macklin, a world authority because of his experimental demonstration of a hitherto misunderstood lung emergency, and his wife Dr. Madge Thurlow Macklin, an authority in the field of human genetics, both worked in cramped quarters at my own medical school at the University of Western Ontario. Their combined annual budget which covered the costs of the medical students' courses in histology and embryology, as well as their research expenditures, was just over $900 a year. They were assisted by a technician (Charles Jarvis) who was offered $60 a month by the dean but who said he had a wife and he could not accept the job unless it paid $80 a month. This he got.

The kind of scientific fervor that existed in the 1930s reminds us of what John Knowles at Harvard observed: "It is impossible to pay a man to do research." The Macklins could not help being stimulating teachers who assigned every student an unusual subject to look up in the library and write notes on and hand in for their correction, and who in their spare time carried on their own investigations in search of truth. I cannot recall either one of them referring to their work as research, nor did they ever suggest that we as medical students might some day go into research. Thinking, reading, and discussing were the logical approaches to medicine they held up to us. They came to our school from Johns Hopkins and stimulated us with anecdotes about that medical school and its faculty members.

In order that the reader may comprehend the richest fruits of research, I have chosen the ten greatest discoveries of the last century. I have inserted short notes through the chapters about these discoverers and some obstacles which they had to overcome to provide the scientific heritage without which we would be as powerless as our frock-coated forebears.

1. Aseptic surgery	Joseph Lister	1875
2. "The magic bullet"	Paul Ehrlich	1909
3. Modern psychiatry	Adolf Meyer	after 1920
4. Insulin	Banting and Best	1921
5. Liver for pernicious anemia	George Minot	1927
6. The heart catheter	Werner Forssman	1929
7. The sulfa drugs	Gerhard Domagk	1932
8. Blue-baby surgery	Taussig and Blalock	after 1937
9. Penicillin	Alexander Fleming	1939
10. Cortisone	Kendall and Hench	1948

These ten great discoveries of the last century were achieved in an estimated total laboratory space of less than two acres. Those laboratories during their most exciting periods of action were used twenty-four hours a day and seven days a week by a few technicians who were badly paid, and by the discoverers, who were usually not paid at all. The combined cost of nine of the ten discoveries did not amount to one million dollars. Cortisone took thirty years and its cost was about $10 million, a mere pittance compared with the billions spent on medical research in the last twenty-five sterile years.

One evening in the spring of 1952 Marvin Pollard, a professor of medicine, and Fred Coller, the professor of surgery at Ann Arbor, were walking towards the hospital parking lot. They paused to view the new $3 million medical research building that was under construction within a five-storey shell. Dr. Coller paused and remarked to Dr. Pollard, "There aren't enough brains in the whole medical school to use that amount of research space."

In the mid-twenties, when the Ford Hospital in Detroit was consolidating its position in surgery and medicine, the directors realized the need for a research laboratory. When Henry Ford was approached about this he quickly gave it his blessing and the laboratory was constructed. Mr. Ford did not forget this venture and two years after the building was completed, during one of his hospital tours, he asked the director of the laboratory to show him around. He was anxious to view discoveries in the making. The building with all the gleaming apparatus pleased him but disappointment soon spoiled the tour of inspection for him and for the director. Henry Ford only asked one question: "What project are you working on today?" The reply did not satisfy him: "We are not doing anything just now, we are drawing plans for an addition to the laboratory." Mr. Ford went to the nearest telephone and (as related to Dr. Chester Keefer by Dr. Roy McLure, his former classmate at Johns Hopkins, who was chief surgeon at Ford Hospital) asked to speak to his plant superintendent: "I am in the research laboratory at the hospital. There's a lot of new expensive equipment here but it's not being used. It will have to be removed. We can't afford to have so much money tied up in one of our plants with no returns." Henry Ford realized that equipment alone would not father original ideas.

The research laboratory facilities in medical schools, hospitals, nursing schools, and private institutes in the U.K., on the Continent, and in the U.S.A., Canada, South America, the West Indies, and Australia now amount to more than 7,000 acres, if we use Paul Ehrlich's definition of a laboratory. All of these laboratories are in full use for only a few hours every week. They are staffed by thousands of well-paid technicians and by directors who are handsomely recompensed for directing rather than for the originality of their contributions. The mass exodus of young physicians from the bedside to work in these laboratories for the acquisition of new knowledge has greatly enlarged the science groups at the expense of the doctors who should be practising and teaching sound medicine.

In spite of all these doctors and technicians and laboratory acreages and many billions of dollars devoted to research, it is a fact that no life-lengthening or life-giving discovery comparable to any of the ten great ones has been made in the last twenty-five years. What has gone wrong? It would seem that the gold nuggets were found by the early explorers and only particles of gold dust are left for this generation to pick up, work over, and publish with any journal editor who is kind.

I have never known any M.D. who went back to medical school to do research who could have been successful in day-to-day consulting practice. There must be exceptions, but for every exception I can point to 100 who would be failures. The research type differs from the real doctor. He plays what is called the intellectual game. Ice-water flows through his veins compared with the milk of human kindness which flows in the veins of the wise, compassionate doctor. Experimenting on lower animals provides him with a secret and complete escape-hatch from the human challenge.

Dr. W. T. Councilman at Harvard noted in 1920 that out of 10,000 students coming into university only 1,000 turn out to be scholars and that, of this 1,000, at the end of four years no more than five would possess investigative or research power. True originality among medical school and medical faculty populations has not changed. Most believe that it has decreased because the resources give the false appearance of action in the acres of laboratories where technicians and gadgets abound but where new discoveries elude the over-paid searchers.

The great breakthroughs in medicine have not been made in elaborate research complexes but have come through the curiosity and the hard work of the doctor who is looking for answers. This is not an argument against adequate research facilities, and what was adequate fifty years ago would now be considered primitive. It is a plea for the research *attitude* rather than the research plant complete with electron microscopes and computers. The really important discoveries are thought about at the bedside or in the clinic and not at the side of a great machine. I want to stress the importance of the perceptive observer who, while he is increasing his knowledge about sick people, is using his eyes and his ears and his common sense, as well as his imagination.

The doctor who is going to make an original discovery that will benefit the sick — and this is all that doctors should be concerned with — will get an idea when he is surrounded by a group of patients who are not doing well under standard treatment. This idea will become an increasing challenge to him, he will worry about it, he will not sleep, and he will go to the library to see whether anyone else has done what he is thinking about or not. If he still believes he is on an original track he will consult his chief who will refer him to the head of the department in which he can do experimental work. When his seniors agree that his argument is sound, he applies for grant money and then leaves his hospital appointment or practice for a year or more to work in the laboratory to prove whether his idea is a good one or not.

A doctor without a solid foundation in post-graduate clinical training who decides that he would like "to do research" should never have gone into medicine in the first place. Research is hard and it must be undertaken with the full expectation of the demands it will make. The seriously dedicated investigators represent a type very different from those who settle for the short week with the team in the laboratory.

Some of the saddest medical histories I take are from "men who went back" and who during their lives have fallen ill and called me. As we go over their personal histories, without exception, referring to their student or intern days, they tell me proudly about having diagnosed an important condition that led to the cure of a patient. Sad, because I know that at the club, in the after-game chit-chat with friends or strangers, this one diagnosis will have been described and re-described through a whole lifetime. Tragic because it compares so ignominiously with the ten or twenty life-giving diagnoses that reward the daily work of the real doctor.

If 1,000 different research ventures are begun by 1,000 investigators in their laboratories, with equipment, grants, and technical and stenographic assistants, 1,000 reports should be expected after one or two or three years' work. If only 10 per cent or 5 per cent or 1 per cent of these ventures lead to something worth publishing, the proposition becomes less attractive. Grant moneys are obtained for *producing*, like every business investment. While the moneys, the lab space, the help, the travel, and the rare published reports do give status to the worker, they bring slight benefit to suffering humanity. When the medical researchers do not engage in research that results in a reduction in suffering, the public's return on its investment falls to zero. It falls below zero because the public has paid for the education of the doctors who left their patients, tried research, and ended up by discovering nothing.

The "cold room" was an aftermath of World War II and it was made respectably urgent by the growing interest in the Arctic. A medical research council chairman who was also a medical school dean noted a $100,000 surplus at the end of a year in the general fund. He was able to procure a modern cold room for his own school with it. In doing so he set the pace for others. A researcher casting about for a new line of action in another centre asked for a cold room and got it. Before ever using it he was moved from research to administration. Two years later whan a faculty member was asked about the cold room's productivity he replied: "We like it because it keeps our coffee cream cold." The first school to get a cold room decided to enlarge. Although nothing original had been done with it in twelve years, the Arctic was still beckoning and so three cold rooms were provided in the new building. Ten years have passed and the rooms have not been cooled down yet; one is used for general storage and the other two for animal quarters.

Dr. Lawrence S. Kubic has observed that "the results of all this science have by and large not been world-shaking discoveries, but they have raised standards of technical skill and of theoretical sophistication for all medical research". We can well ask what the gains have been, when, after so much research for the sake of research, the supply of real doctors has dried up at its source.

Perhaps we should not be critical if the multi-billion-dollar medical research laboratories are allowed to cool off on Sundays. But if these laboratories are all cold on Saturdays and Sundays, and cool from noon Friday until noon Monday, we should call for the efficiency experts. The four months of near-total inactivity during the summer vacation, while the researchers are in the mountains "thinking" about new winter projects, subtracts another big piece of action time from the projects believed to be in progress by those responsible for financing.

True research has never been done in a four-day week. Sir Alexander Fleming always questioned the importance of the research team in the making of medical discoveries.

On-spot studies I have made in the U.S., the U.K., parts of Europe, Canada, and the West Indies have shown me that all of these countries are trying as hard as their monetary and human resources will permit to keep up with or follow the leading Americans on their march into the deepening wilderness of scientific medicine.

My regular query on visits to the directors of laboratories was homely: "what's cooking here?" The replies were surprisingly uniform. "Our chief is attending a cancer meeting in Washington, or we are waiting for the new research fellows to come in, or the animals have distemper and we have had to shut down for two weeks, or our heating system went off over the weekend and we lost most of our rats and quite a few of our rabbits, or we are just moving into our new research building . . .'' The feeling that haunted me as I came away from these laboratories was that the stoves were cold. This is a pity because even the richest donors never see their very own stoves warmed up and cooking.

The number of research projects under way at a given moment is impressive. For example, in the U.S., there are more than forty research institutes devoted to cancer alone. The total cost in money is not known, but some have annual budgets of more than $10 million, and all of them, even the much smaller ones, operate with budgets of more than $500,000 a year. No one is going to start nit-picking and ask what all this achieved on behalf of cancer patients last year. But perhaps it is not unfair to ask this question about the production of the system in the last ten years. It is hardly good enough to learn, each time we ask, ''We are on the borders now of what we hope will prove to be worthwhile extensions.'' We are always on the borders. This is the position after billions of dollars have been expended on space, time, travel, animals, equipment, the multiple skills of the non-medical employees in this huge system, and the hundreds of M.D.s who left their patients to join the quest in the elusive cure for cancer.

If your doctor is doing research in cancer, diseases of the arteries, heart, or brain, infectious diseases, or metabolic disorders, you may be cheated out of what your taxes (and donations) were intended to provide — doctors of medicine and the management of disease.

Dr. Francis Shepherd at McGill stated ninety years ago: ''We must not forget that laboratories, triumphs of architecture though they be, and equipped as they are with all the modern scientific apparatus, will not themselves produce men of science, they will only give them the opportunity of developing. The discoveries of such giants as Pasteur, Lister, Koch, and others were not produced by magnificent laboratories or splendid inducements of fellowships. These men made their opportunities and forced nature, by the power of their intellects, to give up her secrets. Difficulties only stimulated them to still further efforts. Such men are not found at will, but they are born like poets only occasionally. They do most by laboratories who could do much without them, and he that chiefly owes himself unto himself is the substantial man.''

Truly original ideas of importance in medicine are most often conceived in the midst of patients who are not responding to routine treatment. There is nothing antagonistic between the practice and the science, and both approaches complement each other in the doctors who make discoveries.

Dr. Louis Hamman graduated from Johns Hopkins in 1901 and after two years of residency training in the New York Hospital was appointed through the influence of Dr. Osler to the new Phipps Tuberculosis Clinic in Baltimore. With Dr. Samuel Wolman he investigated the possibilities of tuberculin in the diagnosis and treatment of tuberculosis and published the original results in a monograph in 1912. His next original work, published in 1917, involved studies of the blood sugar curve in the human after a calculated amount of glucose had been given. This was extended to demonstrate the very different curve that was obtained with the same amount of glucose some hours after the first curve had returned to normal.

In 1925 Dr. Hamman had his office downtown but was active in teaching in the out-patient clinics and on the private wards of the Johns Hopkins Hospital. The public ward teaching at Johns Hopkins had been placed in the hands of teacher-researchers who did no private practice. These researchers (with their families) spent their summer vacations in the Berkshire mountains "thinking" about research projects for the winter. Dr. Hamman was in charge of the public wards during the summer of 1925 and there made a brilliant and original diagnosis that contributed to the understanding of coronary thrombosis.

A farmer in his fifties from Virginia was admitted because he was coughing up blood. The resident's diagnosis was phlebitis with clots (emboli) going to the lungs. Dr. Hamman sat down with the farmer and listened to his story of experiencing ten days before, chest pains so severe, that he sweated and was short of breath and had to sit down on a log. This description convinced Dr. Hamman that the man's primary trouble was not in his legs but in his heart. He made a diagnosis of coronary thrombosis (quite a new diagnosis in 1925). He stated in his consultation report that this was an unusual coronary thrombosis which affected the right wall of the heart instead of the more commonly affected left wall. He reasoned that a clot had formed on the damaged wall of the right chamber of the heart, fragmented, and passed into the lung, accounting for the coughing up of blood. The attack was too much for the patient and he died. The autopsy confirmed Dr. Hamman's diagnosis which had never been made before. When the teacher-researchers came back from the Berkshires they found that the crown signifying original thinking and clinical reasoning had been placed on the head of Louis Hamman.

The most stimulating teaching event during one long Johns Hopkins period was the clinical pathological conference. At these conferences Dr. Hamman reasoned out before SRO audiences of students and staff his conclusions on cases that had been previously examined by other doctors in the course of difficult diagnostic problems and finally diagnosed at autopsy by the brilliant pathologist Dr. Arnold Rich. These were always great occasions. When he was right (and he rarely erred) and was walking the long hall from pathology to the Marburg Building with his house officers and students, I have heard him exclaim gleefully, "Fellows, wasn't I really hot this morning!"

Dr. Hamman was the first to describe a non-fatal condition often mistaken for coronary thrombosis but which he showed to be only air bubbles around the heart, which occurred with a spontaneous, temporary, and insignificant rupture of the left lung. With Dr. Rich he described the Hamman-Rich Syndrome in which the lungs become permanently scarred after attacks of pneumonia without the usual bacterial causes. All of Dr. Hamman's original observations were made on patients. He never worked with experimental animals although he followed the work of those who did and used their findings effectively in the clinic. He loved youth — its enthusiasm, its eagerness, its boldness — and he never stifled these traits. He loved them and he modified them constructively. Louis Hamman more than anyone I ever knew showed by his life example that the meeting place of the art and the science of medicine is the patient.

Research continues to dominate the dreaming of modern medical educators. Too many medical schools are still operating in the age of improbabilities as indicated by this excerpt from one modern school's 1975 calendar. "The Faculties of Medicine and Graduate Studies have established combined M.D.-Ph.D. and M.D.-M.Sc. programs in which the research curriculum of the Graduate Program is integrated into the program leading to a medical degree. The aim of such programs is the development of future medical teacher-scientists, within an investigative discipline while contact still exists between the medical student and the basic medical scientists."

This implies that medical teacher-scientists can be produced. It takes no note of the fact that the double hurdle of the two examinations for Ph.D. and M.D., accomplished at the end of eight years of education following high school, results in academic fatigue that almost eliminates the possibility of five hard years of post-graduate hospital training, to make a total education time of 13 years. It disregards all of the evidence indicating that those who are partially grey at the temples by the time they get the M.D. rarely proceed to teaching and research. Instead they may subspecialize and enrich themselves. I have never encountered one who became a great professor or who made a truly important discovery, or who reaped the satisfaction of ministering to grateful patients. Many are inveigled into taking various executive positions. Still others, sickened by the memories of all the rats and mice they have slaughtered en route, seek nothing so much as a spot in family medicine. After one year of internship and an apprentice year with a family medicine group that pays well, they are at last able to hang out their shingles. In choosing family medicine, which the would-be scientists once viewed so disdainfully, they become turncoats from the original research band. They also dupe the government (and the people) because the cost of educating a Ph.D. is more than $75,000, which means that as family medicine doctors they have extracted a total of $325,000 for their education by the time they start in practice at the G.P. level.

In fact a large number of M.Sc.s and Ph.D.s are taken as a step towards a better chance of a place in a medical school. Deans of medicine are particularly guilty of encouraging this course of action. Candidates who fail to get into medicine at this stage are destined to spend their lives in a basic science they intended to use only as a stepping-stone. They end up disappointed, disillusioned, and angry.

None of these careers for M.D.-Ph.D./M.Sc. people is as exciting as those realized after two years of pre-medical work, four years in medical school, and five years of concentrated hospital training with an advanced degree in medicine or surgery or obstetrics (for a total of eleven years after high school). Dr. Hamman's example suggests that this type of training will produce not only better doctors but better research as well.

7.

Did your doctor subspecialize?

Specialization is both a product of and a contributor to the scientific information explosion in medicine. It subdivides both doctor and patient, increases the difficulty of attaining a clear sense of medical identity for students and young physicians, and places additional strain on the traditional doctor-patient relationship. Specialization emphasizes the science of medicine and its rational processes in the treatment of disease and contributes to depersonalization, aggravates patient anxieties, and implicitly encourages quackery. It is probably the major factor in disturbing traditional ethical and economic patterns in medicine, and it dominates medical education and research and medical practice, promotes jurisdictional disputes within the profession, and weakens organizational strength and professional power.

DR. WAYNE G. MENKE, 1970
Board of Medicine
National Academy of Science
Washington

A fifty-nine year old decorator suddenly developed a severe pain in his abdomen late one Friday night. His only previous medical history had occurred seven years before when he had been examined by a doctor for high blood pressure. The doctor prescribed pills which the man was to take for the rest of his life. In the intervening seven years this doctor's practice had increased and he had concentrated on blood pressure. The decorator still thought this doctor was 'his doctor', and so got his wife to call the doctor about the pain.

The doctor ordered the man to the hospital emergency where, in the melee of diagnostic testing, a blockage of the small bowel was found. The man landed in the care of a surgeon. At the operation cancer was found.

A short-circuit operation was done for relief of the pain and vomiting. After the temporarily successful operation (the cancer was too large to remove) the patient and his wife were told that he could go home only after the cancer specialist had had a look at him. The jovial cancer specialist told him that he had some trouble in his belly but he would give him a shot every week. When asked about the seriousness of the condition, the specialist replied that the treatment would fix him up for two years at least and with any luck at all he would be good for ten years. The "blood pressure doctor" never came to the emergency room or the semi-private room or the operating room to speak to the man who was by every definition his patient. Three weeks later the man had a chill, with pain and fever and vomiting. His wife called for "the blood pressure doctor" to whom the surgeon had sent the report of the operation, but he was on holidays and a young doctor who was taking his calls saw the man at his home, realized that he was very sick, and sent him back to the emergency. Transfer to the surgical ward was automatic but he only needed treatment for a badly infected wound and "the team" of medical students and interns looked after him during his week in hospital. Two different interns whose names he never learned gave him two mild prescriptions to take if he was ever in real trouble, one for sleep, and one for pain. The cancer man turned up and gave him another shot which made him vomit the day he was sent home.

The course at home was stormy, because he had a lot of pain and could not sleep and was vomiting. His wife, who had no nursing experience, had lost twenty pounds during the month from worry and from trying to do what she could to make him more comfortable. She finally screwed up her courage and with much difficulty got past the switchboard and secretary to speak to the surgeon who had operated, to ask about the diet she should offer his patient. Busy, brusque, and cold, the surgeon said: "He's full of cancer, give him what he wants, he can't live more than a few weeks, it won't make any difference," and hung up.

The incredulous reader may well ask if this can happen in a teaching centre in 1976. It can and it does.

Why have the medical subspecialists been accorded the god-like status that they have enjoyed during the last quarter-century? A major reason is that the rapid increase in medical knowledge has made more and more doctors and students believe that they must specialize because they will never be able to master the vast quantity of information now available.

Even if we accept that as valid, is it reasonable for the subspecialists to have proliferated in such great numbers in the last twenty-five years that at present more than 85 per cent of all U.S.-educated M.D.s are subspecialists?

Out of a total M.D. population of 350,000 serving the 220 million people in the U.S., no fewer than 285,000 of these are subspecialists of one kind or other. By comparison, in the U.K. with a population of some 55 million there are fewer than 12,000 specialists among more than 60,000 doctors.

There are, for example, as many brain surgeons in greater San Francisco as there are in Britain. America now has so many brain surgeons that the average number of brain tumors a neurosurgeon operates on per month is only six. Hardly enough to maintain the deft touch that the public traditionally believes the neurosurgeon will possess.

Dr. Paul Beeson, who moved from Yale to a five-year stint as the Nuffield Professor of Medicine at Oxford, and who is now in Seattle, in comparing the British and U.S. systems points out that the preponderance of subspecialists explains in large measure the excessive cost of American medicine.

In watching the growth of subspecialization and thinking of the future, I have become convinced that this is the primary problem to be faced, beginning now. Since 1950 the medical faculties of the U.S. have been enlarged by the addition of more than 29,000 teacher-researchers.

This indicates an increase in medical faculty specialist teachers of more than 450 per cent. In this same period the total number of medical graduates has increased by about 50 per cent. It is not only these percentages that deserve our consideration. It is the emphasis on research that this kind of teaching stresses. Subspecialization has resulted from the science explosion of the last four decades. The new tests, new techniques, and new medicines have all contributed. We now find that the public and the professionals on medical faculties are equally unsure of the difference between the subspecialists and "the researchers". They are all credited equally in academe!

There is still no sign of a rejection of the research myth. The three policy-makers on admissions at the largest medical school on the continent declared in 1974 that they will take the high-marks candidates against the whole field of applicants because they continue to place science and research and subspecialization first, with patient care and teaching second.

From an historical standpoint, the surgical treatment of the patent *ductus arteriosus* is a fascinating chapter in modern medicine because it formed the opening wedge in the surgical attack on the heart and blood vessel abnormalities that date from birth. The surgeon-in-chief at the Boston Children's Hospital, Robert Gross, achieved this great surgical feat. The year was 1938. Through a very intensely devoted career he continued to make many other surgical and basic scientific advances.

If the emphasis on subspecialization and research in medicine was and still is sensible, it is hard to understand how this outstanding pioneer, who did not regard himself as a subspecialist or scientist should have written in the preface to his textbook, *The Surgery of Infancy and Childhood,* as early as 1953: "In the American system of medical education and practice, there is little if any need of adding further encumbrance by the addition of another specialty; already we have departmentalized and isolated too many areas of our teaching and routine care of human illness."

What the Subspecialists are Doing to our Medical Schools

The worst feature of the sub-specialty business is its effect on medical education. As subspecialists on the faculties increase, good clinical teaching decreases. The number of *gifted* teachers in clinical medicine and surgery and obstetrics is less than 5 per cent of the total U.S. teaching force. In one of the most typical American teaching hospitals, the take-over by the subspecialists has been so complete that there is only one physician-internist remaining on a staff of 225. In such a renowned medical school as Case Western Reserve, with its associated teaching hospitals, it would be hard to find ten physician-internists among the more than 700 teaching faculty members.

From the day he enters medical school, the student is faced with the confusion of subspecialization. Even his foundation subjects of anatomy, physiology, biochemistry, pathology, and pharmacology are taught in departments in which the professors have gained their positions of prestige by devoting their best energies to small areas that rarely have practical relevance to the broad fields of medicine and surgery. The failure to relate these primary subjects meaningfully to the patient at this vital stage harms the student's chance to learn and threatens his future effectiveness as a real doctor. When he passes on to his clinical subjects he again finds that the history-taking and physical examinations are not taught by broadly based physicians but by subspecialists with single-organ interests.

A medical faculty has the fullest responsibility for teaching medical students and interns the important things they must know. In no other four-year period in their medical careers will the students ever need to learn so much so well. The system cannot afford so many subspecialists who refuse to teach students basic techniques and who are too inclined to devote their best energies to wooing and training more subspecialists in their own images.

Too often the teaching subspecialist merely shows the students what *he* can do; he fails to teach them how they can do it. Students are not taught nearly as much as they could be taught about the use of the subspecialists' instruments and techniques, and they rarely develop the confidence to use them in their own practices. The subspecialists clutch their expertise tenaciously and by their attitude imply that every case will have to be referred.

Only when subspecialists begin to teach the students and interns much more about the uses of their special instruments and examination techniques will every graduate have greater competence and interest and confidence in making use of today's standard techniques. This will take business away from the subspecialists, but all of the graduates will be better and more helpful to the public at large. The subspecialists will then be worthy of their status as teachers in medical schools and will be more deserving of the M.D. As most subspecialists now approach medical school, train in their hospital periods, practise, and confer with their financial advisors, many are coming to believe that they should be M.B.s (bachelors of medicine), with subspecialist diplomas, to differentiate them from real doctors with their M.D.s.

In some teaching hospital wards, the fat patients are grouped together "for purposes of intensive study and research", the patients with nervous diseases in another ward, and the stomach-bowel cases in still another. This subspecialistic organization and disease segregation destroys the sensible approach to understanding the patient as a complicated body-mind machine. It renders sound teaching impossible, and the care of patients within this system steadily worsens. This is the kind of narrow teaching today's student is doomed to get. Far from apologizing for the situation, modern medical faculties appear satisfied and even smug about it. The old saw that a teacher might as well be dead unless he is researching is long since *passé*.

The dean of the University of Michigan medical school stated in 1969 that he did not expect five out of more than 200 graduates to become and remain physician-internists. The newest U.S. medical school, on Long Island, boasts that by the beginning of the third year its students will have started their subspecialty training "and will not need to be bogged down by so much general medical and surgical knowledge". In other words, they will get into their subspecialty work without a solid clinical foundation.

Today's medical students are forced into irreversible inferiority complexes by their subspecialist teachers. The unlucky ones who cannot make up their minds quickly and "catch on" in some specialty line must in sheer desperation reach for the vague promises offered by the newest of all subspecialties — family medicine.

Confronted with the long list of subspecialties, the medical student finds himself in a quandary. He feels he must choose a subspecialty as soon as possible, but he has very little experience on which he can base a logical choice. If he consults the family doctor back home, he is likely to be warned: "Don't make the mistake I made — get into a subspecialty fast."

Most of the students who go to medical school do not want to subspecialize. They expect to practise medicine or obstetrics or surgery. But nearly all of their teachers are subspecialists. By following a favourite teacher on his hospital rounds, a student may slip almost without realizing it into a subspecialty. For those who are slow to respond, the chiefs of subspecialty departments have seductive lures in the form of symbols of affluence and the lustre of prestige.

Dr. George Engel of the University of Rochester comments on this early specializing track system: "This may have merit for a few exceptional students, but for most the dangers are narrow parochialism for those who are fortunate enough to make the right choice, and lasting career dissatisfaction for those who make the wrong choice. Unhappy or premature career choices can have profoundly unfortunate consequences for the patients, not to mention the doctor himself."

A top graduate, by the time he reached his third year of residency training, wrote this plaintive appeal: "I want to practise and teach general medicine. I enjoy it — but I do not relish the prospect of settling in a small specialty corner with the understanding that I must apply for grant money, do some research for which I am not fitted, and then publish my findings in the hope of getting a hospital appointment and a place on the faculty if the political climate is favourable for me at the end of another two or three years. I went into medicine because I wanted to be a good doctor. It seems to me that, with more and more intense hospital experience in caring for people, and teaching junior interns and medical students, I shall be a better doctor and teacher. Is there no other way than this subspecialist research way?"

A quite typical example of the new world of medical education is that of the young doctor who has completed five years of post-graduate training and returned to his university medical school to teach and practise his specialty, "diseases of the blood". In the telephone directory he might be listed as Randall, Dr. K. L., Haematology, Royal Alexandra Hospital. This listing protects him from unwanted telephone calls from sick people because his number is only given by the hospital switchboard to callers with the right password. Dr. Randall can never be annoyed by requests to provide succour for a patient with a heart attack or acute intestinal obstruction, or pneumonia. But the same Dr. Randall will never enjoy the deep satisfaction of making life-giving decisions in diagnosis and treatment of society's wounded ones.

In the teaching hospital, the grand rounds is the big event of the week. It is held in the amphitheatre. At a recent grand round attended by more than a hundred students and doctors, a blood specialist was asked for his opinion on a case with pernicious anemia. This was the blood man's chance to demonstrate his clinical virtuosity because such a case will not be presented for general discussion more than once in four years. After the questions from students and house doctors, the chairman turned expectantly to the blood man for a summing up. His reply was a subspecialists' classic: "Well, I only saw the queer blood report and the bone marrow from this patient." He had not been sufficiently interested to go and see what the patient with "the queer blood" looked like in his bed!

The public has become highly specialist-conscious, leading it to insist on subspecialist care. Most of the patients who want to be treated by subspecialists would actually be much better treated by better-educated doctors. Possibly one sick person in fifty requires the attention of a subspecialist and that one in fifty will often need a general physician if he is to be well treated.

The public demand for specialists has kept the specialists very busy, and has made them very rich. Two specialists I know, one a heart specialist, the other an eye specialist, decided to cut down their patient loads, to give themselves more leisure. They doubled their fees. To their astonishment they were overwhelmed with work because the patients concluded that if they were twice as expensive they must be twice as good.

Where will the current rush to subspecialization end? A leader in the eye field announced in 1971 that his specialty in the U.S. now requires 300 medical graduates annually. This equals the output of three schools of medicine!

Sometimes the services of the specialist are of great value. Often they are of little or none. Sometimes they are positively harmful.

A forty-seven-year-old man admitted to a large midwestern university hospital was examined by no fewer than twenty-four specialists without getting any nearer to a diagnosis. One night he took a turn for the worse. Not one of the twenty-four experts was disturbed in his sleep. Their individual interests in the patient were too fractional to make any one of them appropriate to call. A surgeon who was summoned in the middle of the night examined the man's abdomen and pronounced it "not surgical". In desperation, this surgeon suggested that a general physician be requested to see the gravely ill man. Entering the sick room where so many specialists and technicians had preceded him during daylight, the physician examined the patient, checked the reflexes, ears, and eyes, asked for a brain X-ray, and made the diagnosis of brain abscess. The next day, following operation, the patient was able to recognize his wife, and he soon made a complete recovery.

That diagnosis was only part of the physician-internist's eighty-hour week. Had the patient died (and he nearly did) not one of the specialists, forty-hour-weekers to a man, would have had the time or interest to attend the post mortem, and so their future patients with brain abscesses would be in danger of the death this man escaped.

Wise doctors with wide experience reviewing the whole field of medicine in the light of the trend to subspecialization have reached the sobering conclusion that the physician-internist can handle more than four out of five of all the medical diseases over the lifetime of the patient. Is today's medicine unbalanced when more than 85 per cent of all the doctors are subspecialists of one kind or another?

The difference between the physician-internist and the subspecialist calls for careful examination and definition. On the one hand, the subspecialist is looking at the disease while the internist looks at the patient with the disease. The subspecialist is usually immune to the patient's plea for help except in his five-day appointment-packed schedule, while the physician-internist is available whenever the patient gets sick.

A discouraging feature of subspecialization is that most of the unusual diagnoses prove to be hopeless ones. This is disheartening for patients. It is also disheartening for the subspecialists themselves who may not encounter more than three or four patients in a week or a month whom they can treat and make well.

In today's climate where the subspecialists are kings, the G.P.s in their offices and the doctors in the hospital out-patient departments are expected to look hard for the queerest cases, which they send in like bread to be set before the masters on their research tables. The separation of doctor from patient does occur in this situation because the subspecialist often "kidnaps for scientific study" the referred patients for months or years. The doctor who originally referred the patient sometimes gets a letter written weeks or months later explaining all of the examination results — a letter that might as well have been written in Greek so far as the G.P. or his patient are concerned.

I am convinced that dividing patients into parts to indulge the interests of the subspecialists is neither good medicine nor good science. Here are some case examples of diseases I have encountered in modern teaching centres.

> *Bright's disease:* A boy of seven suffering swelling of his face and body was referred to a kidney subspecialist and was studied and treated in hospital. He became still more dropsical and thirsty. His worried parents asked to speak to the subspecialist. When this doctor came down from his laboratory and met them on the ward he told them straightforwardly that their son had Membranous Glomerulitis and was pretty sick. He did not say *how sick*. The disturbed parents called their general physician to interpret the message. He told them that their lad had seriously diseased kidneys — Bright's disease — and that it was very critical. The boy died that night.

The very specialized lab-supported doctors do indeed make the latest and most fashionable diagnoses. But they may not satisfy the patient, or in this case the parents, because they seem incapable of assessing the diagnosis broadly and giving the prognosis or the answer to the burning question, "Will this illness be fatal?" or "How soon will our son die?"

> *Heart:* A forty-eight-year-old office manager was referred by his insurance company to a heart specialist for an opinion. After the examination the two men chatted for a few minutes about

generalities, confidence developed, and as he was leaving, the man, who did not have a doctor, obtained the assurance that this heart man would be willing and pleased to give him a general check-up annually.

When, four years later this man became sick suddenly, he discovered that his heart man was "pure heart" and that he never saw a patient outside his hospital office. The patient got in touch with a physician-internist who came and saw him where he was and examined him. After the examination, which included the circulation in his eyes and the arteries in his feet and the nervous system and the rectum, the patient was puzzled and asked the doctor what he would be looking for in the brain and the arteries, in the feet and the eyes. The physician told him that these were routine precautionary tests for a man of his age.

The man then described his annual check-ups by the heart doctor: "A technician took my electrocardiogram, got a sample of urine, and then some blood for a cholesterol. When these laboratory results were back I was ushered into the examining room where the specialist quickly thumped my chest, listened to my heart, and looked at it under the fluoroscope. In ten minutes, it was all over; he bade me good-bye on the happy note that the cholesterol was pretty good, the electrocardiogram showed no T-wave sagging that would alarm him, the fluoroscope showed no enlargement, and he was sure I would be O.K. until next year."

Which of these two doctors was better for the manager's heart, and which was better for the manager himself?

The "specialist attitude" may show up in medical students or interns.

Coronary thrombosis: An advertising executive, aged sixty-nine, developed a crushing chest pain as he came home from his office after a particularly heavy day. The pain did not go away and his wife called his physician to see him at 6 p.m. At examination the man was pale and cold and breathing heavily and still complaining of pain. Two hypodermic injections of morphine only gave him partial relief. Because he was in shock and because the outlook was questionable a heart consultant was called. He arrived at 6:30. After considering all of the evidence the two doctors agreed that the patient's best chance of survival would be with special nursing in his own home instead of transfer by ambulance across the city to a special coronary care unit in the hospital. They had completed their deliberation and had explained the picture to the wife and were about to leave. At this point the patient's grandson, a junior intern who was working in his hospital's coronary care unit, arrived. This young intern surveyed the situation, looked at the doctors whom he did not know, and very quickly decided that he wanted his grandfather placed under the care of the heart specialist in his hospital at once, in order that he might have all the advantages of modern coronary treatment. In this situation the two physicians were quite helpless and in the face of such insistence on modern treatment they could only wait to see their patient safely loaded into the ambulance. The patient's breathing was supported with oxygen during the ambulance journey. On admission to the coronary unit he was pronounced dead.

Spine fracture: The physician who had been through this experience with the heart patient had to see a fifty-seven-year-old public health nurse two hours later. Her complaint was excruciating back pain that made it impossible for her to move in bed. She told him that when she came home from work and closed the overhead garage door she felt something snap in her back and she had been in agony from that moment.

The doctor, after listening to the story, examined the patient briefly and then came into the living-room to speak to her son. The doctor told him that he believed his mother had sustained a fracture of one of her vertebrae when she pulled the garage door down. The son surprised him by saying that he felt quite satisfied that this was the correct explanation for his mother's pain. The doctor asked how he was able to speak with such assurance. To his great delight, after his earlier experience with the junior intern who was so convinced that the hospital specialists were the only saviours of heart attack victims, he learned that this chap was in the pre-medical course and during his vacations he helped as an orderly in the X-ray department. He replied; "I have seen so many patients come in with this kind of pain whose back X-rays showed fractures that I did not see how it could be anything else!"

These two experiences occurred within hours of each other. They illustrate the difference between experience derived from actually handling patients and experience derived from a dependency on modern machinery — fashionable but not foolproof as we hoped it would be. The intern fresh from the coronary unit who had never ridden in an ambulance with patients connected to monitoring apparatus and oxygen was not as dependable beside this critical heart case as the pre-medical student who had lifted dozens of patients with broken backs from stretcher to X-ray table.

The Specialist Attitude

Uremic poisoning: high blood pressure: The frequent coldness of the specialist's attitude is illustrated by a kidney subspecialist who was phoned by a G.P. from a small town 100 miles distant who had a patient, *a doctor*, with uremic poisoning. The G.P. wondered if the artificial kidney would be helpful for his doctor-patient, who had an enlarged heart, a blood pressure of 240/140 and who was so short of breath that he needed a quarter grain hypodermic of morphine every four hours.

The kidney specialist did not offer to drive the 100 miles to see the critical patient and judge whether the possibility of using the kidney machine warranted the high risk of the ambulance trip. He simply told the family physician, "Send him along and we shall look after him here." The "we" turned out to mean an examination by a junior intern and a foreign medical graduate, the result of whose examinations were given to the kidney specialist when he came down to the ward. The blood chemistry results, duly recorded on the chart, simply confirmed the state of uremia reported in the small-town hospital. The subspecialist did not think much could be done for the patient, but discontinued the morphine, which he thought "could not be doing him much good". This single order was promptly written. The patient had a very bad night, and by the second day looked much worse. Then his wife, who had stayed at his bedside in the absence of a special nurse, was told that the artificial kidney would not be used. The wife begged the subspecialist to let her doctor-husband return to his own hospital. The subspecialist grudgingly consented, but stubbornly refused to allow him any morphine for the journey, which was consequently a nightmare. Back at last in his own hospital where the superintendent of nurses gave up her weekend break to stay with him, the patient next morning died comfortably in his familiar surroundings.

If this subspecialist had known more general medicine he would have concluded from the patient's history, including mention of heavy doses of morphine, that the long ambulance trip was not only unnecessary but likely to be fatal.

In *Annals of Medicine* for February 1973, it was reported that not one patient out of three with coronary thrombosis (where the relief of the pain is the most important first step in treatment) ever received enough demerol or morphine to give that essential lifesaving relief. In this uremic patient, the heart work was greatly increased. Only morphine could give relief from the doctor's distressing fight for breath and relief from pain.

Perhaps the kidney man had never been properly taught about the importance of morphine. When he had stated that the morphine could not be doing much good, he should have been facing up to the fact that his kidney apparatus could not do this doctor-patient *any* good.

Such an attitude in a man who has taken the Hippocratic Oath seems monstrous. Unless we find a way to make the subspecialist more broadly based and more considerate, the patients will be safer if the subspecialist is relegated to the status of technical expert working under the guidance and responsibility of the broadly based physician. Too frequently the present system grants a subspecialist total control of the patient when he is only interested in part of him. Not only is the subspecialist not a dependable doctor outside his specialty, but he may not even be a competent doctor inside it. In this case the kidney subspecialist was not interested in kidney cases that were complicated by high blood pressure!

Contrast the last history with this one:

Strangulated hernia: complications: A seventy-six-year-old man was admitted to the emergency room of a university hospital one Sunday morning because of pain and vomiting. Examination disclosed a strangulated hernia and immediate operation was strongly indicated. But five side conditions quickly became obvious. The patient was very much overweight and he had bronchitis. He had a severe and uncontrolled diabetes that would need correction before surgery. His heart was enlarged, rapid and irregular, and he had very high blood pressure. His mental functions had not been fully normal for six months.

Might an operation on his hernia send him into an acute irrational state? Would he have a stroke? Would his heart give out? Would he develop diabetic complications? Would he be prone to post-operative pneumonia? Ideally, the man required the pooled opinions of five subspecialists and a general physician to decide when operation would be safe.

All the subspecialists were "off service" that Sunday morning. There was not one in the hospital competent to make a "parts evaluation" on the man's brain or heart or diabetes or lung or high blood pressure. Acting alone, on his own judgment, the physician who referred the patient to the surgeon ordered insulin for the diabetes, digitalis for the heart, reserpine for the hypertension, and assumed the risk of the chest condition plus the fact that the patient was a bit irrational. In four hours he had him in safe condition for the operation — which went off very successfully.

How Many Heart Specialists Do We Need?

After 1935, specialization in cardiology began to increase rapidly, and it was not long before the coronary diagnosis could not be settled until the heart man had given his opinion. In 1950, the first World Heart Congress held in Paris was attended by 1,200 cardiologists. It was a memorable occasion. Dr. Helen Taussig held centre stage with her report of 900 cases of blue-baby surgery. Her paper drew a standing ovation as three pink-cheeked little French girls who had been blue babies six years earlier and had had the Taussig-Blalock operation in Baltimore stepped before the spotlight.

Twenty years later, the Fifth World Heart Congress was held in London. By this time attendance had increased to more than 4,000 heart specialists. But this meeting provided only a general assessment of past victories rather than any new discoveries. The surgeons had devised many artificial valves to replace valves destroyed by rheumatic fever, acute infections, or degenerative disease. Many arterial reconstructions were described. The ravages of acute rheumatic fever had been nullified with penicillin and cortisone. Malignant forms of high blood pressure were responding to drug treatment and in some cases to surgery. Some of the acute infections of heart valves were manageable. The shock phase of the coronary attacks was better understood, and the importance of blood thinners could now be placed in a more sensible perspective.

A World Heart Congress is held every four years. In between there is a Hemisphere Heart Congress every two years and there are national and state meetings every year. But in addition there are two dozen or more special meetings every year, held in every tourist-favoured corner of the world. This was the schedule of heart meetings for 1972:

January 18	Geneva
February 21-5	Auckland, New Zealand
March 1-3	Skove, Sweden
March 1-5	Chicago, Illinois
March 13-8	Paris
March 17-8	Florence, Italy
March 23-4	Amsterdam
April 6-9	Bad Nauheim, Germany
April 23-9	San Francisco
May 9	Geneva

May 12-3	Brussels
May 15-7	Paris
May 17-9	Washington
May 20-3	Viareggion, Italy
June 8-9	Lausanne, Switzerland
July 2-6	Barcelona, Spain
July 9-15	Curitiba, Brazil
July 1-13	Bratislava, Czechoslovakia
July 24-30	Rio de Janeiro
August 27-September 1	Sydney, Australia
September 18-22	Copenhagen
September 21-3	Milan, Italy
September 23-30	Madrid
September 24-October 6	Singapore
October 8-13	Singapore

With such a list it is fairly evident that the heart man does not choose his meetings all by himself. His wife has a voice in deciding between Geneva and Rio. Perhaps the tourist-oriented decision is not unreasonable in the light of the massive duplication of information distributed at these meetings. There might be enough important original work going on to justify two such meetings a year — but twenty-four?

The list serves mainly to illustrate how lucrative the heart business is and the light-hearted absenteeism of cardiologists from their patients. One cardiology society in North America has been sufficiently conscience-stricken to reduce the length of its annual sessions from three to two days.

In the 1970s the vast army of heart specialists built up over the past generation has become superfluous. Few heart secrets are hidden from doctors who read. Most heart problems can be solved with sensible use by informed doctors of X-rays, electrocardiograms, and blood studies. Only the occasional patient needs referral to the heart clinic for special investigation and treatment. In view of the easy availability of information about new heart advances, should we be taking a thousand fledgling heart specialists into the North American training system every year? The need for so many heart specialists should be decreasing not increasing. *The effective life span* for the average heart-attack patient statistically is not any better if he is in the hands of a subspecialist than if he is in the care of a broadly based physician. 12,000 attended the American Heart Association meetings in 1976.

Leg pains in a young wife: In 1970 a heart specialist saw a woman patient of thirty-two, referred to him by her G.P. with a complaint of pains in the calves and thighs thought to be due to a circulatory problem. The heart specialist checked her heart, her blood pressure, and the circulation in her legs, sent a blood sample for the fat fractions to a laboratory in California, and finally forwarded his report, concluding that the pains were "nervous", adding that if they worsened he would be glad to see the patient again.

Three months later the woman returned from a vacation with her husband with the pains worsened. The family doctor checked with the heart man and found that his earliest appointment would be in three more months. The doctor then referred his patient to a physician.

The physician examined the woman and found her general condition excellent. She was muscular, with brisk reflexes, and the circulation in the leg arteries and veins was normal. He dismissed the idea of a circulatory disorder, and asked himself the question, how could a nervous pain be worse after a two-week vacation?

The history, rather than the examination, gave the answer. The woman's husband was large, heavy, and impotent. In bed the patient had long sought to arouse his libidinous interest by taking a scissors grip around his sizeable waist. During the vacation she redoubled her efforts, with consequent muscular pain (perhaps accentuated by discouragement). The patient, who was tired and worried but not nervous, was greatly relieved by the understandable explanation.

It was another case of the cardiologist looking at a patient suffering from what he thought was "his disease interest" and the physician looking at a whole patient with a disturbing complaint.

We have been witnessing the current rush of heart subspecialists, and their counterparts the heart surgeons, to advise their coronary patients to have the popular by-pass operation for narrow coronary arteries. This operation continues to be done at the rate of one every eighty minutes in some of the large clinics, despite the fact that medical history and current experimental evidence both point to its risks and frequent uncertain or unsatisfactory results.

If this $10,000 operation did increase the heart's performance power, the ideal surgical candidate should be the labourer who desperately needs every erg of heart energy in order to hold his job. Unfortunately, the coronary by-pass operation rarely returns a labourer to hard work. The executives whose angina (heart pain) is due to high nervous tension want the operation to lessen discomfort and to allow another nine holes of golf.

Can the taxpayer condone this kind of extravagant surgery in our economically disastrous seventies? Can the training programs possibly turn out enough heart surgeons to do all of these long, tedious operations when the results, after more than 30,000 cases, are still in doubt?

The heart specialist who will not make house visits is too far removed from real life in his office suite surrounded by busy technical assistants who run the machines and secretaries who handle his business.

> *Premature exercise:* A regional sales manager of fifty-four had a chest pain that would not go away and he was placed in the coronary care unit of a modern hospital in January 1975. Every test confirmed that he had had a serious coronary attack. Although the pain was still nagging five days later, the cardiologist transferred him to the general medical ward. This heart doctor believed in "early and progressive activity for the coronary patient" and he had the man up in a chair, going to the bathroom, and stretching his legs in the corridor within a week of leaving the coronary unit. During the same week this critical heart victim was dispatched by wheel chair for two prolonged X-ray and radio-isotope examinations. Only two weeks after the attack, he was discharged to his home and told to carry on with increasing exercise, to have his meals in the dining-room from the first week, and then to expand to outside activities around his garden and to "walking the block". As for medicine, he was to take digitalis, potassium pills, two fluid pills a day, four other pills to keep the heart regular, and tranquillizers. Moreover, he was to adhere to a low salt diet, which, with all the medication, was unnecessary.
>
> On his first night at home and every night thereafter he sweated so profusely that he had to shower and change his pyjamas. Nonetheless, he carried on with the regimen ordered by the heart specialist, until a week later when his G.P. was called because he had a shaking chill. (The G.P., with whom the cardiologist should have discussed the case, learned only later, by mail, about the treatment the patient had been told to follow.) He found that the man had a temperature of 103 degrees and that his heart was racing at 120 beats per minute — pneumonia had set in. He called the ambulance and had this very sick man transported to the hospital and placed under the care of a physician.
>
> X-rays to check for pneumonia were taken on this second admission to hospital. These new X-rays turned out to be identical with those taken the day before the man went home. Both showed the heart greatly enlarged and evidence of pneumonia in the left lung. The cardiologist had not consulted with the radiologist about the original

X-rays. He had discharged a man with an enlarged heart and pneumonia and instructed him to adhere rigidly to a vigorous exercise program.

If the cardiologist had conferred with the G.P. in this sick man's home he would have understood the implications of his program of treatment. He would have seen and scaled the long circular staircase he had inadvertantly ordered the patient to descend and ascend at every meal. He could have stepped into the modern kitchen and witnessed the agonies that the unhappy wife was suffering as she tried to maintain the difficult and pointless salt-free diet, which even with her best efforts made her husband shout, "Sawdust!" Of even greater significance, the cardiologist would have seen the $200,000 home with its luxurious furnishings. With interest rates at 12.5 per cent in 1975, and with two boys in private school, this heart victim *had* to recover. He should not have been subjected to the risk that attends any exercise program after such a serious attack.

This cardiologist was very excellent in the milieu of his modern equipment. But how secure were his patients in their own homes, with or without the attendance of a good G.P., when far removed from the specialist's personal care?

The problem of subspecializing was stated very clearly in 1975 in a medical journal: "How can we train enough doctors so well that they will be capable of caring for most of the really sick people most of the time instead of the thousands of subspecialists with their respective skills which are very worthwhile for some of the patients who get to them some of the time?"

Discovery: insulin: Banting and Best
Hundreds of scientists since the discovery of insulin in 1921 have tried in their little ways to minimize its greatness. They have spoken and written about its simplicity and how it could not possibly have remained a locked secret of nature much longer. And yet the student of history wonders.

In the very month of July 1921 when Dr. Frederick Banting and Charles Best discovered insulin, the leading scientific journal and the most authentic textbook had stated that all the evidence pointed away from a hormone like insulin, but that *if* such a hormone existed, it could never be extracted, and that even if it could be extracted the quantity would be so small that it could never be useful in the treatment of diabetes.

Harris Shumacker, in a very thoughtful paper on "Research, Authority, and Publication'', pointed out the deadening influence on the research efforts by young men when pontifical statements by one or several authorities ridicule the ideas of youth.

In Dr. Banting's case, the Canadian authority denying the concept of insulin was Professor J. J. R. MacLeod, in whose laboratory the experiments were soon to be carried out. Professor MacLeod had belittled Dr. Banting's idea in two separate interviews, and had sent him back from Toronto to our medical school in London where he was an instructor in physiology, a very dejected and disheartened man. It was only Banting's conviction that made him beard MacLeod in his Toronto den a third time before giving up. He had found out from some old friends in Toronto that MacLeod was going to spend the summer in Scotland. The lab would be empty. Banting therefore went to MacLeod with three requests:

1. The use of the lab for the two months of MacLeod's absence.
2. Ten dogs.
3. The help of a student in biochemistry who could test for sugar in the urine and in the blood.

MacLeod granted all three requests. In his biochemistry class the next morning he announced the summer opportunity for anyone who wanted to work with Banting on diabetes in dogs. Charles Best volunteered.

Personal experiences had given Banting and Best their determination to find a weapon against diabetes. A high-school girl friend of Fred Banting had died in a diabetic coma, while Charles Best had lost a beloved aunt in Boston with diabetes.

Dr. Banting was the first specialist in orthopedic surgery when he joined the staff of the University of Western Ontario Medical School in 1920. His early training had been in general surgery, and he never relinquished the general approach. Dr. Best has told me that, had it not been for Dr. Banting's skill as an abdominal surgeon, they could not have made the discovery of insulin. Many other experimenters in physiological laboratories in Germany, France, Britain, and the United States had tried to work with the pancreas and to prove that it had some influence on sugar metabolism. But their surgical finesse was not equal to dealing with the delicate pancreas, and their efforts had repeatedly led to fatal or inconclusive results. Dr. Banting was a meticulous surgeon with determination and imagination. Fortunate for the world that he was not satisfied with being a narrow specialist in orthopedics!

Strangulation of the intestine: Two cases in 1973, one in an American and one in a Canadian hospital, demonstrate the work of subspecialists with the support of the most modern operating rooms and intensive care units.

In each of these cases a sharp third-year student should have had no difficulty making the correct diagnosis and in calling quickly for the appropriate help.

Each case was a young patient, one in his thirty-third year, the other in her twenty-seventh year. Each developed abdominal pain and was attended by a doctor. Each was treated as a serious abdominal conditon. In one case the diagnosis was thought to be acute pancreatitis, and in the other, acute inflammation of the gall bladder.

In each case the diagnosis was incorrect. The treatment was the same in both and consisted of hypos for pain, a nasogastric tube to keep the stomach empty, intravenous salt and sugar solutions, and daily lab tests. After several days each patient was in shock and was transferred to the care of a specialist in abdominal surgery.

After prompt examinations and with intensive treatment for shock, each patient underwent major abdominal surgery. Each surgeon had the same work to do because each patient had an acute bowel obstruction with resulting strangulation (gangrene) of most of the small intestine.

Lifesaving treatment consisted of removing many feet of gangrenous small intestine and bringing together the ends above and below the strangulated bowel. In each case the surgeon operated faultlessly and each patient was transferred in fair condition to the intensive care unit.

In the post-operative period troubles developed because so much of the small intestine had been removed that almost no surface for the digestion of food remained. At the time of writing each of these otherwise healthy patients is getting a still new and difficult treatment for providing not only salt and sugar but also proteins and fats in intravenous feedings (a process called hyperalimentation). This hyperalimentation treatment, even when it works well, cannot substitute for the normal digestion in the intestine. It is still a research effort that must be carried out in very specialized surroundings because of the need for so much complicated laboratory checking.

One of the patients was discussed at a surgical grand rounds, and the surgeons and physicians and laboratory authorities all spoke at some length about their individual, specialized parts in the unfolding of this current chapter in surgery. The professor listened through the discussions and then, after congratulating his staff for working so well and so hard, he put his unerring finger on the pulse of the situation in a few meaningful words. "If the doctor who first attended this patient had possessed the knowledge and the touch, he would have recognized the acute surgical abdomen immediately. Had he diagnosed incorrectly he might not have been faulted except that the acuteness of any abdomen necessitates sharing the problem with a surgeon, even when an operation may not be necessary. Had this routine course been followed by the doctor, the strangulation would have been recognized within the first few hours. Curative surgery done at the proper time in any good operating room would have taken perhaps thirty minutes. The post-operative course would have been smooth and short. No bowel would have been sacrificed. The need for the highly-skilled abdominal surgeon, the intensive care unit at $400 a day, and the change in the patient's life's usefulness and duration, would not have developed."

"Perhaps," the professor remarked, "we are not blameless. We did not teach that doctor who first saw this patient the seriousness of the acute abdomen. We are quite wonderful as specialized technical experts but perhaps we are failing as teachers of surgery."

> *An infected hand:* A colleague who always spends a long vacation at his cabin in the Lake District sustained a small wound of his right hand while working on his dock. He touched it up with iodine and forgot it. The next day his hand was inflamed and he went to the regional hospital to seek the advice of a G.P. The specialist "knew what was wrong", but did not think he should treat himself. In point of fact, he was not sure about what was wrong; nor was the G.P. whose judgment was swayed by the specialist's strongly expressed opinion.
>
> The pain and fever and swelling increased in spite of the penicillin he was given. The vacation had to be cut short and the specialist returned to his home centre for special treatment because simple incision and drainage of the infected hand was not carried out at the right time. The condition continued to worsen and eight months later he was still having pain that disturbed his sleep, destroyed the usefulness of his right hand, and necessitated his retirement from practice.

Any doctor can become some kind of subspecialist these days. Most of them do. But an experience like this one emphasizes that the subspecialists without a substantial foundation in medicine and surgery are not capable of dealing with the important diagnostic and treatment principles that should be ingrained in every medical student and intern before the M.D. is granted and certainly before and during the subspecialty training periods, if they are going to be safe with patients, safe with their own families, and safe with themselves when they cannot get a good doctor.

Sir William Osler summed up the specialty lines in medicine as accurately as anyone can do today when in 1905 he wrote: "It is the fashion now for men to go into medicine purposely to become specialists, not that they have a particular aptitude or leaning to their special choice, but because the opportunities for making money are greater and their time will be their own — they only learn enough medicine and surgery to qualify for a degree. Such a training, although it may be a financial success, will tend to bring the practice of medicine down to the mere trade, and the higher and nobler instincts which ought to stimulate a professional man will be no more seen amongst us."

Subspecialized medicine in 1976 seems almost to have reached the situation defined by the religious philosopher Teilhard de Chardin, who — speaking of specialization in general — put it very succinctly: "Specialization paralyzes; over-specialization kills."

Not every reader will believe that, with four years of special training after graduation, the resulting subspecialist should be entitled to twenty-five years of very comfortable living away from the madding throng after 5 p.m., on Wednesday afternoons, and over long weekends. Since this subspecialist's education has been paid for in advance by people who in most instances will never enjoy the advantages of specialist care, it is easier to understand public dissatisfaction with all doctors. The public is asking, quite reasonably, if there should be so many subspecialists while so many people perish.

The patients who are referred to one-organ doctors, or doctors whose interest may only be in a part of one organ, face the prospect of having the specialist order every test he can think of in studying their problem. This may mean scores of very involved tests that are all charged for separately. In the medicare countries this strains the treasury to the breaking point. The average G.P. in Canada's richest province spends more than $250,000 a year in ordering tests and X-rays and specialists' opinions on his patients. In the pay-as-you-go countries it often puts families into bankruptcy. This indeed results in a modern form of quackery, because the specialist with his tests, without assuming responsibility for the whole patient, gains complete possession of him. Not uncommonly, in order to keep the patient, he uses every string in his own bow of tests over and over again for purposes of academic interest, or of self-interest. It is this factor that accounts for one of the most serious cleavages in medicine between the doctors who doctor and the subspecialists.

8.

Did your doctor
reject doctoring?

I solemnly pledge myself to consecrate my life to the service of humanity; I will give to my teachers the respect and gratitude which is their due; I will practice my profession with conscience and dignity; the health of my patient will be my first consideration; I will respect the secrets which are confided in me; I will maintain by all means in my power, the honour and the noble traditions of the medical profession; my colleagues will be my brothers; I will not permit consideration of religions, nationality, race, party politics or social standing to intervene between my duty and my patient; I will maintain the utmost respect for human life, from the time of conception; even under threat, I will not use my medical knowledge contrary to the laws of humanity; I make these promises solemnly, freely and upon my honour.

MODIFICATION OF THE HIPPOCRATIC OATH,
DECLARATION OF GENEVA ADOPTED BY THE
GENERAL ASSEMBLY OF THE WORLD
MEDICAL ASSOCIATION AT GENEVA,
SWITZERLAND. SEPTEMBER 1948

In 1973, the *avant-garde* graduating class in one medical school, where it has been the custom for ninety-five years to administer the oath, decided to become doctors of medicine without taking the oath. But as graduation day approached, class rumblings were heard until finally all of the students, realizing that "solemnly swearing . . ." did imply a different and nobler life ethic for doctors than for the other university graduates, decided that they would be demeaning themselves without proving anything. An urgent request was sent to the most senior faculty member who had charged the previous twelve classes. On the day of graduation the eighty-five new doctors, their families, friends, and teachers experienced the special sense of reverence which only the administering of the Hippocratic Oath arouses.

At a time when the medical schools and their graduating doctors find themselves under a fiercer wave of attack by a disillusioned public than ever in history, would any doctor deny the spirit of this oath? Would any knowledgeable patient be interested in calling a doctor who did not to his fullest ability observe and practise in the spirit of this oath?

After he takes the Hippocratic Oath, the doctor begins post-graduate work in hospital training. He may then go directly into general practice or qualify as a specialist before beginning to practise. One doctor out of three finds practice too tough. One doctor out of three forsakes the oath. One doctor out of three reneges on his care of the sick and finds the daily grind of the consulting room or the operating room just too much. Instead of improving his diagnostic score every day, he comes to realize that he is not being the kind of doctor he admired among his teachers. His patients with unsolved diagnoses increase in number, and his successful cases decrease. He cannot face the human foibles in patient after patient without losing heart and he becomes discouraged. Because every intelligent human being, regardless of his field of endeavour, must have a growing list of successes, for survival and for reasonable life satisfaction, these doctors face the prospect of perishing in the actual practice of medicine.

Surrounded by other, easier ways of using his degree to make a good living, he looks about in such areas as insurance, industrial medicine, and public health. In all of them he finds jobs that do not require across-the-desk consulting with demanding patients and prolonged, difficult discussions with relatives and employers who want the best answers to their questions about diagnosis, treatment, and prognosis. "What does this slight coronary attack mean? Can I carry on with my regular work in the office, in the plant, on the road? Can I sleep with my wife as I have always done? Will this executive officer of ours be capable of picking up his work after this little stroke you have diagnosed? What do you really mean by an early breast tumor in my wife?" Having to answer these difficult questions on which his reputation rises or falls every day may be too much of a strain. If he is not broadly based and cool and committed, the disappointed doctor often faces his awful decision frankly and turns away from the personal care of the sick.

There are many seductive competitors vying for his services. These are represented by executives or educators, or other doctors who have given up practice for non-practice work. The attractions offered by the no-patient jobs for M.D.s include: good salaries, the five-day week, escape from complaining patients at irregular hours, longer and better vacations, travel expense accounts and other fringe benefits. The M.D. who enters a non-practice field almost never returns to practice, and once away from patients he usually stays away from them. He gradually, and with a sense of guilt, accepts the idea that these non-practice fields are worth while in themselves. But turning away from patients forever raises the question: "Is this what the taxpayer expects as a fair return on his investment in the most costly course offered by the university?" The reader must be the judge as he makes his own estimate of these no-patient careers. Here are some fields in which the M.D. dodges the real obligation of doctoring.

Medical Administration

In 1970 the government reported the number of doctors in administrative positions in the United States at 27,500. One very familiar position is that of hospital superintendent. Administrative M.D.s also serve as directors of foundations, research institutes, and other organizations. In such positions they rarely utilize their modest medical knowledge — modest, because it has rarely been braced by intensive clinical experience. Doctor-administrators act principally as figureheads lending the prestige of the medical degree to the organization that employs them. There is no good reason why hospital administrators should be doctors.

Even the full-time dean of the medical faculty should be included in the list of administrators. Much has been written about the wisdom of taking a good doctor out of his role of practising and teaching and making him a college administrator. Cut off from daily contact with sick patients, the dean loses touch with the realities of the profession and finds himself trying to manage the faculty of doctors who are or should be, in the firing lines of practice and teaching. It is often wasteful to make a practising doctor a dean when the job can be so well handled by a professor from anatomy or biochemistry or physiology.

Public Health or Preventive Medicine

This field, dealing with the health of the group rather than the individual, attracts still other doctors who have become weary of looking after patients. According to 1970 statistics, there were 2,800 public health doctors in the United States. Inducements, which appeal to certain doctors, include the opportunity to teach preventive medicine to health workers, nurses, and medical students. The challenge of research is always stressed but important research in preventive medicine by a doctor who has moved from general practice is highly improbable. It is improbable with the scant background for high scientific achievement that the M.D. degree alone confers. The discoveries of the causes and cures of hepatitis, mononucleosis, and the common cold may very well be made, if ever, by scientists with no medical degree. The severe killers have all been beaten — tuberculosis, diphtheria, lockjaw, scarlatina, typhoid, gonorrhea, measles, mumps, whooping cough, poliomyeletis, and syphilis. The research opportunities in public health are consequently very slim for an M.D. who pictures himself making original observations on diseases that have eluded the world's greatest scientists for centuries.

In medical school calendars, public health is referred to as preventive medicine. It has wide applications, but its boundaries are never clearly defined. Actually, the students do not need separate instruction in preventive medicine. Unfortunately it has been generally felt by medical students for generations that student health and public health jobs are usually filled by the professionally anemic members of the medical fraternity.

Dr. David Barr of Cornell has pointed out that "the obligation to keep a person well, to undertake the total health care of an individual (which is preventive medicine) is the function of every physician whether he is a family doctor, internist, pediatrician, surgeon, or obstetrician. It is scarcely believable that any well-trained physician treating a duodenal ulcer, for instance, would be satisfied with prescribing a bland diet and antacid tablets without searching for the life tension factors that must be dealt with to prevent a recurrence." It seems unthinkable that this preventive attitude would not always characterize the doctor. It was not always so, as is illustrated in the story of the cure of syphilis.

Discovery: the "magic bullet": Paul Ehrlich: Salvarsan was Paul Ehrlich's dream of a "magic bullet" that would kill the spirochete of syphilis without killing the patient. When this, the first of all great treatment discoveries, shook the world in 1909, Dr. Ehrlich insisted that it had to be administered by a careful intravenous injection. Otherwise it produced terrible reactions, arms were sometimes destroyed, and it had no effect on the syphilis.

At that time there were very few doctors who could use an intravenous needle. Most doctors lacked the willingness and skill to learn how to use this lifesaving drug. The world was full of syphilitic patients who presented themselves for treatment with sores of every vile description, tumor-like masses (gummata), meningitis, brain defects, kidney conditions, genital ulcers, and heart and blood-vessel diseases. The most disillusioning reaction of the doctors was their stubborn refusal to use this new cure, for fear of losing patients on whom they depended for their income!

The discovery of salvarsan brought about one of the greatest forward strides in medicine and public health. The doctor's shameful attitudes were gradually exposed. The syphilitic cases were rounded up, tested, and given treatment as a routine public health measure. After 1930, patients with positive blood tests for syphilis were required by law to accept the treatment, which cured them or at least insured that they could not transmit their infections to others.

Today most of the routine work of doctors in preventive medicine can be handled by public health nurses who know the needs and enjoy the organizational aspects of inoculations, routine skin tests, routine chest X-rays, and the occasional epidemics that turn up in every community from time to time. Even if serious epidemics do occur, the medical officers of health must always get advice from recognized medical authorities.

The Insurance Doctor

More than 500 North American physicians are employed fulltime by insurance companies. The very much larger figure for those who do insurance work on a part-time basis cannot be estimated. Most of the insurance doctors are well based in clinical medicine, and some are or have been professors of medicine. Therefore, their new employment robs teaching as well as practice. The use of the physicians who do part-time or half-time insurance referee work withdraws a still greater volume of medical manpower from where it is needed most.

The insurance doctor deals with blood-pressure readings, blood-sugar reports, electrocardiogram tracings, and other fixed laboratory measurements. Insurance examinations are always incomplete, although the decisions based on them are nonetheless rigid. The doctor's discovery of a blood pressure slightly above the acceptable figure listed on the insurance table automatically excludes the applicant from getting insurance at a normal rating. Instead of provoking a worry complex for the applicant and his wife — another case of iatrogenic or doctor-induced disease — the insurance referee would be a greater force in medicine if he were employed in treating patients with serious blood pressure problems and in teaching.

Since there is in North America less than one physician-internist to handle the consulting work for 5,000 people, the proper use of these 500 highly qualified full-time insurance physicians would provide 2,500,000 men, women, and children with medical consultation service.

I fully realize that a doctor writing in this anti-insurance-service vein may leave himself vulnerable to attack by that industry, by the M.D.s employed therein, and even by some deans of medicine who lump this insurance work with "medical service".

I must insist that these are the mid-seventies, and that repentance is always good for the soul. In 1934 when I began practice in London, Ontario, the possession of the M.D. degree afforded no surety of an easy living. My gross earnings in the first year, including the honorarium of $250 for teaching, amounted to $835. In that bleak period I am sure that I would have accepted an insurance job of any kind. None was available.

In the 1930s, we could not do much for our patients, the great discoveries had not been made, and practice, even for well established doctors, was quiet. Our total medical-school budget including research when I graduated was below $150,000. The average cost to the student for the two years in pre-medicine and the four years in medical school was about $4,000. Annual salaries for doctors doing post-graduate work in hospitals varied from nothing with room and board and uniforms in the best hospitals, to $600 a year in the non-teaching hospitals.

Now, in the 1970s, doctors can do much more for their patients; medical candidates have a real obligation to serve the sick over and above the obligation they incur when accepting their medical education largely at public expense. With the higher public investment and the greater capacity for healing, can anyone argue that a good doctor should be encouraged or permitted to renounce the care of those in need for a leisurely forty-hour week in the board room environment of the insurance head office?

The following inducements of medical insurance and health insurance were described in an article in the March 1969 issue of a Canadian medical journal with a circulation of 20,000:

There are numerous fringe benefits and the salary is good. Generally a medical insurance director's life is easier than a general practitioner's. Besides regular hours there are paid vacations, paid travel expenses, free weekends, more time for social life and medical reading, and insurance plans.

Few doctors leave the medical insurance business once they are in it. (The insurance doctor being interviewed could only recall one doctor in his thirty years who had returned to private practice.) Not quite as narrow as life insurance, which provides places for G.P.s and internists, health insurance by contrast offers wide scope for surgeons and other highly-trained specialists on a part-time or full-time basis. Working in health insurance, these doctors "police" both doctors and patients' claims.

For the doctor who likes a challenge, wants to increase his income, or has a strong leaning towards the business side of medicine, life insurance companies and health insurance plans present profitable and satisfying careers.

The life insurance industry is one in which the computer is used effectively. Computers can handle the data extracted from the insurance applicant's routine complete medical examination, which is done by his own doctor, with speed and certainty. This could be the computer's most promising contribution to our doctor-short society.

Doctors in Drug Companies

The drug industry employs doctors for four purposes; to edit their trade journals; to answer questions from practising doctors about adverse drug effects in patients; to fill executive positions in order to lend the prestige of the M.D. degree to the company; and to assist very occasionally in research programs. Many more than 600 M.D.s are now employed in the United States by the drug industry.

When more than one bed in twenty in every hospital is filled by a patient who has had the wrong drug, or the right drug too long or a wrong combination of drugs (many patients are taking seventeen pills a day), surely pharmaceutical education should be reviewed.

If the drug industry were to establish professional chairs for teaching medical students how their drugs work in disease (medical therapeutics), many thousands of illnesses would be avoided and thousands of lives saved annually. This approach more than any other would cut down the alarming volume of the doctor-induced or iatrogenic diseases that represent over-medicated or wrongly medicated patients.

The drug industry is as highly competitive as its products are good. Its prime objective however, is more financial than therapeutic. The man who relinquishes the practice of medicine to join this industry is, because of its very nature, separating himself from the personal responsibility of saving human life. Is he not placing job security and regular hours first?

If these non-doctoring fields of insurance and pharmaceuticals are deemed just and good, if the successes of certain corporations depend on the services of full-fledged doctors, should not the cost of educating such doctors be repaid to the medical schools from which the doctors graduated? Or, because the people who paid the taxes to maintain the medical schools did so in the full and reasonable expectation that they could count on active doctors should they fall ill, then perhaps the corporations should pay their governments the anticipated life earnings of the doctors who withdraw from practice to bolster corporation profits.

Psychiatry

At first glance, it may seem strange to include psychiatrists in the list of doctors who have been sidetracked from medicine. Yet most psychiatrists will themselves admit that they have become a breed apart. Even in medical school, the students whose goal is psychiatry are usually recognizable to the seasoned clinical teachers. They stand at the back of the clinic group and when their turn is coming to examine the body of the patient they slide furtively along to avoid the touch. They seem to abhor the flesh. Their very presence slows up clinical teaching at the bedside, because they are not genuinely interested in organic disease.

When psychiatry was evolving in the latter part of the 19th century and more particularly in the first four decades of this century, its developers were remarkably strong characters. They laid its foundations and they experienced the deep satisfaction of seeing it develop into one of the forces of medicine that integrated man's body and mind in an utterly reasonable way. In personality, these early psychiatrists were real doctors, with great compassion that endeared them to their disturbed patients, and commanded the respect of the entire medical profession. I know no better

way of conveying their stature than by relating the story of Dr. Adolf Meyer
as told to me by his famous pupil Oskar Diethelm, psychiatrist-in-chief of
the Payne-Whitney Clinic at Cornell University.

Discovery: Modern psychiatry: Dr. Adolf Meyer: Adolf Meyer was a Swiss.
He was supported during his medical school years by an uncle who was a
country doctor and whom he accompanied on his horse-and-buggy rounds.
Meyer spent three years in the study of nervous diseases in Paris, London,
and Edinburgh under some of the foremost neurological teachers. He then
took a teaching post in neurology in Chicago, where he began his work as a
pathologist. Combining bedside observations with post-mortem findings,
he developed a remarkable knowledge of nervous and mental diseases. He
subsequently became director of the Pathological Institute of the New York
State Hospital for the mentally ill.

The most productive period of his life began in 1910 when he became
professor of psychiatry at Johns Hopkins. Under his direction the Henry
Phipps Psychiatric Clinic was built and opened in 1913, containing
psychiatric wards, doctors' offices, an excellent research laboratory, a
social service department, and a brain-modelling laboratory. In this
laboratory, not only psychiatrists, but all fellows and house officers at
Johns Hopkins who were interested in the nervous system could construct
a model of the human brain during their spare time in the evenings and on
weekends.

The strength of Dr. Meyer's teaching in psychiatry was based on his solid
foundation in brain anatomy, organic brain disease, and neurology. In
teaching, his efforts were directed towards developing adequate and
dependable methods of observation and examination, and it led to an
original plan for obtaining a complete life-record of the patient's illness.
This became the accepted approach to good psychiatry. It was (and still is)
time-consuming, but it is absolutely essential. Every great psychiatrist has
emphasized this approach.

Instead of looking for bizarre explanations for mental deviations from the
norm, Dr. Meyer used a common-sense approach that made his patients
admire him and follow him in the program he helped them to formulate for
themselves. He stressed the importance of discussing the history with the
patient. He maintained that it was the physician's first obligation to leave
the patient after every visit with a sense of how to live in reasonable security
in the interval between that and the following visit.

Dr. Meyer asked if the psychiatrist, the doctor of the mind, could lay all
his cards on the table and still keep his hold on the way they would be used

by the patient. He asked, "Are we not ourselves forced to recognize that our chief card is our life, our nature, that which is never really talked about?" This question implied that the living example of the psychiatrist greatly affected his influence on the patient. Psychiatrists in the Meyerian tradition did not dismay society and the medical profession by their personal explorations into separation, divorce, addiction, and suicide.

Dr. Meyer always emphasized that a psychiatrist must first be a well-trained physician. He laid the foundation that required physicians to take note of the significance of the mental and emotional reactions of patients with medical and surgical diseases, as these influenced the outcome of their illnesses. He went further and showed that some abnormal mental conditions result from disturbed workings of the heart or kidneys or thyroid or other glands, or from structural and chemical changes in the blood itself. He showed that the mental symptoms resulting from such organic disturbances could simulate or resemble the ordinary mental illnesses, and that if the physical part of the problem was corrected the mental symptoms would often clear up entirely. By his broad grasp of medicine and its relation to psychiatry he was able to draw the body-mind fields together; it was his leadership that made psychiatry such an important part of the general field of medicine.

Modern psychiatry has disregarded its history. In spite of Dr. Meyer's teachings, the fashionable swing towards psychoanalysis originating with Sigmund Freud began to spread in America about 1935. The psychiatric fundamentalists all had to spend one or more years undergoing analysis themselves before taking it back to their psychiatry departments. The analytic approach (far removed from Freud's teachings), which consists of eternal listening without doing anything positive for the patient, captivated all psychiatry, and its neophytes still maintain that the "analytic approach and attitude convey the hallmark of authority". This is not an unprofitable work area. Some analysts live handsomely on the fees derived from only twelve patients. The popularity of psychiatry with medical students increased greatly after World War II. Over the last eight years the number of psychiatrists has increased by more than 106 per cent.

Of course, the mental component exists to some extent in every physically sick patient, But the doctor's first responsibility is to deal with the obvious physical ailments before exploring the psyche. When the primary approach to illness is made by the psychiatrist, a critical organic illness is often glossed over. The results are devastating to the patient and his family and to the psychiatrist's reputation.

A forty-two-year-old woman complained of stomach pains. The routine tests and X-rays ordered by her G.P. were negative. He referred the woman to a psychiatrist. Every two weeks over a period of three years she made her visits. They talked, and he explained her stomach pains. One week they were worse because she was worried about her seventeen-year-old daughter. Another week the trouble was her own diminishing sex drive. A fortnight later it was the failure of her son, aged fifteen, in his mid-term examinations. Again, she had suspicions about her husband's late home-comings from the office. During the mother's second year of psychiatric séances the daughter took an L.S.D. trip. In the third year of therapy her husband was increasingly irritable and needed two stiff drinks before dinner. Over the three years, she continued to complain of pain and her weight dropped by thirty-five pounds. At this point her husband insisted on having her see a real doctor.

The physician listened to her story, examined her, and ordered one special X-ray. With the diagnosis of near-strangulation of the blood supply to her intestine by a band of scar-like tissue, he referred her to a surgeon. She was operated on and relieved of the pain. When she saw the surgeon for a final check-up in three months, her weight had returned to its normal level. The surgeon was a quiet man who simply said, "Mrs. Jones, I hope you are as pleased about this as I am." Mrs. Jones said, "I am a normal person again, I can't tell you how grateful I am, and I am just waiting for the pleasure of telling that bastard psychiatrist that my pain and weight loss were not in my head."

The psychiatrist's fees for the three years of interviews exceeded $2000. Much more costly was the neglect, because of her pain and weakness, of this woman's teenagers, the near-dissolution of her happy marriage, and her own physical and mental anguish. The husband must have been a complacent sort. He evidently did not know that lawyers display a sharp interest in cases of suffering that result from medical ignorance and prolonged neglect of complaints by intelligent patients, or he might have instituted an aggressive suit for damages.

The treatment of private patients is expensive. The appointment must be paid for even if the patient cannot keep it, surely the only field in medicine where this can happen. The less affluent patients are treated in groups where they talk with one another, with social workers, nurses, and the psychiatrist who presides. It is a sort of mass-production effort to bring more psychiatry to more people. But "group therapy" can be and often is used to conceal the need of the psychiatrist to escape from the patient, because dealing with a group is a way of avoiding individual human needs and individual human suffering. It is never possible in psychiatry to bring health to the many before the problems posed by the illness of the individual are dealt with. It is claimed that the group approach means progress, but like other fads in medicine it is being ridiculously overdone. Under medicare, psychiatrists charge $300 an hour for conducting a session with twelve patients.

The leisurely pace of psychiatry, the large financial returns, the long waiting lists of patients pushing to get onto a "psyche panel", and the frequent escape from out-of-office or even hospital responsibilities, combine to make it alluring to medical students and graduates who lack the compassion and the clinical touch that stamp the real doctors.

Reminiscent of medical graduates of the early thirties with tuberculosis, who went into chest work to save themselves first, we now see students and graduates entering psychiatry "to get their own thinking straightened out" first. But some are incurable, and many are only partly curable, as indicated by more than six times the incidence of separation, divorce, and suicide among psychiatrists compared with doctors in the other fields of medicine. Most of today's psychiatrists should never have gone to medical school in the first place. If they were interested in the mind they should have tried for a degree in psychology, which carries no responsibility for the care of the sick patient. It is significant that the psychiatrists who have had two years of internal medicine after graduation before going into psychiatry do not behave in their private lives like the ones whose records are so often spoiled.

Many modern psychiatrists maintain that their field is so much more than a medical discipline that their trainees need not spend much of their time on the medical-school curriculum, and that if they do go that far they should not waste a further precious year doing a general internship. "I would not dispute their right to that view," says Dr. George Engel of the University of Rochester, "but I would dispute their right to an M.D. degree. It is a fraud and a deception to pose as an M.D. when one does not have the qualifications for the degree." No student should be granted the medical degree unless he is prepared and capable of meeting the responsibilities of an M.D. Even today's TV soap-operas expect psychiatrists to know what is involved in delivering a baby!

Some psychiatrists seem to want to take a lion's share of medicine.

"Everyone needs his psyche man," is their slogan. Yet they dislike caring for the mentally unhinged. They often relegate these poor unfortunates to the back acres of hospitals for the insane under the care of inadequately trained M.D.s. They only want to help people "who can be helped." They insist that it is quite as natural and necessary for a person to attend his psychiatrist as his ordinary doctor, and that mental depressions and shock treatments are no different from pneumonia and penicillin treatment.

Vice-chancellor Henry Miller of Newcastle-upon-Tyne University's great medical school has written: "Psychiatry is neurology without physical features, a difficult branch of medicine that calls for diagnostic virtuosity of the highest order. The psychiatrist must be first and foremost and all the time a physician, expert certainly in unravelling the complexities of mental symptomatology, but also at least as adept in general medicine as his colleagues in cardiology or neurology. In fact, the psychiatrist whose knowledge and experience of the many disguises of serious organic disease are too insecurely based is a danger to his patient."

There may or may not be too many psychiatrists today for the needs of the emotionally disturbed part of the population. But what is certain is that there are far too many as a proportion of the total medical force. To permit the displacement in medical school of increasing numbers of students who want to be real doctors, by those who want only to be armchair or couch psychiatrists, is inexcusable in our doctor-short society.

9.

Is your doctor too interested in fees?

The people will never deny a good doctor a good livelihood.
VICTOR JOHNSON, M.D.

After 1965, political pressures began to threaten the secure financial position of doctors. The reason for these pressures originated with the doctors themselves. They had been putting their own pecuniary interests and advantages ahead of their art, so that in 1974 Thomas C. Chalmers, dean of New York's Mount Sinai School of Medicine, advised them to pay less attention to earning and more to learning. With even more acrimonious admonitions from the public, doctors now find themselves compared with the money-changers in the temple rather than with their forebears descended in the true Hippocratic tradition.

When doctors return to class reunions after twenty or more years of practice, a quarter of them say that if they had to choose their careers again they would not pick medicine. Half of the members of some classes have become bored with the monotonous daily grind of practice, and, comparing their satisfactions and disappointments with their classmates', say they would have chosen some other field in medicine if they had only known more about the possibilities at the time they graduated and began their post-graduate training. Too few remain enthusiastic about their work. One specialist, a doctor's son, had hated medicine from his first day in medical school, until he retired at the age of fifty-nine.

138

The kinds of dissatisfaction expressed by so many M.D.s could only mean that medicine for them had not been rewarding. If there are so many discontented doctors, the simplest arithmetic points to much larger numbers of unfortunate patients who could not have been well cared for by M.D.s who were never doctors at heart.

Cannot to-day's doctors find a rewarding life in medicine if they put the profession ahead of the purse? The problem is not new; more than a century ago the Edinburgh professor who became the world's greatest surgeon believed the subject called for stern mention: "Gentlemen, it may seem to you that these imperfect pieces of advice indicate to you that there lies before you a somewhat steep and thorny path; and truly, if we had nothing but pecuniary rewards and worldly honours to look to, our profession would not be one to be desired. But in its practice you will find it to be attended with peculiar privileges; second to none in intense interest and pure pleasures. It is our proud office to tend the fleshly tabernacle of the immortal spirit, and our path, if rightly followed, will be guided by unfettered truth and love unfeigned. In the pursuit of this noble and holy calling, I wish you all God-speed." Today's doctors, considering the rewards in medicine and surgery, can do no better than heed the advice from Joseph Lister's graduation address in 1876 at the Edinburgh Medical School.

In October 1932 a very frail woman was referred to the Marburg private pavilion at the Johns Hopkins Hospital under the care of Dr. T. R. Brown by her own doctor in South Carolina. She complained of weakness, loss of appetite, loss of weight and severe diarrhoea. She was anemic and she weighed seventy-two pounds. Dr. Brown made his examination and then gave his pronouncement to the husband.

"Your wife is critically ill. I do not think she has cancer. She cannot eat enough to recover and we shall have to feed her intravenously and also by a tube in her stomach. We should be able to control the diarrhoea with medication. My intern will be her doctor and he will see her by day and night to give the intravenous sugar and water. Of more importance, he will pass a small tube through her nose and gullet to her stomach so she will get all the fats and carbohydrates and proteins she must have. If one side of her nose gets sore from the tube he will change it for her. We should know in six weeks if she is going to recover. You will see the improvement as soon as we do."

The husband was a wealthy tobacco jobber who idolized his wife. They had no family. After Dr. Brown had given him the outline of treatment and left the room, the husband took the intern into his confidence: "Our life together has been extremely happy. If you devote your skill and attention to her and she can come home again you will not find me niggardly. I shall count on you, Dr. Sharpe."

The patient responded to the treatment and was able to go home with a special nurse by the end of November. She weighed ninety-six pounds. She had never weighed more than 102. Both patient and husband were ecstatic. When she came into hospital she was sure she would die and she went home well.

From the Johns Hopkins post office off the main hospital corridor, word leaked on the morning of December 21 that a heavy one-inch pine box 12" × 12" × 8" had arrived from South Carolina. It was addressed to Dr. John Sharpe. The interns gathered after five in the residence bedroom with hammer and chisel to uncover the gift from the tobacco jobber. Before the opening the betting was well under way. The consensus was gold because the box did not shake and it was heavy. Every bet was off when the packing was removed. Only John Sharpe stood his ground: "I can't tell you fellows how thrilled this cake makes me . . . to think that little Mrs. Ramsay is well enough to bake a cake makes my Christmas." Mr. Ramsay was a keen observer and he had estimated his man Sharpe exactly.

Louis Goodman, at that time a fellow-intern with Sharpe, coined the phrase, "G.P.P." to denote Sharpe's grateful private patient, and the Christmas cake in the pine box became another Hopkins anecdote. Goodman later co-authored *Therapeutics in Medicine,* the best textbook on the subject.

It would be misleading to have the reader assume that the interns at Johns Hopkins did not need gold. Goodman and Sharpe, like other interns in the 1930's, got room and board and uniforms but no dollars for their services. The hours of their work were unlimited. Most of their time was spent on the wards, in the out-patient clinics, in the clinical-pathological conferences, at the Journal Club sessions, and in the Welch Library. It was considered a privilege to be in a good teaching hospital, and money was never the primary consideration.

During the hospital training period, young doctors had to make the same important decisions then that they do today: to go into general practice in a large or small city? to do post-graduate work for five years and then choose the city in which to practise as a consultant? to try for a faculty position in a teaching centre with the hope of being a consultant and a teacher? or to take more post-graduate work and do research and aim for a professorship with higher academic prestige and with or without personal responsibilities for patients of his own? All these career possibilities in medicine still carry their separate monetary returns and more especially their personal rewards for the individual doctor.

Medical practice in the 1930s, the time of the Great Depression, was slow for all the doctors. Money was so scarce that it was hailed as the greatest medico-political triumph of the time when the Ontario Medical Association executive at its annual meeting in 1936 announced that the government payment to a doctor for attending a patient on welfare was to be increased from $1.00 a month to $1.35 a month. Very different from 1976 when $7.50 is paid automatically by medicare for a two-minute office call to any M.D. for any sort of service.

In 1936, some of us who hoped to practise and teach heard that one of our group who had decided to practise in a city in Oklahoma and not to teach at all was grossing $1,000 a month in his second year. We could not believe it! The doctors who decided to practise with medical school connections had to be content with less — much less. Most of the doctors who were fortunate enough to get junior teaching positions were given honorariums of from $250 to $800 a year that committed them to caring for charity patients and teaching on the public wards of the hospitals every morning. They spent their afternoons in their offices and in the evenings they consulted with doctors on patients in their homes.

At that time, although practice and income came slowly, most of the doctors were better informed. They did have more time to keep up with the medical journals. Nowadays, with the feverish rush all the doctors are in from the time they begin practice, their journals pile up and are rarely touched. Eventually stacks of journals are sent off to be bound so that they can be used occasionally for reference. Practising without an up-to-date knowledge of what is new in medicine cannot be gratifying for the doctor who is honest with himself.

Today, with high fees and few non-paying patients, there are few Dr. Robin Hoods who over-charge the rich to cover their services to the poor. Medical and surgical tariffs are now settled by arbitration between independent insuring agencies or government health services and representatives of state or provincial medical associations.

Doctor-arbitrators often argue that plumbers and carpenters and TV repair men earn as much for an hour's work as they do, or more. This is not quite cricket. The M.D. has been provided with the costliest education by the governments acting in the interests of people. More is naturally expected of him. His reward should be beyond money and beyond price, because he is a member of a privileged profession. The minute he quibbles about fees as if he belonged in the market place, the professional image is tarnished and the public's natural admiration for the doctors takes a drop. It is impossible to compare doctors' incomes with those of other professionals, politicians, executives, and skilled artisans. The more highly trained the doctor becomes before he starts to practise, the more money he will have spent, and the older he will be before he begins to pay off his debts. The doctor with integrity will deserve what he earns and will use it without ostentation if he is wise.

Busy practising doctors do get richer faster. But they tire out ahead of time. Their keen clinical edge is blunted from dealing with picayune items on demand by patients who try to get as much as possible for their fees or medicare premiums. The doctors must take longer and costlier vacations to escape exhaustion. But the luxurious vacations rarely recharge them for the grind for more than a short spell. Like the tired doctors in the U.K., by the time they are fifty they want nothing so much as retirement, and practice for too many of them becomes a matter of putting in time. Their satisfaction with medical practice is not high.

When I was the youthful physician of one of our local businessmen with a bad heart, I was impressed with his description of this ideal consultation at the Mayo Clinic: registration at Kahler Hotel; the reception centre in the Clinic; the week of tests; the several specialists using their individual instruments for checking all his body organs; and, finally, the consultation with Dr. Howard Burchell.

It wasn't the length of the consultation but the way in which Dr. Burchell wove all the evidence together while making his own examination, answering the man's questions slowly and completely — giving answers that were meaningful that day and for the rest of the man's life. The patient lived for fifteen years confidently and very productively. He had consulted a physician who exemplified what every doctor, whether generalist or subspecialist, should aspire to be at the consultation.

The greater reward for the physician showed up well in this man's case. Not only were all of the subspecialists' examinations "negative", but the patient had not remembered one of them!

A prosperous American in his later years retired in Niagara Falls and built a magnificent home on the Canadian side of the river just above the gorge. With very clear insight he phoned a Dr. Hadley, a physician with a well-regarded local record, and said: "Doctor, it is not unknown for a man who is well at seventy-six to unexpectedly have a sickness befall him at night. I can assure you that my health is excellent. I just wish to let you know that I am living here in the event that illness should strike." Dr. Hadley's reply was direct: "I don't go out at night."

I had occasion to visit this man later, to renew an old acquaintance. Life had been good to him and with a remarkable appreciation of art he had surrounded himself with more than $2 million worth of paintings and sculpture. When he told me about his non-experience with Dr. Hadley I felt sorry — for Hadley!

The doctors who will not make night calls on very sick patients never experience the reward of appreciation that radiates from one who is suffering and from the worried members of the family. I am sure that most doctors are not too lazy to make night calls. They cannot be money-grubbers because medicare pays handsomely for a night visit. It must be that they are too insecure to deal with a serious illness when unsupported by all of the hospital techniques and specialists.

The release of the "gross take" figures from computers makes the citizens and the other professionals aware of the incomes of doctors in general and of certain doctors in particular. Should it be possible for any doctor after one year of general internship to honestly gross $51,000 in his first or second or third year of practice as a G.P.? Can any health system that puts no premium on growing professional experience and knowledge be a good one? It is no secret that the general surgeons and the surgical subspecialists do have much higher incomes than the G.P.s and the physician-internists.

When the age of medical miracles came after World War II, it led to the subspecialties in quick succession. Each one involved one or more highly marketable techniques that set the man who could use them apart from the doctors practising general medicine or surgery. The experts who used these techniques became very busy and very wealthy. The people had prayed for subspecialists to bring them relief from their "single organ complaints" and their prayers had been answered.

There is less financial inducement for the doctor to specialize in countries with socialized medicine. The examples of Britain and Scandinavia show that socialized medicine and heavy taxation combine to make subspecialization less inviting and to increase the number of more generally trained practising physicians of the sort so badly needed in the North American medical systems, where millions of people do not have doctors whom they can call their own.

With medicare people no longer feel that health is a personal treasure, largely determined by the manner in which the individual curbs his appetites and follows established health rules. They feel it is a right. Such insistence places a heavy burden on medicare and on doctors. Taking the single example of alcohol — billions of medical dollars are spent baling out drinkers from acute binges, temporarily treating the resulting brain and liver wrecks that occupy large numbers of hospital beds, and comforting the wives and children and parents whose sorry plights call for quite as much of a good doctor's time and effort as his treatment of the liver failure that follows grain alcohol abuse. Yet this is an unavoidable and ubiquitous problem that every doctor in practice must deal with.

After Christmas 1971 a G.P. was called to see an intelligent wife and mother of sixty-five because of a bad spell of bronchitis. Her husband in the adjoining bedroom was still in a deep alcoholic fog at 11 a.m. on December 28. They had just returned after having spent Christmas in another city with their children. In conversation on the long distance telephone with the one son, the doctor found that the three days had proved to be catastrophic. The father was a quiet drinker and had been advised two weeks previously about the risk of going to a new environment when his daily alcohol requirement was so great. This advice he had not accepted.

The wife's condition was one of utter exhaustion and frustration and humiliation as a result of the three days with her children and grandchildren and daughters-in-law and their relatives. She had not sustained another stroke but she had a headache, her heart was bothering her, and her blood pressure was 230/120. The solution to this problem was hospitalization not of the wife but of the husband. The general physician prepared the large dose of sodium amytal that an alcoholic of this grade requires to put him to sleep. The man had begged for a night's sleep and the doctor gave the medication by intravenous injection. The patient fell asleep immediately and the ambulance was called. He awoke in hospital where he was kept for two weeks. He improved so much that he was confident that he could live without alcohol. Three months later he was in better health than he had been for five years. The wife's cough disappeared within a week.

Many doctors at graduation can give a direct intravenous injection confidently. Many cannot. Many shake visibly when they give it. Very few know what drug and how large a dose to use under these circumstances. Every responsible doctor should be capable of resolving such a common problem on the spot because these patients are cantankerous and difficult and often refuse to be dispatched to the emergency room of a hospital.

The doctor who handled this husband-wife situation was not a neurologist or a liver specialist or a psychiatrist. He was a G.P. who knew what he had to know to help the wife and the man himself. It was a very worthwhile call. "Not just drying out another drunk." Both patients got better, and, because people are quick to forgive the alcoholic who puts up a good fight and gets back to his work, the outcome was worthwhile. His two sons who had excelled in university both held responsible positions. By doing all that could be done for their father, that doctor steadied their careers through difficult times.

As a sidelight on drinking, this man remained on the wagon during the last three years of his life. After an illness lasting a week he died unexpectedly. The autopsy showed extreme hardening and narrowing of all of the coronary arteries and the brain arteries. Alcohol had not protected him against arterial disease.

Is it expecting too much of today's medical students and interns that they collect the personal experience with the intoxicated clientele of our emergency rooms to enable them to act with the same kind of confidence this doctor demonstrated? The fees for this part of practice are no higher than for giving B12 shots, but there is a greater personal reward.

Geriatric Practice Is Rewarding

The doctor's character is revealed in medical school and throughout his life in practice by the way he handles older patients. I have never liked the way patients who persist in living past some arbitrary age are allotted to the geriatric slot. Many people at eighty are younger in mind and body than others are at forty. The line between the old and the young is too hard to draw. So many people will age overnight following a little stroke, a heart attack, or a cardiac arrest if the reserve squad has been a few moments too slow in starting up the heart's action.

"Geriatrics, the new specialty" might be expected to attract either a young doctor seeking an exciting challenge, or a burned out M.D. who wants a lighter work load. Both approaches are unfair to the patients. The young man would be incompetent because of lack of experience, and the burned out M.D. would lack the optimistic resilience on which these patients thrive.

The elderly patient is likely to have trouble in several organs at once, compared with one-disease-for-one-patient, which is the average incidence during the first half of life. Therefore, the doctor who handles elderly citizens should be many times as experienced as the young doctor is likely to be. Caring for these patients makes a more balanced doctor and with this approach he can build up the sound judgment and compassion that will qualify him to know when is the sensible and humane time to turn off the resuscitating machine, not only in the old but in the young as well.

The *Atlantic Monthly*, in 1957, added this note of caution to doctors: "There is a new way of dying today. It is the slow passage via modern medicine . . . if you are going to die it can prevent you from doing so for a very long time."

The doctor who hasn't got it in his nature to accept the privileges and advantages of maturing with his patients will miss many of the most satisfying rewards in the practice of medicine. The older patients can all be helped in little ways and often in very big ways.

> A woman of seventy-one visiting in Florida in Janaury 1974 began to lose her grip on life. Her husband brought her home and within ten days she became totally paralysed and incoherent. As her family doctor observed her downward course, he maintained her fluid balance and arranged for good nursing care. One day, having decided to leave no stone unturned, he talked the problem over with a consultant and finally persuaded him that he was not just dealing with another old woman with a hopeless stroke. To everyone's amazement a large clot was localized and successfully removed from over the left side of the brain. She responded slowly but made a wonderful recovery. "This was the most rewarding case I have cared for this year," was the doctor's description of his experience.

Any doctor who cares for older patients reveals his skills to the most unexpected people, and in the process he becomes a real person with whom the older patients gladly share their accumulated wisdom. The extensions of older patients' families or business or political connections are endless

and the doctor who is kind and keen and concerned makes some of his
happiest associations because of the size of the human family.

This seventy-nine-year-old man had not been eating for three weeks,
he was generally uncomfortable, and his bowels were loose. The
ward doctor making his rounds twice a week never did anything more
than place a stethoscope over the man's heart before moving on to the
patient in the next bed. He did not ask the nurse about how the bowels
were working because for two weeks the absorbent pads had always
been soiled and smelly.

When the old man's nephew, a surgeon, whom he had financed
through medical school, unexpectedly flew into town, he called the
doctor in charge from the airport to tell him that he had come to see
the uncle to whom he owed so much. The doctor agreed to meet the
surgeon in thirty minutes at the hospital information desk. On the way
to the ward the doctor filled the surgeon in on the steady downhill
course of his uncle's condition.

As the nurse escorted them to the bed the surgeon observed that his
uncle was thin and frail and in misery. His voice was weak, the bed
was soiled. The surgeon casually recited Dr. Osler's yarn about the
doctor consultant who forgot to put his finger in the rectum of a
patient with unexplained symptoms and who one day "put his foot in
it" because he had neglected to examine the rectum! He asked the
nurse for a glove, courteously passed it to the doctor, and with a
gentle but peremptory nod motioned him to turn the patient on the left
side and insert his gloved finger in the rectum. The unfortunate doctor
turned beet red. The rectum was full of impacted stool which
accounted for the patient's general uneasiness, loss of appetite, and
the constant soiling from the brown liquid which leaked around the
hard fecal mass. With the removal of the impaction followed by a
cleansing enema the patient's uneasiness soon subsided. There was
no more soiling which had kept the nurses changing the linen. The
appetite returned and he began to take an interest and live again.

The wise doctor will never sell a patient short — not even if the patient is
deaf or blind or just constipated.

An eighty-nine-year-old spinster called a young faculty lung doctor
her friends had insisted she see when she caught a chest cold. He was
too busy to see her (implying that she was a bit beyond the time when

she could expect him to do very much for her). Disappointed but undaunted she called one of the senior faculty doctors, who said he would gladly drop by on his way home after his afternoon office hours. The bronchial cold did not turn out to be pneumonia. The patient was bright, interested, and anxious to help others. She was especially interested in helping young men who wanted to become good doctors. She wondered if he could interest the dean in using $1.2 million for the medical school. He was able to make arrangements very quickly according to her wishes. When the announcement of the gift appeared in the local paper, one young faculty doctor developed a new and persistent symptom. Insomnia. House calls don't pay much but sometimes rewards are not realized in fees.

The twilight period of life is good and it is good to live it through when the body is kept in working order and the mental outlook is brightened by the visits of an interested doctor. I have always done work in chronic hospitals and have enjoyed it. In my time as a consultant to a community hospital in a country district, where the people seem never old enough to die, I have learned a firm lesson from one doctor in particular. The hospital office often criticized this doctor for admitting so many older patients to hospital. By consulting with him I was subtly made to feel that I was collaborating in this crime of keeping oldsters well for nothing! One day this admirable doctor put his feelings into words: "I believe I should do all I can to make these good people as fit as possible to enjoy the months or years they still will face."

With increasing life expectancy, the number of chronic patients, most but not all of whom are beyond forty-five years, is increasing every year. This large group of patients accounts for a high percentage of visits to doctors' offices and to "health centres," that latest of all panaceas for providing health care. But these health centres fail to provide good service for elderly and chronic patients. They also fail to take advantage of the educational benefits of caring for older people.

It is a cruel custom when older patients, who account for more than one-third of medical practice, are sent off for lab tests and X-rays day after day from these centres, and told to come back again and again to get the results. They are often so tired, and transportation is often so difficult for them and their busy relatives. Moreover, the volume of trivial work in these centres with patients from infancy to old age is so great that by training and by the daily work routine the doctors only learn how to practise "slip or requisition medicine" by ordering tests on every patient. They do not have the skill that only comes with the laying on of hands.

In 1933-4, as an assistant resident in medicine at the Baltimore City Hospital on the Johns Hopkins and University of Maryland Services, I realized the high importance of learning in a chronic hospital environment. Besides the new general hospital with 400 medical and surgical beds in which the resident staff spent most of its time, we were responsible in the century-old hospital for its nearly 2,000 patients suffering from diseases affecting the blood vessels, brain, spinal cord, heart, liver, kidneys, abdomen, bones, and joints. Cancer, tuberculosis, and syphilis in their advanced states were common. All of these patients required whatever supportive medical care was available at that time. The density of disease on those wards was always high. In an adjoining house of incontinence there were fifty unfortunate patients who spent their days on commode chairs because they had lost the control of their bowels and bladders. Any doctor who ever worked in the Baltimore City Hospital, if blindfolded and transported by some magic force back to the huge foyer of this hospital, could identify his position instantly. The experience that was available for learning at that hospital was unmatched.

There are hundreds of thousands of chronic hospital beds in North America that are available for teaching and for the service that accompanies good teaching, but are not now used for that purpose. Clinical medicine can only be mastered by caring for large numbers of people with organic diseases, under the influence of good teachers.

Fees and Rewards with Medicare

In spite of editorial entreaty, I had purposely avoided any reference to medicare. However, with the costs of socialized medicine continuing to double by the year, I feel compelled to allude to some of the obvious errors. Socialized medicine in the English-speaking world began in Britain in 1948. Before that time the medical care of the poor had been the moral responsibility of the local doctor and the community. Dr. Will Pickles in his book on general practice has given this description of medical care in Britain before social legislation was introduced:

> Before 1911, patients without means and the unemployed and old people whose sole means of support was the old age pension of five

shillings a week, called on the "parish doctor" when they were seriously ill. This doctor, whose official title was District Medical Officer, was paid about fifty pounds a year by the Local Authority and usually carried out this work in addition to running his own practice. Not all of them gave the time and care to the destitute and old that they gave to their better-off patients. The next class of patients going up the social ladder was the "club" patients. Club patients at that time paid three or four shillings a year, sick or well, to the doctor. Special mixtures compounded of the more economical drugs were provided for them and issued in unwrapped bottles. Above them, in the hierarchy, came the private patients. They had pleasant-tasting and rather expensive flavouring materials added to their medicines, which were issued in wrapped bottles and they were charged "what the traffic would bear". In a city practice, this was usually quite modest, two and sixpence for a visit with perhaps a shilling extra for medicine. It was customary to visit private patients in their homes. When they came to the doctor's house, those above a certain subtle social line were admitted to the doctor's drawing room instead of the surgery, and the doctor's wife would engage them in a few moments' conversation while "the doctor" was being fetched from the surgery.

With the introduction of the National Health Service, everyone was to be considered equal and entitled to the same kind of medical attention. Every patient was to be treated like a private patient in the old system. The National Health Service provoked strife and inefficiency from the beginning and the problems have never been more critical than in 1976. It is a question of money. How can the melon be sliced to please all of the doctors and the patients?

Britain's Health Minister Barbara Castle in Britain's Labour Government was incensed about the glaring inequities of their bankrupt National Health Service. She vowed to close private hospitals where the rich still receive care. She determined "to erase the obscene spectacle of affluent people pushing past the poor" in the long queues leading to doctors in their surgeries (or offices) or in the hospital emergencies. But we doubt that the Health Minister had much faith in this system she talked about. When she had an attack of sinusitis, she insisted on having a surgeon see her as a private patient.

Canada launched its Universal Medicare Program in 1969 without having completed careful studies of how the experiment was working out after twenty years in the U.K. Like Britain's plan, it guaranteed equal care to the loggers in British Columbia, the farmers on the prairies, the mine-workers, the stockbrokers, the business executives, the professionals, and the fishermen in Newfoundland. Well, of course the country's geographic features alone ruled out any possibility of applying the universal feature of the plan.

In the United States in August 1974, after years of wrangling, the House of Representatives Ways and Means Committee members were split into at least three factions, each group backing one of the dozen or so national health proposals that had been introduced, but all refusing to compromise their differences. Dr. Jessie L. Steinfield, former U.S. Surgeon General, has written:

> Government at all levels has become more and more involved in the health problems facing the American people. Government is not only financing a significant portion of medical research, medical education, and medical practice, but through laws and regulations is reshaping the very structure of the organizations involved in these activities. Government has no rational plan, no design, no program, but rather a multiplicity of categorical programs aimed at solving specific problems that frequently create new problems and exaggerate others.

This is the state of affairs before any co-ordinated plans for medicare are agreed on for the United States.

Regardless of how or where any medicare system works it increases the demand for more doctors. The demand is always greater in the wealthy nations. Medicare, by paying for every item of service, lessens the lustre of the professional image and tends to make doctors dishonest. The volume of work is too great and the doctors are too busy.

A mother with bronchitis goes to her doctor and without anyone to care for her children she takes them with her. After she has been examined she asks the doctor to check Sammy's ear and Susan's throat and Tillie's cough. Medicare pays $7.00 for the mother's bronchitis but should the doctor extract an extra $21 for three one-minute peeks at the childrens' symptoms of the mother's infection?

Medicare practice does not encourage continuing education. The time spent by the average G.P. in study alone or at meetings amounts to just over twelve hours in twelve months. Even more surprising, the study time that the new family medicine doctors must put in to maintain their standing in this newest specialty is one hour a week.

Everyone who can, pays his medicare premium, or has it paid for him by his employer. While these payments do not defray a quarter of the actual cost of operating the system it does make the patient believe that he is entitled to everything that the private patient in the old system could afford. This means that the poor, the middle class, and the well-to-do, whether their premiums are paid out of welfare or by cash, are instantly transformed into demanding private patients (D.P.P.s). It is this transformation of the entire population that defies economic solvency in every government-operated medicare system.

Medicare makes cash-on-the-barrelhead medical arrangements illegal. But no business transaction is ever completely protected from corruption. Various influences can determine the speed and quality of medical attention. The individual doctor chooses the path he will follow.

> In March 1974 a public ward patient, a young twenty-seven-year-old mother with a heart condition suddenly worsened unexpectedly at 2 a.m. and Code 7 — the distress signal — was announced over the P.A. system. Only one final-year medical student responded. The condition got worse and the head nurse in desperation went to the coronary care unit to try to find at least a senior resident in cardiology. A quick glance explained the shortage of staff on her ward. Three doctors and two nurses were all working feverishly over an old-looking woman of eighty-three who had a cardiac arrest. Once they got the heart beating again it was reckoned that her chances of survival would be better if a pacemaker was inserted. This was accomplished promptly even though this woman (regarded as senile) would never know her own name. The eighty-three-year-old patient was the favourite aunt of a senior government official whose influence in medical politics had to be given due consideration even if his aunt had become brainless moments after her heart stopped.

From its beginning, medicare's originators had to make the plan as attractive as possible for the doctors, who feared that the take-over of medicine by government would bring with it a deterioration in quality of care. It was never a question of money, because, in every program in America to date, the doctors have come out ahead financially.

The medicare experiment in Canada has proved to be exorbitantly expensive and its cost has increased by more than one billion dollars per year since its beginning. In Ontario with its population of 8 million, where the figures are carefully tallied, the health minister reported in 1974 that medicare for that year cost nearly $3 billion. In spite of the spiralling costs, the quality of doctoring is decreasing. Although claimed to be universal, medicare leaves more than two million Canadians without access to any medical attention because of the shortage of M.D.s who actually doctor the sick and the maldistribution of the doctors. Too many of them practise in the cities. The increased demand for medical services, brought on in part by medicare, results in a host of substitutes for competent doctors. The near-doctors cannot do more than the foot work when the patient is really sick.

A fifty-seven-year-old tobacco farmer was referred to the professor's service for an operation after X-rays revealed a growth in the stomach. During the stormy post-operative days the patient complained of shortness of breath and a dry irritating cough every time the professor and his interns made rounds. They routinely left the prevention as well as the care of this post-operative complaint to the paramedical physiotherapists who pummelled the man's chest twice a day and checked the results of their work with their stethoscopes to make sure the air was getting into his lungs. Finally, on the sixth day, a junior intern was called at 7 a.m. because the man was gasping for breath. The intern removed the surgical dressings and examined the abdomen only to discover that it was distended with fluid. He got the okay from the senior resident and did a painless tap, which removed more than a gallon of fluid that had been pushing up the man's diaphragm and compressing his lungs. There was no mystery about the cause of his shortness of breath.

This farmer's story stresses the fact that all the paramedical workers and nurses in the world cannot safely treat a patient who is critically ill unless the nature of the illness is settled by a capable doctor.

More mechanization of medicine cannot solve the need and it carries its own risks. It has been estimated that more than 5,000 deaths occur in the intensive care units on this continent annually because orderlies and nurses and technicians and doctors do not understand the complexities of the machines.

For medicare to succeed we shall need to return to a more clinical style of medical education that will lessen the doctors' dependence on computer tests, X-rays, and other gadgetry. They will need to know how to use these, but they will not be helpless without them. Too much sickness always occurs away from the newest machines.

With medicare, everyone becomes a selfish and often uninformed D.P.P., as the politicians and doctors in the U.K. and Canada have found to their embarrassment. Medicare can never be universal because the social handicaps of ignorance, timidity, hopelessness, and poverty interfere with the proper utilization of free medical care. It is still the rich who have the knowledge and often the political connections to take the greatest advantage of medicare services.

If medicare is to work, the doctors who will reap the richest rewards, though not the highest incomes, will be those who know that every patient is interesting to doctors who take an interest. When this happens, most patients' attitudes are likely to change and the D.P.P.s will behave more like John Sharpe's Grateful Private Patient. When patients, regardless of money or employment or origin or race or creed, realize that a grateful attitude on their part brings out the most conscientious work their doctor is capable of doing, their dissatisfaction, which stems from so much irresponsible doctoring, will be reduced, and medicare, which is here to stay, will be better for patients and doctors alike. The result would be a different patient and a better doctor.

Discovery: Liver extract: Dr. George Minot: In one of Dr. Henry Christian's medical clinics at Harvard a patient with an undiagnosed anemia was under discussion. None of the professors, residents, interns, or final-year students — not even Dr. Christian himself — could solve the case. A third-year student in the back row named George Minot made the right diagnosis. The feat proved to be no lucky hit. Dr. George Minot went on to become a leading authority on anemia and blood diseases.

In 1921, when he was thirty-five and had just been made chief of medicine at the Huntington Hospital in Boston, this brilliant young doctor developed severe diabetes. The only treatment for diabetes at that time was diet. His wife Marian, under the personal instruction of Dr. Elliott Joslin of Boston, the foremost authority on diabetes, weighed every bit of food he ate on a little scale that was always kept at the table. They did not succeed in controlling the diabetes and George lost twenty pounds from an already spare frame, and his life outlook appeared bleak. But just then, insulin, discovered by the Canadians, Frederick Banting and Charles Best, became available and George Minot was restored to a very active life.

He at once resumed his researches on pernicious anemia. His own difficult experience he now turned to growing account. "You know," he told friends, "I am always thinking about diet. It is food that makes different people different, and I have a good notion that the bone marrow in pernicious anemia needs food of some special sort." The blood-forming bone marrow, he decided, was the key. At certain times the bone marrow did not produce enough red blood cells. One of his associates, Dr. George Whipple, had found that anemic dogs regained their blood faster if they were fed raw liver. Dr. Minot decided to try raw calves' liver on his anemic patients. A half-pound of liver, ground up and flavoured with tomato ketchup or lemon juice, was prescribed as a daily diet for an Italian immigrant patient, who, by good fortune, liked raw liver. He (and all of the other patients less keen on the cuisine) showed immediate improvement. By 1930 Dr. Minot was able to report his findings on thirty-four cases of pernicious anemia who had regained their health.

Liver extract was later substituted for whole liver and ultimately the liver fraction required for production of red blood cells was isolated and identified as vitamin B-12. In 1935 Dr. Minot and his associates, Dr. William P. Murphy and Dr. George Whipple, received the Nobel Prize.

In addition to his achievements in research, George Minot was an outstanding teacher who inspired more than fifty professors of medicine and 300 physicians from all parts of the world who worked under him at the Boston City Hospital. His biography is appropriately entitled *The Inquisitive Physician*, because he was the kind of physician who worried about patients who were not progressing under standard treatment.

Dr. Minot experienced the high rewards that come with teaching, research, and the practice of medicine. Amid his heavy academic duties and the care of his own health, he was not too busy to make house calls, even on children with leukemia (in that day a totally hopeless disease), whom he cheered and whose parents he befriended.

10.

Is your doctor still
waiting for lab reports?

*The ability of the doctor to use his eyes and ears and hands —
all his senses — to gather information, and the development
of his thinking power to interpret that information is what he
must be taught. Mechanical machines, like the X-ray, and all
the methods of the laboratory will help him, but they too
must be interpreted.*

DR. GEORGE MINOT

More than 2,000 years ago, ailing Greeks were accustomed to going to the
marketplace in the hope of encountering others with worries or complaints
similar to their own for which they had found cures.

Today, with the predominance of laboratory-dominated medicine, the
patient is again often on his own, left with a diagnostic word or a laboratory
or X-ray report that he must match with that of anyone he can find who will
listen at the club, at work, or on a jet. The doctor seems to lack the time, or
the ability, or the kindly technique to explain the meaning of the tests to the
patient, who is left dangling with a report of the blood cholesterol, blood
sugar, heart murmur, increased eye tension, thyroid gland tests, or
sometimes with five pounds of X-rays in a fat envelope.

Thousands of normal people and their relatives are made miserable every
week when they are told that their blood sugar is a few points too high and
are put on diets and pills to prevent the dreaded complications of diabetes.
The normal level of blood sugar after fifty years of testing is still not
uniformly accepted. This is another typical example of doctor-created
sickness (iatrogenic disease), which grows by the day.

156

So many lab reports are just not quite "normal". The average general practitioner or subspecialist, who cannot possibly know the meanings of all the tests, finds himself in a confused position. Instead of being able to say positively, "This means nothing, carry on with your normal way of life," he is more likely to build a hedge against the one-in-100 chance of some day being criticized for not having started to treat the patient's test before the patient had a disease.

Dr. Richard Cabot, the famed medical teacher at Harvard between 1905 and 1930, found and taught that the greatest diagnostic accuracy was likely to be reached when 60 per cent of the total evidence was made up of a history of the patient's chief complaints supplemented by personal and family medical history, when 30 per cent came from what the good doctors had found on the physical examination, and when 10 per cent was provided by the laboratory reports on body fluids, the electrocardiogram, and an occasional X-ray.

In today's uncertain, mechanized, automated medicine, the history may involve as little as 10 per cent of the total examination time. The thorough physical examination in a day when it is one man for one organ may occupy 15 per cent of the doctor's expensive time. Too often 75 per cent of the time which should be devoted to making the diagnosis and outlining the treatment is spent in ordering, waiting for, and considering the X-rays, laboratory results, and subspecialists' reports.

A male teacher, twenty-five, was taken to the emergency room with concussion and lacerations, the result of an auto accident. X-rays of the skull were normal but those of the kidney were reported as showing a stone. The urine report was "albumen and casts and blood".

The man and his family were seriously upset because his sister had just been operated on for a uric acid stone in her kidney, and, according to the report, he not only had a stone in the kidney but also Bright's disease! A kidney specialist was called at once. It turned out that the lab report was in error, as are 25 per cent of all lab reports. In this case another patient's urine report had been attached to his chart. The X-ray stone was just a calcified gland overlying the kidney but not in it. The false alarm from the laboratories would not have happened if the doctor, before pronouncing such a serious and improbable diagnosis, had taken five minutes to glance at the X-ray and check a sample of urine in the lab himself.

Mistakes can be made in the laboratory by the machine, by the technicians, or by those who transcribe the results. Even when the reports are accurate they may be misinterpreted or misunderstood by the doctor who ordered them. Testing has become so highly sophisticated that very few doctors can possibly keep up to the minute in biochemistry, in nuclear medicine, in enzyme studies, and in the highly theoretic and uncertain field of immunology. The output volume of all the laboratories of the Western world has dangerously outstripped average medical knowledge.

The most expensive area of laboratory testing involves X-rays. They have become a universal panacea, giving satisfaction to both patient and doctor. "Your X-rays are all normal, the pain must be in your head," is a too-frequent diagnosis after a long series of visits to the radiologist has been completed. Eighty per cent of them could be dispensed with if competent doctors were available to examine patients before the X-rays were ordered.

In the emergency room of the hospital a doctor on duty who is called to see a motor-vehicle accident patient makes a "glance examination", and fills out an X-ray order that may be carried to the X-ray desk by the patient himself. It is a large order for X-rays of the skull, chest, neck, spine, abdomen, hips, thighs, knees, legs, and ankles. The reason for so many X-rays is that there might conceivably be a suit for damages at some future date, and the doctor must feel "protected". He lacks the confidence to rely on his own clinical skill. The cost of such an X-ray series will exceed $150. The waste of the X-ray specialist's time and talent, the overuse of the too heavily worked department, the time-waste of numerous technicians and secretaries, and the cost of storing the X-rays in carefully filed individual envelopes in a special hospital area can hardly be determined. This overuse of X-ray film goes on by the ton in every department around the world every month.

X-ray medicine unsupported by the skilful clinical examination in the emergency room is not good medicine, and it is certainly not safe defensive courtroom medicine. Doctors who practise this way sooner or later experience dreadful embarrassment or end up in court. When the doctor, instead of really examining the patient, merely signs the order form for so many X-rays, he is still committing himself to responsibility for the safety of the patient after he leaves the hospital.

I had to see a patient in our emergency room at noon on Sunday, April 22, 1974. While waiting for an examining table I stepped into Number 1 operating room to see a young woman who had just been brought in unconscious. She had been mugged. Blackened eyes, dilated fixed pupils, heart rate 170, blood pressure 50/40, bruises on face, neck, chest, pubis, and extremities. Calls went out for the intern on call; for a respiratory technologist to support breathing and administer oxygen; for lab technicians to draw blood for counts, chemistry, drug levels, and clotting factors; for the senior medical resident to consider the shock state; and for the neurosurgical resident.

In all the confusion of orders for every conceivable diagnostic possibility, I was most impressed by the way this neurosurgical resident palpated the skull through the dirty greasy hair all matted with clotted blood as he examined for evidence of scalp injury, a running ear or gross fracture, all the while employing his great skill in estimating the factors that might account for her critical state. So different from the sort of doctor who orders X-rays without getting his hands dirty.

One case that came to court in 1973 concerned a woman who had sustained four rib fractures on the right chest and two on the left. The doctor had ordered the routine X-rays but had not examined the woman then or afterwards. She died because one lung had been punctured by the end of a broken rib. Had the doctor just touched this patient, he would have perceived the air under the skin (surgical emphysema) and been directed to the damaged lung.

The cases that lead to litigation are the ones where the doctor — with his hands in his pockets — has never examined the patient but only ordered the X-ray technicians on duty to take X-rays for the X-ray specialist to interpret the next day.

Routine X-rays usually show fractures, but not always. With head injuries they do not show death-dealing blood clots. They do not demonstrate muscle and tendon injuries, heart injuries, spinal cord and nerve injuries, liver and spleen and bowel and kidney and blood vessel injuries. Any of these may prove fatal. Most of them can only be spotted by a doctor who possesses skill in doing a thorough examination.

A doctor's wife in our county sustained a fall from her horse and complained of a lot of back pain. She was taken to the best hospital where X-rays of the hips and pelvis and spine were taken. The reports were all normal. In keeping with modern teaching "to get the patient with back pain moving so it would not get stiff", she was urged to get out of bed and move about the following morning. The pain increased. A more experienced doctor was called to check the patient and the X-rays. Everyone involved was horrified when the examination of the woman's back showed not only a fracture but a dislocation. The evidence was all there on the first set of X-rays but the doctor who had listened to the story of the back pain had not examined the back. He had looked at the level of the back in the X-ray where he thought the pain was. The fracture-dislocation was six inches higher up.

Because of the over-use of X-rays, X-ray specialists, and especially the good ones, are in shortening supply. Thirty years ago the X-ray man was a real consultant to the physicians and surgeons in his hospital. His department was the hub of the wheel to which all staff doctors and interns went before making the big decisions about their patients, to operate or not? what type of surgery? what would be the safest time for operating? what kind of pneumonia? how large is this heart and what is its shape?

Now, more than 90 per cent of busy doctors never consult the X-ray chief in the average hospital department to review the X-ray pictures with him. They only take a quick look at the written report of the X-ray on the patient's chart. This downgrades the radiologist to the role of service man. His job is to keep his department running in order to handle the ever-increasing flow of requisitions. Actually, there is no shortage of good X-ray specialists. There is only a growing waste of their time and energies. My X-ray advisors assure me that more than three out of four of all the X-rays they turn out are unnecessary. They are done because sufficient time has not been spent on history-taking and the examination of the patient by the doctors who ordered them.

Recently, I had occasion to visit an excellent X-ray department in one of our modern hospitals after an absence of three years. Adjoining the reading room where the radiologist was reporting the previous day's X-rays, I noted a new, enlarged storage room where formerly the stands for filed X-rays could have been estimated in cubic feet. Now the stands went to the ceiling and they could only be estimated in cubic yards.

It is not unusual for the X-ray department to receive a requisition about a patient complaining of pain in the abdomen that reads: "Do X-rays of the stomach, and *if* negative do gall bladder. *If* this is negative do X-rays of the colon. *If* this is negative do X-rays of the kidneys and bladder." Such an order means that the patient must fast before all four examinations, take pills for the gall bladder test (and if six do not give a good shadow of the gall bladder he will have to double the dose and go back a second time), take castor oil at least once and probably twice to ensure good colon and then good kidney pictures, and take a brisk laxative after the stomach-colon X-rays to avoid a serious and never-before-experienced constipation. He will lose two or three days or half-days from his work. He will not feel normal for a week.

Besides the ordeal for the patient, overloading the X-ray department means astronomical costs. If the X-rays are not skilfully done they are only confusing to the doctor who ordered them and alarming for the patients who are told about them. The carelessly demanded and often needless X-rays cannot be carried out *harmlessly*, especially during pregnancy.

Other lab tests are more over-used than the X-rays. Blood counts and bone marrow examinations, blood gases, blood electrolytes, blood chemistry tests of more than 100 kinds, and the isotope studies which apply nuclear medicine to diagnosis have increased the volume of laboratory work incredibly. In teaching hospitals especially and on certain lab-dependent doctors' services it is routine practice to demand every test that has been mentioned in the latest medical journal.

Full lab sheets are believed by the uninformed doctors to indicate "a real good work-up" of the patient. Some doctors may have a personal interest in the laboratory or may order tests when they are too busy or too tired to examine their patients properly. Frequently the doctor just cannot figure out what is wrong. Since it is all paid for by insurance, he does not stop to consider the total cost in bed time, in the overwork of laboratory personnel, in the inconvenience to the patients, and he resorts to ordering tests as time-saving, short-cutting, or delaying devices in patient management.

In recent years, the electrocardiogram, because of the heavy reliance placed on it by physicians, surgeons, life insurance companies, and people generally, has taken first place among all tests for patients over thirty. The heart specialists rely on it just as doctors in earlier times relied on the clinical thermometer. And yet the electrocardiogram cannot give the diagnosis of angina, heart failure, a weak heart, a strong heart, a heart with a murmur, or an enlarged heart.

When abnormal, it is of considerable value in completing the diagnosis of coronary thrombosis, many types of irregularity, and digitalis poisoning. The electrocardiogram does not provide 20 per cent of all the evidence required for the accurate assessment of a difficult heart case. In the light of this fact it is sobering to note the place this one examination holds today. If the electrocardiogram is normal, patients with positive clinical warnings of heart trouble may be cleared for surgery. Life insurance companies sell billions of dollars of personal coverage on the basis of good electrocardiograms. Men re-marry, begin new business ventures, or take round-the-world cruises after the doctor calls and says, "Your electrocardiogram is O.K." The heart may stop that very day. Sometimes the brain may be softening, or a growth may be under way in the patient's vitals, but everyone has become so heart-conscious that all other reports take second place to the electrocardiogram.

> A farmer, aged seventy-one, had been admitted three weeks previously with a heart attack. He was making a satisfactory recovery in the small community hospital when he unexpectedly developed a new pain in his chest and vomited. During the man's three weeks in hospital twelve electrocardiograms had been done. The laboratory sheet was dotted with blood counts, blood-enzyme reports, and blood electrolytes, all of which were normal. No medication was ordered when the patient got this new pain, which was accompanied by anxiety, sweating, and shortness of breath. The patient's doctor, an executive type of man who always treated by getting more tests, had ordered yet another electrocardiogram, a chest X-ray, and another complete round of blood tests. They would have to be mailed to the city for the electrocardiographer's interpretation and the results then mailed back while the patient languished. The doctor's treatment without the E.C.G. was "no treatment".
>
> Meanwhile a consultant was called in. He was more concerned with the patient's distress and the intensity of the pain than with the E.C.G.'s and blood reports. He found that the heart action was laboured, and that the blood pressure was below 100. The bedside diagnosis of a bad coronary attack is often the surest. The pain and anxiety were controlled with a hypodermic injection of morphine. With the killing pain relieved, the man survived the attack. Two months later he was back managing his 300 acres. If this patient's executive-type doctor had just used his stethoscope with precision or even placed his finger on the pulse below the blood pressure cuff he could have treated his patient quickly and properly.

The greatest number of tests are performed in the general laboratories. Unlike X-rays and E.C.G.s, they yield evidence about blood, urine, stools, body fluids, and biopsies of tissue samples from every organ. They include the rapidly expanding field of nuclear medicine with its very helpful isotope techniques.

The doctors in charge of the laboratories try to support the doctors who order tests by the thousands. But like the overworked doctors in X-ray departments, they vehemently decry the overuse of their services (referred to as the practice of "order slip" or "requisition" medicine) by doctors who do not examine their patients first.

> A boy of fourteen was admitted to a hospital as a case of "stomach flu" with severe vomiting and diarrhoea. His blood was immediately sent to the laboratory for the routine list of tests. The lab reports of the blood taken when he was sick came to the ward the following day. They were all normal except the blood salt which was abnormally low, the usual consequence of severe vomiting. The nurse telephoned the reports to the doctor. The doctor, feeling that he had to do something, ordered an intravenous of a highly concentrated salt solution.
>
> Meanwhile the boy had recovered because he was eating and drinking normally. He was given the intravenous salt treatment ordered by the doctor and he died.
>
> His death was due to acute swelling of the brain caused by too much salt. The doctor had been a day late in his treatment. He was treating the test, not the boy.

Dr. William Bean, professor of medicine at the University of Iowa, gave today's situation a sensible perspective when a younger medical professor asked him if he did not agree with the current practice of allowing students and interns to order as many tests as they wished on their patients. Dr. Bean replied, "I would be happier if I knew that my students and interns could make a diagnosis on a sick patient and treat him when the power went off and the laboratory lights wouldn't come on."

The massive use of machine-generated laboratory information that became the fashion after 1948 led to the most fabulous medical information explosion in history. This has resulted in a progressive overuse and overreliance, and confusion caused by "unsolicited" bits of lab information.

A doctor who only needs to know a patient's blood-sugar level, will automatically receive a report of twelve different blood tests, amongst them the blood sugar (with the automated machines, twelve tests can be reported as cheaply as one). If one or two of these other "unsolicited tests" is abnormal (even if unrelated to the patient's condition) the doctor feels obliged to seek an explanation. It is the lucky patient these days who, having come to the hospital with one disease, does not depart with three or more.

Laboratory medicine has carried everyone from deans through faculty chairmen, professors, instructors, researchers, hospital residents, interns, students, and practitioners, down the road to self-extinction as good doctors. The patient is bled, his health suffers, medical teaching deteriorates, and the taxpayers go bankrupt under the rising costs.

With today's heavy emphasis on tests, it can be stated categorically that scarcely any living man over the age of forty can submit to a routine laboratory screening with twenty tests along with the chest X-ray and the electrocardiogram and then be told *without reservation by the average doctor* that every examination is normal and that he is healthy. Having gone to the doctor *as a person* he is completely tested and he emerges from the ordeal *as a patient*.

"Multiphasic laboratory screening" or mass-testing of normal people has become the magic slogan in the last ten years. The fascination of multiphasic screening for doctors, laboratory scientists, and public health professionals has left unanswered the crucial question: "Will the person who is lab-diagnosed before symptoms develop live longer or as happily or as usefully as the person who seeks help when he gets a new pain or swelling or bleeding?"

> One of America's greatest doctors underwent a prostate operation when he was seventy-two. The operation was a success but the pathological report was cancer. In spite of every modern treatment this cancer spread to all the bones and two years following this operation he died. One of his close associates recently gave me the full history. Twenty-five years before the 1969 operation this doctor had had his first prostate gland operation in one of Boston's very excellent hospitals and the pathological report was "no cancer". The surgeon who operated in 1969 requested that the gland that had been removed in 1944 and that was still preserved in a bottle of formalin be re-examined. This meant re-cutting the gland for many more microscopic sections. Careful study showed that there was cancer in some of the sections. Had the cancer diagnosis been made in 1944 this doctor, much of whose greatest work was done after this, would undoubtedly have been treated with one or several of the new medications for prostatic cancer as they were being tried. These would certainly have destroyed his feeling of good physical and mental health and shortened his life.

With the ultra-special testing of our time, more and more healthy people are being converted into patients unhappily every day. Doctors need to be very broadly based and wise if they are to protect their patients from so much unproven laboratory nonsense. The multiphasic screening facility of the Kaiser-Permanente Foundation in the San Francisco area is the locale of the best-known and most thoroughly studied of all major multi-test screening programs. After some eight years of follow-up, no difference in sickness or death was found between the people screened every year by their elaborate procedures and corresponding control groups who merely went to their doctors when they developed symptoms.

"Broadly speaking, the direct and indirect effect on health care of multi-chemical screening has been harmful, seriously harmful," says Dr. Murray Young of Toronto General Hospital. And Dr. Edward MacMahon of Boston, reminds us that, "The investigation of disease can be more grievous than the disease itself."

One of the most popular routine laboratory tests is the annual Pap test for detection of cancer in the female cervix. This test requires taking a simple swab from the mouth of the womb. This is examined in the laboratory — not by the doctor himself. The Pap test has become routine with gynecologists, general practitioners, and the general surgeons doing pelvic surgery. In many offices and clinics the test is taken by nurses. The Pap smear is taken by any one of these professionals but it is always *interpreted* in a sub-department of pathology as being "positive", "suspicious", or "negative".

Cancer of the cervix is most likely to occur between the ages of twenty and sixty. Only the very rare case shows up after sixty. Beyond sixty, abnormal bleeding will likely mean trouble in the ovaries or womb or elsewhere but rarely in the cervix. Doctors argue that if any woman, regardless of age, will make it a habit to go to her doctor every twelve months for a Pap test, then in the course of the examination some other condition may be found that can be treated. This may be true and important because breast cancer for example is at least 200 times as frequent as cervix cancer.

But because cervix cancer is so rare after sixty, the doctors' time doing "routine examinations with the Pap test" in women in the sixties and seventies and eighties could be spent more effectively in other ways. This would reduce much of the anxiety in women who are always worried until the doctor's nurse calls and reports that "the Pap smear is normal".

These Pap programs have been pushed very aggressively. In a public health program in British Columbia 20,000 women were examined with the idea that they would be re-tested every year. But patients do not like submitting to impersonal tests; only fifty of the original 20,000 turned up in the fifth year of follow-up. This poor response is typical of many screening programs.

One wonders whether it would not be more rational for doctors to simply ask their patients about abnormal bleeding or for the patients to report any unexplained bleeding between menstrual periods to their doctors.

> A woman of sixty-seven had been in the habit of visiting her gynecologist every six months since her menopause. At every single visit a Pap smear had been taken and reported "negative". Five months before her operation she had made her regular visit, but it was a busy day and the gynecologist did not do any more than say "Hi". The nurse took the Pap smear and it was reported negative. Five months later this woman felt a pressure low in her left side. She was given an appointment within a week when she phoned the office nurse. The gynecologist was shocked when he made his examination. He found a tumor of the left ovary. At surgery a spreading malignancy was found. No one can say whether it would have been discovered had a pelvic examination been done five months earlier. No one can deny that with this tumor developing the Pap smear gave no evidence of it.

The Pap test, like any other test when done routinely at all ages without a meaningful history and a careful pelvic examination, usually turns out to be an inadequate if lucrative substitute for good doctoring.

The more the doctor comes to rely on a mass of laboratory evidence, the greater the shrinkage in his true doctoring power. Every time he orders another test or X-ray without having taken the history and done an examination to justify the test, the excellence and accuracy of his clinical touch declines a little. The more the laboratory services are demanded, the less dependable they become. The right diagnosis is often completely obscured by a multiplicity of lab reports.

> A healthy man of 64 had an attack of pneumonia from which he made an uneventful recovery. Two weeks later he was complaining of weakness in his legs and was given tranquillizer pills because it was believed that he was suffering from a nervous upset. Within ten days he had lost the use of his legs and the continued application of tranquillizers in large doses landed him in an emergency ward of a

larger hospital in a state of acute delirium. He was then transferred to a teaching hospital.

The patient was now showing paralysis of his face and his four limbs, and was quite unconscious, with attacks of arrested breathing. He was put in the intensive care unit and had numerous blood examinations, one of which suggested slight kidney trouble, another slight diabetes, another a change in the working of his lungs.

Because the paralysis and mental condition could not be accounted for, a carotid artery injection with dye to show the arteries of the brain by X-rays was carried out on both sides, in a search for something like a brain tumor or an aneurysm. The X-rays were normal. Attention next focused on the weakness of his legs. It was felt that he might have pressure on the lower part of his spinal cord and a myelogram, or X-ray of the spinal cord outline, was done. The cost of these studies had now exceeded $1,200.

Among all the tests, a spinal fluid examination at the first small hospital pointed to the diagnosis. A second examination confirmed the original test but this team of specialists decided there was too much conflicting evidence. A young consultant who had been mystified by all the lab reports as they came along wrote this note on the chart on the fifth hospital day: "Indeed in spite of all these conflicting opinions and laboratory reports this man does look like a case of neuritis."

He was right — the man had neuritis, and he recovered completely. The interpretation of the spinal fluid report from the first hospital should have settled the diagnosis.

Any keen final year medical student would have been able to make this diagnosis using his eyes, his ears, his head, and the spinal fluid report, if his head was not cluttered up with all the misleading lab reports. The charge for the laboratory examination of the spinal fluid was just five dollars.

During the last quarter-century, technology has contributed so heavily to diagnosis and treatment that it is no longer believed to be possible for a doctor to work effectively without the newest apparatus in a modern hospital with its army of technicians and subspecialists. With all this gadgetry, the threat of dehumanization of personal relationships between the doctor and the patient undoubtedly occurs and the excellence and the satisfaction of good practice decline.

A man forty-seven was seen by a senior physician in the out-patient clinic of one of our best hospitals. In the previous four years he had been seen by many senior medical students, interns, busy doctors, and specialists. He had had chest pains, cough, headaches, dizzy spells, indigestion, diarrhoea, and pains in his shoulder and hips and back. Because of these many complaints he had been sent for a new test or X-ray or a specialist's opinion every time he came. The complaint that brought him to the hospital the day this physician saw him was inconsequential — ''smelly sweating feet.'' The physician was interested in the thickness of the chart with its numerous negative specialists' opinions, X-ray reports, and laboratory test sheets. He sat down with the students and the patient and took the man's history. The man had not succeeded in his Grade 8 examinations in public school. His job history was inconstant, and he had never held a job for as long as a year. He was unmarried. He had no responsible relatives and no friends. The only place he got any attention was at the hospital out-patient clinic. To continue visiting he had developed different complaints, each of which was recorded as a separate story.

No doctor student had taken the time to put this unfortunate man's story together. It was found that he had been in a mental hospital on several occasions where the diagnosis of schizophrenia had been made.

All this poor man really needed was a little time and sympathy, and some guidance about his living. For patients like him the real doctor must act as a crutch who gives support along life's difficult path. Laboratory tests are often useless and they are sometimes compared with giving stones to patients who need only the bread of healing exemplified in the skilled sympathetic touch.

The many laboratory advances should have acted as checks and balances to make doctors more exact as practitioners and as teachers. Unfortunately, the substitution of the lab reports for the laying on of hands has produced a generation of doctors who are unsure of themselves, and who would not dare trust their clinical skill in a patient's home or in a community hospital, where most sick patients are found. These doctors, when unattended by their supporting casts of lab technicians, X-ray experts, and specialist consultants, are quite helpless. They completely miss the satisfaction of practising real medicine. They are afraid to meet the disease on its own battleground.

11.

Is your doctor up-to-date?

To serve the sick is an exacting privilege.

ANONYMOUS

So far we have talked mainly about doctors who are "not there." Some are not there because our bad methods of recruiting kept them out of medical school. Others are not there because they got sidetracked into research, subspecialization, administration, or some other non-doctoring area.

What about doctors who are there, but who give their patients treatments that are outdated or unsound?

A new article appears in some medical journal on the average every twenty-six seconds. No one could expect doctors to keep abreast of all the medical literature. But lacking a confident familiarity with the proven new medical developments, the practice of medicine for many of them becomes frustrating and disheartening — a fast defensive game played with highly informed patients. How much should they know to be safe?

With increasing frequency, the patient now dictates his own course and his own terms. He may insist on an electrocardiogram, a brain-wave tracing, a vitamin B-12 shot, an operation, a blood test, or a consultation with some specialist whom he or his friends think he should see. Obliging the patient has been made so acceptable, and the expenses are so frequently underwritten by public and private insurance carriers, that the doctor has found himself going along more and more with "the demands of the customer". He is going to have to return to across-the-table consulting and to teaching the patient. He cannot be a man of putty, who acquiesces to every complainer who gets his information via the news media, or a spongy mat on which his patient steps to squeeze out an order for a newer antibiotic.

From earliest times people have sought cures and with every cure new hopes have come and have led in turn to still newer cures. Reports continue to flood the media and the people press doctors for the newest treatments. But it always takes a long time for any treatment to be carefully assessed and accepted or given up entirely and relegated to the category of the outdated.

> An impressive correction of a 300-pound fat woman was achieved with the by-pass intestinal operation. This works by shunting most of the food away from the absorbing surface of the intestine. Within a year of a successful operation this young woman, who began with the appearance of a sad tired tub of lard, became vivacious and beautiful. This was very dramatic. Unfortunately the bowel by-pass disturbed her body chemistry so much that the normal course of nature had to be re-established.
>
> We would have expected that with the happiness of renewed vigour and beauty this patient would never again indulge in gluttony. Sad to relate, within a year of the time of return of the bowel's working in nature's own way, her weight had returned to the original 300 pounds. A modern surgical miracle had been performed but the patient did not have the willpower to maintain her beauty. This by-pass operation has a substantial surgical mortality and soon will be discarded entirely. This woman may now request the very newest cure for fatness and have her teeth wired together!

Quite a few of the medical and surgical breakthroughs within the last three decades have followed this pattern. Here are some of the surgical miracles of the last thirty years which have been discarded:

- The sympathectomy operation to release nerve muscle tension of the arteries for high blood pressure. Now medicines are used.
- Surgery on the brain for Parkinson's disease. Now the L-Dopa series of tablets are superior.
- Frontal lobotomy surgery, for mental agitation. The tranquillizers and mood elevators are better and safer.

- Operation for toxic goitre. Now it is radio-active iodine.
- Tic doloreux. Now the tablets are often better than this delicate brain surgery.
- Coronary by-pass surgery for severe angina. Of very doubtful value and on the way out. The cost of X-rays and operations would exceed $4 billion a year if this treatment were used routinely. This is more money than the tax structure should support for one disease.
- Transplants of livers, hearts, and kidneys are decreasing every month. The rejection factor is insurmountable.

The stature of the doctor diminishes every time a visit or a call extracts the demand item. This is a good time to refer to some of the areas in which the over-busy doctor is cornered by his patients. The doctor yields, because to yield seems so harmless, because the patient is so insistent, and because the doctor is not up to date to the point where he can say with assurance: "This is nonsense, it will do you no good, and I shall not be a party to it."

The B-12 Shots

The most common example of drug by patient demand is vitamin B-12, the replacement for liver extract. Like liver extract, it controls pernicious anemia. More than 99 per cent of these injections are given to patients who do not have pernicious anemia and who are not measurably helped by them. The only yardstick of gain is the crude and totally unscientific one that "the patient feels better for it". Many patients go to the doctor for a B-12 shot two or three times a week because of low blood pressure, or nervousness, or fatigue. Some doctors use it for the treatment of undiagnosed forms of neuritis, bursitis, and arthritis. There is no reasonable proof that improvement follows its administration for any of these vague conditions.

This is all wasted medical care. It does no good. It may do no direct harm except by serving as a substitute for proper treatment. The use of any medication that makes over-busy doctors buy disposable syringes by the thousand and whose patients enter the waiting room "with sleeves rolled up at the ready" is humbug.

When the probability of the patient's being helped by visiting a doctor in 1910 was no more than 50-50, handing out a bottle of pink medicine to the patient carried visible and usually unpalatable assurance that the doctor expected his patient to get better or to come back if he did not get better. That was the essence of what is now referred to as "continuity of medical care." The doctor was able to study the development of his patient's sickness. Some got better and some got worse. When surgical conditions showed up they could be spotted and treated. For the time it was pretty good practice and it did little harm. Most diseases were incurable anyway. Modern surgery was only beginning and medical cures were almost non-existent. Multitudes of patients with symptoms but without disease kept going back to their doctors for months and for years. The doctors dispensed concern and hope *and* a bottle of pink medicine with a little something extra for the latest nerve strain or pain.

Today, most patients can be cured or greatly helped by the wise prescribing of the right medicines. Reliance on the old doctor's pink medicine and now the pink B12 shot is rarely justified. The doctor should be making the right diagnosis and ordering the right treatment in the 1970s.

The Blood Thinners

In 1929, a student in engineering at the University of Toronto sustained a critical injury to his left arm and shoulder which tore the main artery carrying blood to the arm and hand. He was rushed to the emergency room at the Toronto General Hospital. The surgeon called was young Dr. Gordon Murray who was developing his meticulous techniques for the repair of blood vessel injuries. Dr. Murray deftly stitched the torn artery together, but the next morning the hand was black from gangrene and amputation had to be carried out.

While the operation was a technical success, the blood had clotted in the injured artery. This was the bugbear of blood-vessel surgery in those days. Dr. Murray went to his chief, Professor Edward Gallie, and told him the story. He insisted that if something could be used that would prevent blood from clotting in repaired arteries, limbs could be saved.

A substance called heparin had been discovered in 1916 at Johns Hopkins by Drs. Jay McLean and W. H. Howell. When used in tiny amounts for experimental purposes it prevented the clotting of a few drops of blood in a test tube. It had never been used on humans.

Dr. Murray got in touch with Dr. Charles Best in the Department of Physiology and Dr. D. A. Scott at the Connaught Laboratories and urged them to produce heparin in quantity. After years of trials and disappointments they developed a preparation made from beef lung that had no unfavourable reactions and prevented clotting when given after the repair of injured blood vessels. Its most immediate and widespread use turned out to be for patients with phlebitis (clotting in the leg veins). In the first large series treated, Dr. Murray found that the pain and fever of phlebitis would usually disappear within forty-eight hours after heparin was started.

There were difficulties that slowed the easy use of heparin in the 1930s. The patient had to be in bed with a continuous intravenous drip running into his arm with the heparin added to the intravenous solution. The number of drops per minute had to be regulated in order that the clotting time of the blood was prolonged enough to prevent clot formation, and this required a special nurse to count the drops per minute frequently, for if the intravenous ran too fast there was a risk of bleeding and if it did not run fast enough the drug did no good.

With increasing knowledge of phlebitis and later of disease of the coronary and brain arteries, it seemed reasonable to think that, if a person was beginning to have clotting in any important artery, the early use of heparin might prevent the blockage from becoming complete. Before many years, the routine use of heparin in the early phases of treatment of heart attacks and stroke became standard and in some centres it still is. Heparin made heart surgery, kidney dialysis, and the entire transplant chapter possible. It is still the best treatment for acute phlebitis. However, it does not protect against impending heart attacks or strokes, and Dr. Murray himself insisted from the beginning that heparin would never dissolve a clot once it had completely formed.

Because of the cost, the necessity of frequent laboratory checks of the clotting time, and the need to have the patients in hospital with special nurses, a search began for some comparable drug that might be taken as a tablet. The story of sweet clover disease in cattle was described by F. S. Schofield of the Ontario Veterinary College in Guelph in 1921. It was later found that spoiled sweet clover could be extracted and a material obtained that could be put in tablet form. This was called dicumerol. Given in large amounts, it always made animals bleed to death. It was reasoned that a smaller dose would alter the clotting mechanism in the human patient and prevent clot formation. This approach was developed at the Mayo Clinic in 1940. In the next ten years it gained world-wide popularity, until it constituted the standard treatment for many heart and brain and phlebitis patients. During the years from 1945 to 1970 many of the most renowned heart specialists firmly believed that it was possible to prevent future attacks of brain and heart and leg thrombosis by the prolonged use of dicumerol or allied drugs in tablet form. But in the last ten years critical assessments of many series of cases treated with and without these drugs, known as "blood thinners", have proven that they do not accomplish the specific effects that had been claimed for them. There is a constant and unpredictable risk of hemorrhage with the standard dose, which is sometimes critical and too often fatal. Whenever hemorrhage occurs it invites infection. Hemorrhage around nerves may lead to paralysis.

It is now known that the estimation of the dose of any blood thinner is very inaccurate when the patient is also taking drugs for rheumatism, infections, insomnia, or heart, liver, or kidney conditions. It is always dangerous to use the blood thinners in older patients, in those with high blood pressure, or in patients with stomach or bowel ulcers.

A few doctors gave early warnings about the blood thinners — notably Dr. William Evans and Dr. Edward Bartram of London, England, and London, Ontario, respectively. Despite Dr. Evans' assertion that "this stuff is nothing but rat poison", the use of blood-thinner tablets became widespread.

Most doctors who were anxious to do something for their heart and brain and phlebitis patients used the blood thinners routinely. There has never been any solid experimental proof that the blood-thinner tablets do influence blood clotting predictably and safely. The patient has been the experimental animal while the doctors without familiarity with the published unfavourable results have continued to prescribe.

A man of fifty-four was referred to a cardiologist because of an acute coronary attack. He was hospitalized, treated with demerol for pain and his blood was "thinned" with dicumerol. It was a bad attack and he was sent home to his own doctor's care after eight weeks with instructions to keep on taking the dicumerol and to return to work gradually. In six months while still having his blood thinned he was sent to the cardiologist after another attack, which was not quite so bad as the first one. He was discharged after four weeks, still taking the dicumerol. One year from the time of the first coronary attack he was re-admitted with heart failure. The student who took the patient's history found that his business had gone into bankruptcy and that his wife was working. The history further brought out the fact that the man's ability to calculate had been destroyed after the first heart attack and this explained his loss of business acumen. He was one of the coronary patients who had sustained little strokes following the heart attack that had occurred in spite of dicumerol treatment. The cardiologist, preoccupied with thinning the blood, had neglected the much more serious changes that were taking place in the man's brain. The dicumerol had not saved his heart or his brain.

Every reader will have known patients or relatives of patients who had phlebitis and whose doctor prescribed tablets for thinning the blood.

A store manager of fifty-six had tolerated increasing pain in his right hip for more than ten years and had reached a point where he had pain using the brake and accelerator pedals in his car. He was seen by a very excellent orthopedic surgeon. The X-rays showed hopeless arthritic changes in the hip joint, and an operation that consisted of complete replacement of the joint was undertaken successfully. On the second day after the operation the patient was up in a chair and he continued to increase his activities every day. On the ninth day he had a sudden pain in his right chest, he spat blood, and examination revealed slight swelling of the calf of the right leg. The diagnosis was post-operative phlebitis with loosening of a clot in the leg vein and a resulting pulmonary (lung) embolism. This kind of phlebitis is an unpredictable and unpreventable complication of any kind of pelvic operation, and of many abdominal and hip operations.

The patient was treated promptly and effectively with heparin. In two weeks he was home. He was gradually taken off the heparin and placed on dicumerol blood thinner tablets, which he took every day. Five weeks after the embolism he felt very well and went back to his store, halftime. Every Monday he went to the hospital laboratory where the clotting effect of the tablets was checked.

On a Sunday evening ten weeks after the operation, two friends came to dinner. As he was bidding them good-bye he lost his speech, slumped to the floor, and lapsed into deep coma with heavy breathing. The next day he died as the result of an extensive brain hemorrhage from too much dicumerol.

It is almost impossible to use any blood-thinner tablet effectively or safely. Every month we see patients admitted to hospital because of hemorrhages that have been caused by their quite unpredictable effects. It will never be possible to estimate the prolongation of hosptial stays because of unfavourable complications, or the mortality figures directly attributable to this treatment.

The blood thinners should not be taken by patients who are using aspirin, sleeping pills of any kind, anti-cancer medications, blood pressure medications, anemia medications, or tranquillizers. They should never be used in patients who have hepatitis or cancer or stroke or pericarditis or pleurisy, or who are past or current alcoholics.

Any doctor who contemplates using blood thinners must first consider whether his patient has evidence of any of these serious diseases. The elderly patients are always placed at risk with blood thinners.

The Antibiotics

Since the development of penicillin in the 1940s and streptomycin in the 1950s, antibiotics have increased in numbers at a fantastic rate; they rarely remain on the market for five years before something new and better is developed by the drug companies. *Yet most of all the antibiotics prescribed are not needed.* In many instances the patients have no infections at all and the drugs are given as preventatives although they have little value as preventatives, except for rheumatic fever patients. They do not work in virus infections, which account for most of the influenza-like illnesses. When used for streptococcus, staphylococcus, pneumococcus, and venereal infections, their use must be concentrated and controlled by a doctor who is well versed in their effects. The employment of the antibiotics in an uncritical routine way carries many risks, and may permit other serious infections to develop that are not responsive to any kind of treatment. Their abuse is reflected in the fact that one patient in twenty in every acute hospital bed in America is there because of the over-use or the wrong use of drugs. The antibiotics are the most common offenders.

The busy practitioner, beleaguered by requests for a shot of penicillin or "some capsules to control the flu bug", is tempted to acquiesce without taking the time to check the temperature, look at the throat, listen to the lungs, and do the appropriate cultures — not to mention checking sensitivity of the offending bacteria to the drug.

The Brain-Wave Tracing, or the Electroencephalogram

Brain-wave tracing was developed as an experimental tool in the 1930s. Its primary use was in the study of epilepsy and it brought about a new understanding of the electrical activity of the brain. Besieged by large numbers of patients with seizures or epileptic attacks, doctors pressed the manufacturers to produce machines that would record brain waves for the nerve specialists to study. Over the last twenty years, and particularly in the last ten years, brain tracing or electroencephalography (E.E.G.) laboratories have been set up in all the large hospitals. But the E.E.G. is not an efficient tool. Perhaps one case of epilepsy in fifty will show significant changes in the yards and yards of record paper that enable the reader (usually one man in one city or one large hospital) to give a report that will actually help the patient's doctor. This is a very low score. The E.E.G. does not permit the most experienced reader or electroencephalographer to differentiate a brain clot from a tumor, abscess, or blocked artery or vein, or from a case of migraine. The E.E.G. exemplifies a test for which the average M.D. is often pressed by his demanding patients and that only rarely has any measurable importance in his management of the patient. In getting the report, the doctor is never any wiser about how his medicine for epilepsy is working. In bowing to the patient's pressure he is only downgrading his diagnostic skills and adding to the waste of the taxpayer's money.

Reading tracings and dictating their interpretation into a tape recorder is an absurd waste of the valuable time of the small number of active nerve specialists who should have much more important work to do dealing directly with the patients who need their skill. The referring doctors are often required to wait too long for the more important opinions on acute brain cases. Sometimes they must wait indefinitely for the E.E.G. report and when it finally comes they are no wiser, and their patients are no better. The E.E.G. readings should be done by Ph.D.s in electrophysics who do not have to care for patients and who might do some worthwhile investigation on the miles of records that flow every day from these over-used machines.

A boy of thirteen was presented at a surgical conference recently. While wading in a swimming pool his legs had given way; he had gone under and was drowned. Prompt treatment restored breathing and he was transferred unconscious by ambulance to our emergency department. The junior intern who examined him noticed a weakness in the left arm and a reflex change in the left foot. He thought it was more than drowning and he called our brain surgeon to see him. More history was obtained from the family and it was learned that the boy had been treated by a pediatric team for migraine headache during the previous six months. The pediatric team was sure of the migraine diagnosis because the brain-wave tracing (E.E.G.) supported it. He was treated with aspirin but the headache had continued to get worse. The brain surgeon, using his ophthalmoscope, saw at the back of the eye evidence of pressure on the brain that dated back over a period of months. An X-ray of the skull showed a large benign tumor at the base of the brain. The intern was the bright doctor on this case "because he looked a second time" and called for appropriate help. The pediatricians had been carried off course because they had relied on the E.E.G. (which is never exact for diagnosing migraine) and because they neglected to examine the eyes and X-ray the skull in a boy with a bad headache. Reliance on the E.E.G. almost cost this boy his life.

Tablets for Diabetes

Fifty years after the discovery of insulin, its proper use is still not understood by most doctors. A real diabetic whose before-breakfast blood sugar is high, who is subject to infections or coma, and especially on whom surgery is to be performed, can only be accurately treated with diet and correct doses of insulin. The doctor who prescribes insulin must first be familiar with the diet his diabetic patient is to follow. There are over four million diabetics in North America; because so many doctors are overworked and do not understand the insulin effects, and because so many patients dislike using the necessary needle, it was inevitable that when non-insulin pills for diabetes appeared they would be extremely popular. The diabetic with complications cannot be adequately controlled with any anti-diabetic tablet. The combination of diet with tablets, used over a five-year period, does not appear to be as safe as diet with insulin, because arterial and heart disease occur more often.

For many years, before the introduction of the pills, less than 10 per cent of all diabetics under average medical care were adequately controlled. This meant that diets and insulin doses were not correctly regulated. This is serious because diabetes now accounts for one quarter of all cases of blindness in North America. The only factor that is likely to prevent this blindness is the best possible treatment of diabetes. The same holds for a great many cases of gangrene of the feet.

Ellenberg and Riskin, in their textbook entitled *Diabetes: Theory and*

Practice, state the case in a very sensible perspective everyone can understand: "It has been our opinion for some time that the average control of diabetes in this country falls short of all goals, mainly because the busy doctor cannot give sufficient time to educate and inspire the diabetic patient, particularly the young one. Because the average patient rebels against regimentation, unless he can be sufficiently motivated, which means a combination of firm belief and sustained effort, the life management is not what it should be. All too often enthusiasm at the beginning of treatment wanes with the passage of time".

Diabetic tablets taken without a proper diet and adequate meals may produce a prolonged drop in the blood sugar level, which can be followed by permanent brain damage, according to Charles M. Gaitz, in *Aging and the Brain* (1972). Such a serious possibility emphasizes the need for the doctor to be certain that the older diabetic knows enough to obtain, prepare, and eat his proper diet. Dr. Martin G. Goldner of the State University of New York Medical School has stated it well: "Insulin is effective in all types of diabetes all of the time. The tablets are effective in some types of diabetes some of the time".

The Cholesterol Craze

It can now be stated that no doctor who has examined hundreds of hearts at post-mortem and seen the narrowed coronary arteries through which only a trickle of blood can pass will ever waste time trying to convince his patients that they must spoil the months or years left to them with low cholesterol diets. He will know that the narrowed arteries can never be opened up again by any diet. And yet the story of hardening of the arteries and blood cholesterol and blood fat has captivated both doctors and public for more than three decades. For years no medical meeting was complete without a series of reports on the blood fats and their control, and the results when they were left uncontrolled. It was fashionable to send samples of blood to a special laboratory in California for the exact estimate of the different fat elements. After a small stroke or a heart attack, patients have been put on the most outlandish diets aimed at lowering blood fats. Heart doctors have now become disillusioned and have begun to realize that nothing is gained by tinkering with the fat contents of a diet in an individual who has developed arterial disease. Nor is it possible to prevent arterial disease by adhering to a low-fat program from youth. In the Korean war, routine autopsy studies on healthy young American soldiers at an average age of twenty-five showed evidence of coronary arterial disease in 75 per cent of them. Changes in the arterial system do begin in early life and they cannot be altered by the employment of any low-fat program so far devised.

In 1935, Dr. Edward Hall began experimental work on the heart at the Banting Institute in Toronto. His work attracted the attention of Dr. Paul Dudley White in Boston and he was asked to present his findings at several important American heart meetings. Heart disease had claimed the lives of both of Dr. Hall's parents. When he reached his middle fifties his own heart began to give trouble and he saw the handwriting on his own life wall. In my last conversation with him we talked about heart troubles in general and turned to the cholesterol story which at the time was at its height. This man, whose family history compelled him to think about coronary heart disease for more than thirty years and who in his own person experienced the most incapacitating features of the disease, made this statement: "If there is any possible relation between coronary disease and cholesterol it would be necessary for everyone who wanted to avoid a coronary attack to live on a cholesterol-free diet from birth. Of course this would be as unreasonable as it would be impossible to achieve."

One heart specialist told a patient with a coronary attack who had asked him about diet, "I can make your life miserable with a real stinker of a diet without fat, or I can let you live happily. You must make the choice." A heartless and senseless decision to force on a patient. Why could the doctor not just request a reasonable low-fat diet from the dietitian if he believed in the low-fat idea — or even if he did not.

In the heyday of the cholesterol chapter, a sixty-year-old surgeon was buttonholed by one of his medical colleagues just back from a meeting on "hardening of the arteries". An enthusiastic convert to the concept that any increase in cholesterol calls for active treatment, he pushed the unsuspecting surgeon into the lab for the test. The report came back 262 (with the normal being between 150 and 250). The surgeon asked what this meant. The medical man replied, "Well, it's better than 500, but I'm glad mine isn't that high. I will start you on a diet right away."

This news upset the cool-headed surgeon, who saw many coronary attacks in his patients and among his friends. He spoke with another physician, told him about the 262 and the diet program he was headed for. This physician described the reading of 262 as too close to normal to worry about, and asserted that the effectiveness of diets was still unproven even in high-cholesterol cases. Relieved, the surgeon scrubbed up for his next operation, and five years later was at the operating table doing his eighty-hour weeks.

> In 1969 a woman of seventy-two was admitted to our hospital with high blood pressure and signs of a threatening stroke, but otherwise vigorous and healthy. Her history brought out the fact that she was a cream addict and for more than thirty years had taken one-half pint of rich cream daily. Routine examinations were done, and one interesting finding was a normal cholesterol reading. "For the sake of science" and with the co-operation of special nurses, this woman's cream was withheld from her diet for two weeks. At the end of that time she was allowed to return to her one-half pint. That day, following the heavy splash of cream in her diet, her blood cholesterol was tested again. It was found to be below normal.

Never a month goes by without some sad patient asking if he can risk one egg a week or a teaspoonful of cream in his coffee. The question is ridiculous.

During the past few years some of our foremost pathologists, examining the coronary arteries of patients who have come to post-mortem because of non-heart deaths have found them to be entirely normal. Leafing through the hospital charts of some of these patients with perfectly normal coronaries, they have been dumbfounded to find that in life the blood cholesterol done in the best laboratories may have exceeded 1,000! They have asked the simple question: "If high cholesterol has any constant effect on the coronary arteries, how could this happen?" The cholesterol craze has been an assumption, not a fact.

The American College of Cardiology met in Chicago in 1972 with 3,500 heart specialists in attendance. The college requested that the Conrad Hilton Hotel prepare meals low in saturated fat and cholesterol and at the request of the college the spread served was margarine.

The cardiologists behaved like sheep on this occasion and, with a scientific program that did not contain anything really new or lifesaving, most of those specialists would have returned to their practices with nothing more for the patients with coronary disease than advice about cutting down on the fat in their diets.

Three years later, at the 1975 International Conference on Arterial Disease, the conclusion was reached that there is no scientific proof that cholesterol-lowering by drugs or diet alters the life outlook after one or more coronary attacks. The five-year mortality rates in treated and untreated patients were exactly the same.

Should the reader have a very with-it doctor or cardiologist he will not be worried by the cholesterol reading in his blood. That is old hat in 1976. He may be like this poor fellow:

> A high-ranking insurance executive of forty-eight working under the usual strain of this occupation developed low discomfort in his chest. One doctor said it was "stomach nerves", but to be dead sure he referred him to first one and then, for final confirmation, to a second heart authority.
>
> These are the exact words the executive was given after two weeks of thorough hospital investigating:
>
> "Your triglycerides are high and this means that you have hyperlipoprotinemia Type IV. Triglycerides are the main factor in coronary disease. You have biochemical diabetes because one blood sugar after that double slug of glucose you were given was above normal. This often occurs when the triglycerides are high. This all means that you are a very high-risk candidate for a coronary attack. If you take off fifty pounds, quit smoking, keep drinking, stick to this diet which has no natural fat in it, take a spoonful of corn oil before breakfast every morning, don't touch sugar in any form, exercise every day to the point of fatigue, and sort out your life priorities, you *may* escape a heart attack. You have some gout, so take one of these tablets every day so long as you live. You should feel better if you follow these rules. If the triglycerides come down you may have a chance. Come back for a re-check in eighteen months, and we will know how you are doing."

I have listened to so many stories like this with cholesterol and now with triglycerides that I believe that doctors who practise this way are producing a sort of "mental castration" on their innocent patients.

We could not be critical of these doctors if the diets they order did reduce the blood fats and if reduced blood fats did eliminate the risk of a coronary attack. But we have absolutely no proof that they do.

The Diet Treatments

Diet fads date from the beginning of man's history. With the better understanding of kidney disease, gout, stomach ulcer, colitis, gall-bladder disease, sprue, liver failure, obesity, undernutrition, allergies, diabetes, toxic goitre, heart failure, and deficiency states, rational diets constitute many of the important foundations of good medical treatment. These diseases will often be better controlled by thorough diet-planning if the diagnosis is certain, if the patient can adhere to a program he can understand and afford, and if the intelligent preparation and serving of the diet are assured.

When the patient is a husband with overweight or ulcer or diabetes, the likelihood of his following the diet very often depends on his wife's willingness to provide *and to eat* the same diet. Human nature being what it is, the wise wife will accommodate herself peacefully to his diet instead of making the dining-table a battleground over which she harangues her husband-patient for not following the rules set down by the doctor or the dietician. "To doctor" means to teach, and the dietary aspect of any treatment requires the doctor to fill his teacher role as he convinces the patient of the need to stick to his diet. This requires encouragement and time in the original consultation and at later visits when details must be checked with the patient and often with his wife.

In kidney diseases, depending on the stage in which the patient happens to be, and where one stage merges into another during the usual course of Bright's disease, the diet will have wide variations. At first it is sugar and fat and some fluid with no meat. Later on more meat than the average normal diet contains is ordered, without salt but with a limited water allowance and some sugar. In the chronic stage the patient needs a great deal of fluid and sugar and fat and a reduced allowance of meat. The doctor must understand kidney disease and take considerable pains in managing his patient from one stage to the next.

The Low Salt Diet

In the early 1940s, Dr. L. H. Newburgh of the University of Michigan demonstrated that the majority of patients with old-fashioned dropsy could be helped by "drying out" if the salt in the diet was rigidly curtailed or eliminated. Patients who had been swollen from heart failure or kidney disease or liver disease got rid of the swelling, breathed better, and lived again. This diet was one of the medical breakthroughs that did more for many patients than drugs had ever done. During the next twenty years the doctors, with the tireless co-operation of dieticians who were called to see dropsical patients, always instructed them meticulously about the low-salt diet. The results were very good for patients with the intelligence, the willingness, and the kitchen co-operation needed, but not all patients were so fortunate and even those who were had to put up with unappetizing meals. Now, drugs that help the body and the kidneys to get rid of large amounts of water have been developed and improved. These "fluid pills" are harmless tablets which, when taken once a day six days a week, prevent the storage of excess water by the body. This has improved the lives of millions of patients.

The tendency to persist with something that has proved its worth very often becomes deeply rooted in medicine and many doctors in practice and interns in hospitals, confronted with dropsical patients, continue to order a low-salt diet as if from habit. In nine cases out of ten the tablet does the work better without all the trouble.

Jogging to the Undertaker

The current fad of jogging was originally suggested by the heart specialists, and in 1964 at the Inter-American Heart Congress several papers were presented that intended to show that exercise after a heart attack is good. Now, more than ten years later, and after many deaths on this jogging course — often under the careful supervision of experts — we know that a person who has had a real heart attack places himself in grave danger by jogging or push-ups or any other vigorous exercise. The enthusiasts claim that there is a great morale-building boost in achieving a track program (which the patient probably never attempted in his youthful days) after a big or a little coronary attack. It is supposed to prove to the patient that he still has a lot of steam and that he need not look back to the pain and sweating and short breathing of the coronary attack but only ahead to normal vigorous living.

We all regret the deaths of three doctors while leading their respective jogging packs of coronary patients along three different Florida courses. It is now becoming more customary for doctors to prescribe jogging than to indulge in it.

I think of two fathers and sons who presented contrasting images. One father and son in 1970 were thirty-seven and thirteen, respectively, as I watched them jogging along the beach. They went a mile up the beach, turned and came back, jogging more slowly, the father panting noticeably. They could not converse, they had no breath for talk. I could not help wondering if that father would make it to fifty.

The other father-and-son image goes back many years. I saw them on the main street in Stratford, Ontario, the father forty-five, the son in his twenties. They walked, hands clasped behind their backs, to the east end of the city and back. It was an hour's stroll, and as they walked they talked, the father sharing his wisdom with his son. Fifty years later the son consulted me for a minor complaint. He was still going to the office daily at seventy-five and enjoying life thoroughly. He had always walked for relaxation during a very busy and happy life.

After studying hundreds of hearts at autopsy following coronary attacks, and having been amazed by the fact that the subjects had lived so long with such badly diseased coronary arteries, I have been convinced that the jogger who tries to make his narrowed coronary tubes carry as much blood to the heart muscle as these tubes did for a two-mile run when the jogger was twenty years old has been badly misled. Doctors who acquiesce in the jogging fad, out of a lack of autopsy experience on heart patients, push their jogging patients into early coffins, without ever knowing why they died.

In out-patient and office practice I see patients every week who have absorbed the current teaching on exercise by the heart doctors. Men and women of sixty or seventy walk six miles a day to avoid heart disease. Everyone beyond forty will have some coronary artery changes and such changes, from all the evidence available, cannot be prevented or reversed by exercise.

The exercise enthusiasts recommend enough exercise to make the heart beat pretty fast, and with this speed-up in heart action the blood pressure always goes up. They believe this to be good for the patient. Actually he does this every time he answers an important phone call, because every call induces some tension, the adrenalin effect occurs, the heart beats faster, and the blood pressure rises. All this while the man is sitting in his easy chair! If it is relaxation the busy man (with or without a bad heart) needs, he will get it much more certainly and safely by walking without exhausting himself.

It is the fad now with many men and women to jog to get the weight down. This is nonsense because in order to lose one pound net it is necessary to go thirteen miles. After this much exercise the appetite becomes ravenous and the jogger just cannot resist more calories. No pills have yet been made to neutralize this hunger. After all the articles for and against jogging, it can be stated that no man at fifty will ever run as well as he did at twenty-five. Nor will he be as good a bed partner.

When a doctor tells a patient he has angina pectoris, it is just like beaming the radio-TV slogan at him, "heart disease is the number one killer". The wiser physician takes the time to point out that changes take place naturally after middle life in the coronary arteries which supply that muscle which never rests — the heart muscle — with a fast flow of blood which has just been filled with oxygen after it has passed through the lungs. When heart pain develops it is nature's protective warning for a man to slow down, to avoid danger, and in some cases to desist from strain.

The diagnosis of angina should not be regarded as the equivalent of a death warrant, for much of the important work of the world is done by men with this condition. The average life outlook in these men, when it is not cut short by cancer or high blood pressure or accident, when they follow a moderate life program, is more than ten years.

I have never known a patient who jogged to the point of conversational breathlessness regularly attain the age of 62 before getting angina. I have known a great many who died coronary deaths many years before 62. I am saddened when I watch the jogging executive groups in their many-splendored trappings doing their two miles downtown in the lunch hour. They are indeed flooding their leg and chest muscles with blood at high flow rates but they are depriving "that great muscle of the mind" with which they do the thinking act.

There can be little advantage in having well-circulated muscles in the legs if that great muscle of the mind is deprived of its blood supply. It is so foolish to suppress or suspend thinking completely in order to keep praying the prayer of all joggers, "Lord may I not drop dead in the next four miles."

For the heart specialist, the critical point is whether or not a physical conditioning program, maintained during the remainder of the patient's lifetime, will prevent future attacks and assure longevity. The question so far remains unanswered and the available evidence is vague.

High Blood Pressure Pills

Blood pressure reading is the most common single examination that a doctor dealing with adults carries out. The great majority of people who are told they have high blood pressure will live and die with it, but not because of it.

> A woman of fifty-three came to see her doctor in 1935 for a check-up and was found to be in good health, with normal weight, heart, arteries, and kidneys. The blood pressure was 190. No treatment was

ordered. She was seen at intervals thereafter and her blood pressure gradually increased. However, the lower, more important (diastolic) reading was always within the normal range between eighty and ninety. The upper reading increased to 220 and 230, and in the last five years of her life it reached 250. This woman died three days after she fell and broke her hip when she was seventy-six. After all the years with "high blood pressure", her heart at autopsy was normal. She might very easily have been made into a blood pressure invalid if her doctor had been an alarmist during the twenty years he cared for her.

People who are made aware of their blood pressure usually worry because they identify themselves with other blood pressure people who have had heart attacks and strokes. There are more than twenty different kinds of blood pressure. Most of these are not serious or life-threatening. Never a week goes by but a worried patient comes in because he or she has been told that "your blood pressure is over 200". Such blood pressure information can usually be "absorbed" by the knowledgeable physician and not inflicted on the patient, who may live for many years in good health with a blood pressure of 200. Every patient is different and there is no common denominator. It is the doctor's business and his responsibility to diminish the patient's anxiety if the blood pressure machine reads high. He will usually do more for most if he treats the patient rather than the pressure.

Pills prescribed for lowering blood pressure are frequently given to people whose readings are just a shade over normal in the hope that heart failure and stroke and kidney trouble may be prevented.

No more than 15 per cent of all patients who are told that they have high blood pressure need these medicines. Their proper use should not as a rule be commenced without a careful assessment of the kind of blood pressure, the state of the heart, the blood, the brain, the thyroid, and the adrenal glands, the weight, the sex, and the duration of the high blood pressure.

In severe cases of high pressure, hypotensive drugs (drugs that reduce pressure), when ordered with care, have great value. Their use in most blood pressure cases does not do any good. In many cases they make the patient utterly miserable and dizzy when he rises from his bed or chair, often to the point where he may fall and sometimes break a leg or his back. Unless prescribed with experienced clinical discretion, the resulting advantages are slight, and the unpleasant side effects are many. Drugs that lower blood pressure may aggravate mental symptoms in elderly people by reducing blood flow through the diseased arteries supplying the brain or by predisposing to strokes. Medications for lowering blood pressure are costly.

Only the soft, uninformed doctor abdicates his true role as health teacher in managing difficult and demanding patients. The real doctor is capable of holding the line against requests for the nostrums that appear, like the latest vitamins, in new packages every day. The real doctor, sometimes at the risk of incurring an occasional patient's disfavour, will be so well informed and so up-to-date that he does not encourage practices that may be harmless, may be harmful, may even be lethal, but which are for the most part unnecessary.

12.

Did your doctor retire early?

*Don't think of retiring from the world until the world will be
sorry that you retire. I hate a fellow whom pride or cowardice
or laziness drive into a corner and who does nothing when he
is there but sit and growl. Let him come out as I do, and bark.*

SAMUEL JOHNSON

A secure retirement seems more and more to be the goal to strive for.
Should it be the main life-objective of the doctor? Perhaps in some
occupations it is natural, but if what a man is doing is intrinsically worth
while, and if he derives satisfaction from doing it, what is the point in
retiring when he still has the physical and intellectual vitality to keep going?
Pope John XXIII set an example for everyone when upon being elected
pontiff at seventy-eight, instead of accepting the papacy as a mere caretaker
interim, he set about reorganizing the entire church and living his own life to
the fullest while contributing mightily to history.

When should a man retire? When should a man for whom society has
provided its richest education be pushed into retirement?

Kingman Brewster, Jr., president of Yale University, observed in 1968:
"Almost without exception it is the elders (those who do not retire early)
who are productive up to and well beyond retirement." These are the
people who never stop growing and who never comprise the dead wood of a
university faculty. The committed "natural" in a particular profession
cannot resist entering the profession in the first place and, once in, he
cannot stop. He will never retire. The successful doctor, like the

189

independent business executive, lawyer, union leader, actor, politician, or publisher, whose mental and physical health are sound, becomes busier as he approaches seventy. Medicine is one of the professions that permits prolonged freedom for doing what needs to be done.

The real doctor, having practised medicine all his life without a fixed retirement time, has no reason for giving up his work. If he has taught part-time in a medical school he will have maintained and enlarged his clinical power. If by policy he should be retired from his teaching at sixty-five, he will then find himself with as much consulting as he may wish to do. The real surgeon whose mind is nimble and whose knuckles are not stiff can continue to operate on a year-to-year extension of hospital privilege as long as his peers believe he is competent. Should his knuckles stiffen, he can direct the organization of a new surgical department in a new hospital, or act in an advisory capacity in medical education. His is the voice of experience.

How different is the man who says, "I'm fifty-five now — I'm beginning to look around for things to do that will take the place of my regular work because I don't want to put my feet up when I'm sixty-five." There has been much thought and writing devoted to this type. He may be the full-time medical teacher, dean, or administrator, the insurance referee, or drug company executive. All of their jobs are finished at sixty-five and they go on pension.

Current medical planning, supposedly aimed at protecting doctors from the tensions of practice, is being developed around the forty-hour week with mandatory retirement at sixty-five. The doctors in this system will actually begin to retire in spirit before they have ever experienced the satisfaction of practising medicine.

There is a malignancy about the sixty-five figure. The smart man begins at fifty-five to bank the fires and to build his hedges against retirement. This reduces the productivity of numberless M.D.s who should be committed to medicine for life. This happens every day in the U.K., where almost every doctor retires at sixty-five.

The effective successful doctor will face greater demands on his time and talents at forty than at thirty, at fifty than at forty, at sixty than at fifty, and, with full health, at seventy than at sixty. The young man entering medicine must know that the reward for work well done is more work, and he must love it. Medicine is not for the weary ones. The best doctors are usually the busiest doctors. Retirement can never be the life goal of the real doctors. There is too high a satisfaction in bettering or saving patients' lives.

These remarks do not, of course, refer to doctors who have become victims of nervous or physical ailments, and to whom the admonition: "Physician, heal thyself," must apply.

The prematurely retired doctors I have observed did not often burn out and retire so often with physical disease as from breakdowns in the nervous balance. They were just not cut out to be doctors in the first place and they lacked the strong instinctive urge to deal with ailing human beings. They wore out early because the practice of medicine for them was always an unhappy defensive game they were forced to play with their very well-informed patients. Certainly, no work can be any harder or less satisfying than medicine if it is practised under the strain of uncertainty and if the patient holds little respect for the doctor, whom he can badger for the newest fad in diagnosis or cure. It is only with a really substantial educational base, and with the ingrained habit of learning, that a doctor can maintain his nervous balance.

In medicine, the keen, the balanced, the energetic, and the optimistic spirits are the ones who are likely to stay happily in the race for life. These are the perpetual learners with knowledge and wisdom. They will have been so well educated during their eight years of medical school and hospital work and so well sustained through their lifetime by critical reading habits, and visits to good hospital centres that they cannot be pulled off course by the preliminary reports and the explosions of knowledge. They know that not more than one published medical journal article in 200 has important relevance in the doctor's day-to-day work, and they have the critical faculty that empowers them to pick the pearls quickly and disregard the unessentials.

History is well stocked with outstanding examples of great physicians and surgeons who did not wear out at the conventional age. Here are four examples of medical giants who continued to grow by the year long after they turned sixty-five. The reader will have personal knowledge of doctors who contributed mightily to the good of their patients and the world by their labours to and beyond the age of seventy.

> Dr. P. L. Tye of Milverton, Ontario, after sixty years of active practice near my home town, made house calls and hospital calls over an area of 200 square miles by day and by night. He wore out at eighty-five. He once remarked that any doctor who did not go when he was needed was not worthy of the Hippocratic Oath. Dr. Tye was a living proof that within the medical profession itself there were real doctors, "and then there were the rest".

Dr. Robert Zollinger of Ohio State University Medical School had trained more professors of surgery than any living surgeon, but at sixty-five he faced retirement. The chair, which his occupation for more than thirty years had made illustrious, was not easy to fill. The dean finally requested Dr. Zollinger to continue for another two years. He agreed, but, on the day he agreed, he called the younger members of his department together. He told them that his letter of resignation to the dean was on the dean's desk and that it would become effective on the day when he could no longer out-teach, out-operate, out-investigate, out-speak, and out-influence in the highest circles of American surgery, not one but all of them together. At seventy Dr. Zollinger was still at the helm. He had always worked a ninety-hour week. When he took his vacation in 1967 his next-in-line found himself working 120-hour weeks.

Ohio State School of Medicine was less lucky in its handling of Dr. Charles Doan, who as professor of medicine and dean had charted its course through its most illustrious years. Even his time ran out and at sixty-five he retired. The rules did allow him to continue admitting private patients, and he carried on his heavy practice in blood diseases with patients from all parts of the world, without considering the passing years. He was stunned on his seventieth birthday when, on going into the medical department, without having received one warning word from a single faculty or hospital source, he found that the lock on his office door had been replaced. He realized that he was finished. He called his assistant and set off on his last hospital rounds to bid good-bye to his patients and formally place them in the care of his assistant. Every patient expressed keen regret.

One man from New York was very incensed and said that he had been so pleased with his improvement that he had written out a cheque for Dr. Doan that morning to use for improving his laboratory. Dr. Doan thanked him but had to refuse the offer. This New Yorker, a man sixty-seven, could not understand why a great mind like Dr. Doan's should be removed from his patients and his work, and suggested that he should go across town, join the staff at the Riverside Methodist Hospital, improve its laboratory, and carry on with his practice. Dr. Doan was moved but said there would be no place for him at Riverside because of his age. This man was disgusted to learn that medical people could be so stupid. He was about to tear up the cheque, and then paused and said, "Dr. Doan, I want you to try to break professional tradition, go to the director at Riverside, and simply ask him if he would be interested in having his laboratory service updated." Dr. Doan agreed to do what this stubborn patient requested. He found the request easier to fulfil when he opened the envelope and looked at the cheque. It was made out to him personally in the amount of $4 million.

The old quotation, "Man's inhumanity to man make's countless thousands mourn", applied here. The impatience of the faculty to get Dr. Doan out of the hospital proved to be the greatest gaffe in the history of Ohio State. Dr. Doan was still caring for a steady stream of patients in Riverside Methodist when he was seventy-five.

Dr. Herman Blumgart completed his term as professor of medicine on the Harvard service at the Beth Israel Hospital when he reached sixty-five and then served a long term as chairman of the committee on admissions to Harvard Medical School. Then, doubly retired, he became physician in charge of student and faculty health services for Harvard University. He told me later that he had never known happier days. He was seeing sick individuals of all ages with streptococcal throats, pneumonia, leaky heart valves, emotional trouble showing up under the stress of university life, acute appendicitis, mononucleosis, and more. He was visiting some of his old patients in chronic hospitals. At seventy-five he was a very busy and very valuable staff member at Harvard.

It is clear that there should be an honourable alternative to the dread spectre of forced retirement at sixty-five when the salaried doctor is alert and willing.

As we have seen, many thousands of older people in our good chronic hospitals badly need the attention of doctors, and most of them never get it. Geriatrics is interesting and important because it represents a patient population that is worthy and wise and highly grateful for medical services. I know no patients who are more likely to thrive on good doctoring. In this enlarging field mature doctors have a wide-open opportunity to serve well and profitably in terms of patient and personal satisfaction. If the care of these patients was available as a second career for full-time teachers who had quit at sixty-five, it would be good both for the patients and for them. Doctors who have not been happy in a purely academic career could look ahead eagerly to this field, maintaining their self-respect instead of anticipating retirement at sixty-five or earlier!

If this practice was combined with an extended policy of teaching in chronic wards, the otherwise retired doctor would also have the stimulus of student contacts.

All medicine is not new, and fresh discoveries do not outdate what is known every five years. Every hospital service is strengthened if it retains its senior members for consulting. Their stored wisdom is irreplaceable, and it is kept updated because in partial retirement they can keep up with the journal articles that the younger men do not have time to read. From their large experience they can quickly pick the wheat from the chaff in the hundreds of journals published every month. Dr. Alan Gregg of the Rockefeller Institute said: "Of any and all facts that bear upon our relation to the future, I would be inclined to attach the highest importance to the fact that the learning process goes on incessantly, from cradle to grave."

Here are three typical cases, out of hundreds I could cite, that illustrate the advantages of long medical experience:

A fifty-four-year-old woman was admitted to the hospital in 1968 with very painful feet and black tips of the right great toe and the left second toe. The general examination showed she was normal above the knees. The shins were cool and the feet were cold. The diagnosis was arterial disease with critical changes in the feet. The blood examinations for sugar and cholesterol and the other fat fractions, and the uric acid, were all normal. The X-rays of the legs showed extreme hardening of the arteries which looked "like bone" due to the presence of so much calcium in their walls. Similar arterial changes were seen in the X-rays of the arms from the fingers to the shoulders.

The pain became so severe in hospital that aspirin, codeine, and demerol afforded poor relief.

The consultant heads of the medical and surgical sub-departments of heart and blood vessel diseases were called to give their opinions and to add their suggestions about treatment. They pointed out the grave risk of infection and spreading gangrene and death. Their unanimous opinion was amputation of both legs through the upper thigh level. They were unrelenting in their insistence on this course of action.

The woman's physician was a doctor past retirement age who had cared for his patient for a long time. He knew that the patient's father had died of gangrene "before they could cut his legs off", and she was terrified of the disease. The doctor discussed the proposed amputation with the woman's husband, who was horrified and felt sure that the thought of amputation if not the performance of the operation would finish his wife. Carefully weighing all of the evidence in history and physical examination, the X-rays, and specialists' opinions, the physician decided against the double amputation and settled on a program of nursing care, antibiotics to control infection, and different medication for the relief of pain. The course was slow but it was upward. Over a period of months the black areas diminished. One and a half years later the second toe was removed without complications by a general surgeon. Good healing followed this operation. Five years later the patient was still pain-free. She had her feet. She could not walk but was up in a chair and she could stand. She was in excellent spirits, enjoyed company, her bridge club, and weekend visits at home.

A man of thirty-four had experienced severe weight loss. He stood 6′2″ and his weight was just over 100 lbs. He was sent by his family doctor to the university clinic for study by a specialist. The physical finding that attracted the attention of the interns and residents and the specialist was a murmur or bruit in the patient's upper abdomen. Quite mystified by this finding, they decided that the man should have an arteriogram. This is an X-ray done by using an iodide mixture that casts an X-ray shadow when it is injected into an artery. The injection is made through a small catheter introduced into the artery in the groin. One of the senior physicians, hearing about this proposed investigation, raised a cautionary note for two reasons. From his experience he felt that the murmur was a normal finding without any relevance to the patient's illness, and he feared that some injury to the man's artery in the groin might occur if this examination was carried out. However, the weight of the group prevailed and the X-rays were carried out. They revealed that everything in the abdomen was normal.

That same evening the leg and foot became pale and cold. The head of vascular surgery and his team had to operate for four hours through the night, repairing the injury to the artery that had been caused by the X-ray catheter. The leg was saved, but only by superlative surgical skill.

Another man, twenty-one, with ulcerative colitis came to hospital for complete study. He was thin, pale, fevered, and, among other findings, had a murmur over the upper part of his abdomen. This patient was to be presented at a Grand Medical Staff Conference and it was felt that the murmur would have to be accounted for. The medical resident determined that its significance could only be settled by an arterial X-ray study involving the arterial catheter. This examination again only proved that everything was normal. Tragically, a serious injury to the artery resulted from this test. The leg and foot turned white and cold, gangrene set in, and the leg had to be amputated above the knee. A classic example of iatrogenic, or doctor-induced disease.

These three patients' problems were not well handled by the professors and their associates, who were all intent on investigating every little detail at the risk of the patient's total welfare. Only the clinical experience of a doctor who had seen gangrene in all its forms, and who had witnessed the advantages and tragedies of special X-ray techniques could say: "I think this woman can best be managed without operation now," and "This kind of X-ray investigation in young men in my experience is hazardous and has rarely demonstrated anything that helped the patient." When the clinical experience of the senior physician was followed, two legs were saved, and when it was rejected, one youth's leg was perilously threatened, and one was lost for life.

Would the reader, after having entrusted the health of his family to his doctor for ten or fifteen or twenty years, feel satisfied with this doctor and with the doctor image if he received notice that his doctor was going to retire at sixty-five or sixty or fifty-five? Might he be likely to ask the incisive question: "Was my doctor in medicine because he liked caring for us, or did he care more for the good life?"

The story of the two men who discovered cortisone gives us the best example of great achievement in the "retirement years".

Discovery: Cortisone: Dr. Edward Kendall and Dr. Philip Hench
Prior to 1928, Edward Kendall, a biochemist working at the Mayo Clinic, isolated the thyroid gland hormone in crystalline form. Then in 1930 he began an entirely new quest for the adrenal hormone. His previous experiences with thyroxin provided the foundation for this exceedingly difficult task, which required rigid self-discipline, perseverance despite failures, and sustained creative work in the face of distracting tensions provided by keen competitive research efforts elsewhere.

During several years of this contest Kendall's laboratory was operating three eight-hour shifts a day. Nine hundred pounds of the small adrenal glands from beef were used every week in the quest. Early in World War II it was reported that German flyers were being converted to supermen by "cortical extracts of the adrenal glands". These rumours were soon disregarded and the search continued for the elusive "compound E" hormone that was still only a conviction in Edward Kendall's head. But by 1948 two more black clouds loomed before him. As a pure research worker, the sixty-two-year-old Kendall faced obligatory retirement in three years. His time was running out. So was the patience of the Mayo Clinic's research funders and the Merck Laboratories in New York. After all, Kendall had been on his adrenal quest for eighteen years at a cost of about $10 million — more than the total money spent on all productive research in the history of medicine.

Meantime, another dedicated man had been working in the Mayo Clinic. Kendall knew Philip Hench well. Since 1926, Hench had been in charge of the department of joint diseases. A physician who endeared himself to thousands of patients, Hench was the greatest teacher and writer on rheumatic diseases of all time. Always on the lookout for a clue to the mystery of the worst joint disease, rheumatoid arthritis, he made two very important observations.

The first was that rheumatoid patients who got jaundiced noticed that their painful joints felt better as long as the jaundice persisted. He therefore tried to produce jaundice artificially in some of his patients but without success.

The second observation led Hench to formulate a new concept about rheumatoid arthritis. He noted that his rheumatoid patients who became pregnant always got relief from the joint pains while they were pregnant. After delivery the joints got bad again. Sometimes they were even worse than before the pregnancy. Hench asked himself what could be happening in the glandular system during pregnancy that removed the pain and often the swellings of this disease.

These observations, made in the period 1928-38, led Hench to predict that a hormone would be discovered that would relieve the joint inflammation just as pregnancy did.

While Hench was working with the rheumatic patients, in another part of the clinic Kendall was continuing to unravel the mysterious chemical formula of the adrenal hormone. Each was aware of the other's deep interest. The question was, could Kendall isolate the hormone, and in a quantity sufficient for a clinical trial, before his time and money ran out?

In the spring of 1948, a conclave of American physicians and scientists expressed a distinct lack of interest in the properties of Kendall's promised "Compound E", and the Mayo Clinic, after eighteen years of support, questioned the wisdom of further commitments. At this critical moment, Kendall was able to obtain from the Merck Laboratories the first small supply of Compound E available, for Dr. Hench to use on one of his patients.

Dr. Kendall estimated that a daily dose of 100 milligrams might produce some effect. He prepared the first sample and advised that it should be given in two daily injections at twelve-hour intervals for seven days. Every day for a week Kendall, the scientist, prepared the medicine, sent it to Dr. Hench's ward, and waited anxiously for a report. The first patient who received Compound E was known only as "Mrs. G." Her name was kept secret.

He knew that if the treatment succeeded it would be evident in four days. Finally on the seventh day, Christmas Day 1948, he could control his patience no longer and telephoned Mrs. G.'s ward doctor to ask her condition. "Oh, I forgot to tell you, she's better," was the laconic reply. Four other patients, given the same treatment, confirmed the beneficial results. Compound E, now known as cortisone, has proven to be one of the most remarkable therapeutic and research tools physicians, surgeons, and basic scientists have ever had, capable of favourably changing the course of over 100 diseases. Drs. Kendall and Hench did not begin their careers with the object of making enough money to retire. They did not slow down when retirement age drew near — quite the contrary. After the discovery of cortisone, both kept right on going. Dr. Hench worked ceaselessly until a combination of diseases overcame him at sixty-seven. Dr. Kendall was still active in his laboratory at Princeton when he was eighty-seven.

Women in Medicine

Early retirement is, regrettably, characteristic of women doctors, and the fact that a growing number of women are being admitted to our medical schools is an unpopular but real reason for the decrease in our total doctor power. This may be startling and unacceptable to many people, but the evidence and statistics show that it is all too true.

No study has given an accurate estimate of the average working life of a woman M.D., but pooled evidence suggests that it is not more than one third that of a man. Many attempts have been made to upset this disturbing figure. Recent studies of the lifetime performance of the average woman doctor claim that this can reach 65 per cent of the male performance. However, those who have gathered these data have assumed that the woman doctor is to be considered as scoring 100 per cent on the performance scale if she works as much as forty hours a week. Compared with the seventy-hour week that the real doctor will devote to active practice and study, this standard automatically places the women in the grey zone of professional performance. A forty-hour week examining healthy school children, doing laboratory work, public health, psychiatry, or research is scarcely medical practice at all. And yet between 10 and 30 per cent of all medical students in the United Kingdom, the United States, and Canada are women.

The newest medical school on this continent has announced that fifty-two out of its 100 seats have been taken by women. There were only forty-eight men in the class beginning in September 1975. If one accepts that the average life performance of all women medical graduates is one-third that of all men doctors, then these fifty-two seats in this school will yield the equivalent doctoring power of seventeen male M.D.s working a full career. This medical class will produce sixty-five M.D.s (net) instead of 100. A survey of women medical graduates of Oxford University in the years following World War II produced some devastating statistics:

- 80 per cent of those surveyed had married and 14 per cent of these did not wish to work.
- Over 60 per cent of those who married non-doctors ultimately gave up their careers.
- Of those who remained single, and continued to practise, half were specialist consultants, only a quarter were general practitioners, and two (out of forty) were surgeons.

Equally compelling were the less statistical conclusions of the survey. Married women doctors were frequently seriously worried that their families were suffering because of their careers, or were frustrated by the restrictions imposed on their careers by their family responsibilities. Those women who had interrupted their careers after a minimal amount of post-graduate education to bring up a family had great difficulty re-entering the practice of medicine. The practice of medicine, surgery, and obstetrics is a continuous learning process requiring both experience and study. It cannot be interrupted by child-bearing and the family responsibilities that follow without being seriously weakened.

A recent survey of women doctors in the province of Quebec shows that regular participation in the practice of medicine was about half that of male doctors, and, of those who were practising, just over a quarter were in general practice, and half were working in psychiatry, anesthesia, and other subspecialties.

Women do not comprise even 1 per cent of the best clinical teachers in medicine, surgery, and obstetrics. They are not even giving the lead in family medicine where they might be expected to excel. It is argued that more than 75 per cent of the doctors in the U.S.S.R. are women. The Soviet example has been influencing deans and admissions committees unreasonably in the Western countries. Whether a system that is allegedly working in the U.S.S.R. could ever be feasible in America is an unanswered question. All of the available evidence belies it. Few people will question the present superiority of Western medicine over Soviet medicine.

Harvard's most distinguished physician, Dr. George Minot, has remarked: "Women are not strong enough to be doctors. As soon as they marry, the time and money spent on their education will be lost, and only a few will be able to carry on in laboratory work, and even a smaller number in practice." Can 25 per cent or even 5 per cent of the seats in medical schools be given to women who for the most part marry, have families, and have to live with the unalterable biological variations between the menarche and the menopause?

The *average* woman with husband, home, and two children is said to work a seventy-seven-hour week. If she undertakes a medical career, can she be expected to add another seventy hours to equal the successful male doctor's performance in practice? If she excludes the normal social obligations, if she has abundant energy, and if she can secure one or two dependable domestics, she may be able to do this. But it will be a heavy load.

Even in her student days she is faced by the choice of answering emergencies in her own household and those at the hospital. Her male classmates will take the calls for the absent housewife but it becomes increasingly objectionable for them when she takes it for granted that her parenthood or household management is the unspoken reason for her absence from duty.

Almost all women doctors leave practice temporarily at some point in their careers and the average time amounts to four years. This not only means a loss of four years of practice. It also means a loss of basic medical skills that can only be maintained by constant use; appreciating the significance of heart murmurs and sounds, recognizing the feel of the abdomen over the acute appendix, identifying the unusual pregnancy, are everyday examples. A woman doctor who has "temporarily" left practice is often afraid to re-enter it, because she has lost her confidence.

Birmingham Medical School in England made a deliberate attempt to retrieve for medical practice the large number of women doctors who had stopped working for some years to raise their children. An elaborate retraining program was established but there were no takers.

"Prejudice against women compounds doctor shortage" was the headline for a recent article in a medical journal by Dr. Harold Kaplan, professor of psychiatry at New York Medical College. He sets out his figures, which advocate the acceptance of married women by admissions committees to medical schools. He urges maternity leaves during the four years in medicine, alternate examination dates to allow for pregnancies, and child-care accommodations. He suggests that medical mothers should be able to deposit their newborns in the medical school's infant metabolism research centre, but he does not mention the cost to the taxpayer of about $100 per day.

Dr. Kaplan is a psychiatrist who has been turning out women psychiatrists at a higher than average rate. He reports that forty-two physician-mothers were trained in the psychiatry residency training program at his college. All forty-two went on to complete the training requirements of the American Board of Psychiatry and Neurology. Over-zealous in his own non-doctoring field, Dr. Kaplan sees no reason why the flexibility he introduced in his psychiatry course for women could not be applied to all branches of medicine, "to permit not only the recruitment of more women for medicine but to facilitate the completion of the additional three or four years of their post-graduate training in hospitals". In fact, Dr. Kaplan's plan is an admission that motherhood duties do interrupt women in medicine from completing the necessary three or four post-graduate years to qualify as well-trained doctors after they receive the M.D.

The study of female M.D. graduates from Johns Hopkins showed that 67 of those "who were not in practice" had been in the top third of their classes. I cannot forget a recent visit at the Case Western Reserve School of Medicine. The one distraught man at the lunch table that day was the professor of medicine. He told about the brightest student in his clinic group during the four-year course. On the last clinic day when the students were discussing their internship plans he waited eagerly to hear where this bright girl was going to start her post-graduate studies. Instead of announcing an excellent hospital internship she bowled him over by flashing a diamond ring for him to admire. Never again will he be so enthusiastic about women in medical school.

Professor George Whitfield of the University of Birmingham Medical School, in his study of women doctors published in the *British Medical Journal,* describes a similar instance: "Marriage in some instances also appeared to have precluded the fulfilment of a professional career of brilliant promise. One graduate who achieved six prizes and scholarships and an honours degree and who was awarded two distinctions has obtained no higher qualifications and is engaged in the school medical service and maternity and child welfare, where doubtless she is doing most excellent and valuable work, but her intellectual and personal qualities are sufficient to carry her to the heights of the profession."

There can be no argument about the superior interviewee finesse displayed by the average young woman coming to a medical school's committee. If she is bound and determined, politically astute, and possessed of a pleasing personality and appearance she will certainly displace male candidates standing in the same long line of applicants. In order to counteract male susceptibilities and to provide a deeper perception of female candidates' long-term promise, Professor G. L. Montgomery of Edinburgh suggested that a chairwoman who is a living example of the successful woman in medical practice and teaching should interview women applicants along with the male members of the committee on admissions. As a committee member for many years himself, he realized that the choosing simply could not be done by an all-male committee.

In medical school a woman is always at a numerical disadvantage. She can and does surmount this by hard work but it involves stress and it is often interrupted by critical emotional upsets. Not only must she equal the average standing of the male members of her class, but she must exceed it in order to live at ease and thereby remain emotionally stable.

Women certainly have the brain to study medicine, but they rarely have the brawn required for a lifetime of practice, and too often not enough persistence to complete their training. The attrition rate for men in medical schools is 8 per cent but for women it is 15 per cent and their reasons for giving up are usually non-academic. Is it right to fill the top places in the first-year classes with women candidates who are less likely to complete their training? One medical school dean has stated: "If we accept a woman we had better make sure she will practice after she gets out. This year I had to insist that we accept only the better-than-average women." It is not stated how he picked "the better than average woman candidate".

While women can study medicine with distinction, the sheer physical demands of most of the medical work are beyond their capabilities. Surgery is a case in point. Dr. Blalock had only one woman who interned in his surgical course at Johns Hopkins, and no woman ever went the full five years to become a surgeon. There has been one distinguished woman surgeon in Canada but her health suffered irreparably and at the age of fifty-five she was forced to give up her practice. The American Board of Surgery has stipulated that "the residency in surgery is a full-time endeavour". This effectively excludes women from general surgery.

We are at present suffering from a serious dearth of master general surgeons. (The crisis over malpractice insurance premiums reflects this in part.) Large numbers of surgical subspecialists have rejected general surgery "because it is too tough". When a quarter or more of the available medical students are female, the possible candidates for surgery professors to choose from is in effect cut by a quarter. We cannot afford this loss of potential prime surgical skill. The same factor reduces the physician-internists, because of the length and intensity of their post-graduate work. If a woman can and does put her career first, if she puts in a seventy-hour work week, if she can consistently practise her profession until she is sixty-five or seventy, then she has a perfect right to compete for one of the limited number of seats in the medical schools.

Recognizing the inescapable limitations most women doctors will have, the medical educators who have done so much to encourage women to enter medicine are now advocating that they be directed into "suitable medical subspecialties" such as psychiatry, lab medicine, eye, skin, and so forth. Is this sound advice, when what the public needs above all is dedicated doctors? Moreover, there is only one outstanding female eye surgeon in the United States today, and she specializes in retinal detachments. No cataracts, no glaucoma, no squints.

Some of the women doctors have specialized in anaesthesiology, but modern anaesthesia is highly complex and even when anaesthesiologists work in groups their hours are irregular and normal social contacts are very hard to maintain. The newest idea for women is emergency medicine, where a woman can actually work continuously for twenty-four hours and then have seventy-two hours off duty. Again, this is very strenuous work that requires a great deal of preparatory training in medicine and surgery. This life is emotionally draining. Not many women can persevere at it for long.

Post-graduate work is always difficult for women, and few top residency training positions are ever held by them. Women rarely become senior professors of medicine. Only occasionally do they persist in obstetrics.

In January, 1976, the *British Medical Journal* attempted to grapple with the problem of women in medicine in relation to new legislation against sex discrimination in employment. The editorial acknowledged that despite the high academic standards of women medical students, they were at a disadvantage in competing with men who were willing to give 100 per cent of their effort to their profession. Clearly it is undesirable to lower standards in order to make the most demanding specialties more manageable for women doctors. Instead the editorial sought lamely for a practical provision for women doctors unwilling to make a maximum commitment to medicine, but "who wish to combine medicine with marriage without doing damage to the standards of either." An impossible dream!

The reader may point out quite rightly that some very important medical discoveries have been made by women. But the numbers are low. I have always admired these six women doctors, four of whom were among my best mentors.

- Maude Abbott of McGill University, whose work provided the foundation of modern knowledge of congenital heart disease.
- Madge Thurlow Macklin, a pioneer and world authority in the study of genetics.
- Dorothy Reed of Johns Hopkins, the pathologist who made possible the diagnosis of Hodgkin's disease.
- Florence Sabin, a medical scientist of wide-ranging accomplishment.
- Jessie Boyd Scriver, an outstanding pediatrician at McGill.
- Helen Taussig, who devised the blue-baby operation.

Discovery: Dr. Helen Taussig: The blue-baby operation
In 1930 Dr. Edwards Park, the professor of pediatrics at the Johns Hopkins Hospital, asked Dr. Helen Taussig to develop a children's heart clinic. At that time, she recalled in a recent letter, she was not particularly interested in the congenital (present from birth) heart malformations, but Dr. Park told her she could not have a heart clinic without learning about them. He referred her to the lifetime study of more than 1,000 post-mortem specimens of congenital hearts by Dr. Maude Abbott at McGill, and as he blithely assigned her the position he added: "When you do this it will be a great day."

In the new clinic Dr. Taussig was provided with a fluoroscope, an electrocardiograph, and a social worker. Her annual budget (including her salary) was less than $4,000. Dr. Park suggested that she write down her own examination findings on each patient, get an X-ray and an electrocardiogram, and personally fluoroscope each one.

Following this routine, Dr. Taussig one day examined a very unusual blue baby and when she put all of the evidence together it added up to the diagnosis of a congenital heart condition that had not been recognized before.

Later, when the infant died, the accuracy of her diagnosis was established at the autopsy, and the case was published.

As Dr. Taussig studied the blue babies that were brought to her clinic, she observed that many of them went along on a straight line and then became much worse as the blood flow to their lungs was critically reduced when a small artery called the *ductus arteriosus* spontaneously closed. Before these babies got worse, this artery had been carrying just enough blood to the lungs to maintain a fairly adequate circulation.

In 1938 Dr. Robert Gross of Boston had published his account of closing this abnormal artery in children where it was threatening life by carrying too much blood to the lungs when the heart was normal. This pioneer achievement set Dr. Taussig to ask the question: "If this artery can be closed, might not a surgeon be able to build an artificial ductus in a blue baby?" She was so convinced of the reasonableness of her idea that she went to Boston and asked Dr. Gross if he would consider such an operation in a blue baby. He was not in the least interested.

She returned somewhat dejected to Baltimore and decided to wait until Dr. Alfred Blalock became the new professor of surgery at Hopkins, because he was interested in chest surgery and in experimental techniques. After watching him do his first routine ductus operation in 1942 at Hopkins, she said: "Dr. Blalock, I stand in awe and admiration of your surgical skill, but the really great day will come when you build a ductus for a blue baby instead of doing today's operation in a child with too much blood going to the lungs." Dr. Blalock gave a great sigh and said: "When that day comes this will seem like child's play."

Dr. Blalock took the problem to the experimental laboratory and, with the tireless assistance of his trusted technician Vivien Thomas, he was ready to tackle the first blue baby that Dr. Taussig asked him to deal with exactly two years to the day after her request. This operation, in a puny infant, at ten months of age only weighing ten pounds, carried a frightful risk for such a heroic first attempt in an entirely new field. The operation was a success and the infant showed an improvement in colour, gained weight, and was able to leave the hospital a month later. That was 1944.

When their third patient came through the new operation successfully, with a fresh pink complexion in place of the ghastly blue appearance, with weight gain and increased energy, and without the unnatural clubbed fingers, Helen Taussig saw her dream of nearly ten years come true.

This most original concept of Dr. Taussig's revolutionized the approach to heart surgery. At that time the latest textbook stated: "There is no treatment for any congenital heart disease except tying off a *ductus arteriosus*." In her clinic position at Hopkins, Dr. Taussig could easily have kept up to date by explaining to distraught parents the hopelessness of their blue babies' hearts. She might even have prescribed digitalis drops when the infants began to get worse. Instead she continued to make careful observations and not only kept up to date but forged a totally original path that led to life and usefulness for thousands of children.

Not many doctors will repeat Dr. Taussig's feat, and yet every doctor's diagnosis of every patient is always a discovery and every treatment he prescribes or does is always an experiment.

With the examples of these six women in mind, I maintain that 5 per cent of a medical class should be women, in order to allow everyone with scientific fervor (which is a world apart from a student with exceptionally high marks) to have the opportunity to study medicine. I must underpin this statement with this tribute to Dr. Florence Rena Sabin, who, more than anyone before her, opened the doors of medical schools and hospitals to women seeking to devote themselves to a career of scientific investigation. Florence Sabin had no intent of opening those doors to women who would enjoy the kudos of getting the medical degree and then settle into a short, cozy work week with husband, home, and children.

There are occasional happy two-doctor households, where the careers complement each other and do not involve a perpetual competition in excellence. Unfortunately, these are exceptions. In one of the best medical schools, more than 50 per cent of these marriages had ended in divorce by the finish of the internship year.

The woman doctor who marries outside her profession encounters hazards of a more terrifying nature. Medicine when well practised does have its glamour, and doctors who excel are highly regarded. The spouse must be willing to accept his wife's night calls, her night meetings with other doctors, and the everlasting studies she must keep up with. It used to be argued that a man was wedded to his career and a woman was wedded to her man. This adage does not always hold today when there are so many couples, each member having a successful career, sometimes with the wife being the more prominent breadwinner. In medicine, however, the doctor must be wedded to the medical career, with family and household taking second and third place. For any woman this is likely to be difficult. For her non-professional husband it often becomes intolerable and the incidence of divorce among such couples is cruelly high.

Successful women doctors all stress the fact that it is a big help to have "great husbands". Well, there can be no question about the advantages of a male cook and housekeeper and child-care expert at the home base while mother works as a doctor. But the fox has a habit of turning, and when some of these compliant husbands find other female interests and the marriage falls asunder it is a cruel life in which the doctor-mother is left.

> One highly intelligent woman slipped through the male committee net, graduated with honours, and went directly into a medical specialty. She married and had a child and by dint of hard work and an understanding husband she pleased her charming chief so much that he encouraged her to go for an advanced degree. She achieved the degree but in the effort to please her chief she lost her husband. When she opened her consulting suite with a four-year-old son to support, her remarkable achievements seemed much less important.

Many non-practising doctors have become naïvely enthusiastic in urging women to enter medical school. These doctors simply do not know the demands of practice and they are not qualified to represent medicine as it is. It is not acceptable to hear a woman doctor explain, "I could not get to my Saturday-morning clinic because I had no baby sitter." Some doctors just have to attend clinics.

When nine female scholarship doctors were asked why they had taken seats in medical school that might have been assigned to men, the average answer was: "I just loved getting high marks, or pleasing my teachers, or beating the fellows in my class." Only one of the nine possessed the "healing power" and four frankly admitted that they were not clinically assured or comfortable when caring for patients. In most cases they were apologetic about their marriages. They all manifested signs of guilt because they had not kept growing professionally after graduating.

A very clever daughter of a dentist early decided that she would be a doctor. Her marks through college and medical school were excellent. She qualified easily and paid for her licence to practise. Just after this, she met her Prince Charming and they were married. Within a year she had her first son. One day when her father was leaving her house after visiting the young family, he asked, "Where are you hanging your diploma, over the kitchen sink?" Eighteen years later, her conscience still smarting, her children in high school, she began teaching in a lab four half-days a week.

What of the bright M.D.s who marry bright M.D.s?

One brilliant female M.D. had scooped up every medal and every scholarship during her four years in medical school. After her graduation she obtained the most sought after internship in the country. Soon she married an intern. He was bright but not quite as bright as she was. He did well and was absorbed into the faculty. She had one child and then did some work. But after the second, third, fourth, and fifth child, she became bound inextricably to the home base. No hospital work. No practice.

In the medical-business section on tariffs in a 1973 journal, the author argued that doctor-fathers are criticized by society when their children do not go straight in life. Since the volume of a doctor's practice squeezes out family time, those doctors who are forever pressing for higher fees have now suggested that this is one of the prices a doctor must accept and that higher fees should be charged to offset this absence from the family, which other workers do not have to contend with. If such an argument has any possible merit, how much more would it apply to doctor-mothers whose children go astray because their family time is inadequate?

Katherine Hepburn, in a television interview with Dick Cavett, said that she had decided at the beginning of her career to have no children. As she said, "You can't have it all." She wanted to be an actress, but to the children in her life she decided to always be "Aunt Kate." Women who contemplate a successful medical career should bear Miss Hepburn's example in mind.

People always keep asking girls entering medicine how they will be able to manage a medical practice and a family. One female student did substitute practice for two months with a woman who was in family medicine. This woman proved to be a wonderful inspiration to the female medical student, who said, "She and her surgeon husband had four children. They were involved in scouting. She was a pianist who practised daily and who gave a concert while I was working with her that summer."

Would the reader be satisfied with a doctor who practised on the piano every day to a point where she could give a concert, was the mother of four children, was an interesting wife for a busy surgeon husband, and was actively involved in scouting?

The women's liberation movement furnishes a weak case for getting more women into medicine. For the most part women do not band together to improve the status of women in medicine or in society. They have to curry the favour of their male teachers, their male classmates among whom they will most likely find their mates, and the male doctors with whom they will spend most of their lives in practice. They inevitably place their profession ahead of their gender in the big life situations.

In 1930 the women in medicine decided to found the *Journal of the American Women's Medical Association*. At first the articles were written only by women. When submissions began to dwindle the editors had to seek articles by prominent male physicians and surgeons and obstetricians. The original purpose of the journal faded. In 1970 this publication ceased even though the number of women in medicine in the forty years had trebled.

At the present time, none of the women's hospitals are completely staffed by women doctors and many of the senior appointments are held by male M.D.s. When more than fifty million American citizens live and die without ever seeing a doctor, when more than 100 million citizens could not call and get a competent doctor on a weekend, is it right to displace 25 per cent of male applicants from medicine by women who do not go the limit in practice?

Early Retirement

Early retirement and the philosophy of retiring men or women doctors early does not reflect favourably on the medical profession. The public's criticism of this trend is much harsher when its doctors quit practice to live at ease. Doctors may assume that they are no different from the moneychangers in the market place, but maybe their patients have higher expectations of them.

In spite of the people's belief that doctors are different from artisans and financiers, they continue to hear doctors boast that because of good performance by portfolios of stocks or shrewd real-estate deals they are going to be able to retire five years or ten years earlier than they had expected to. Should these M.D.s have been accepted for medical school in the first place? Ought a perceptive population of patients to wonder how important such doctors' practices have actually been? Might still other patients begin to ask why specialists are often the early quitters?

I have never known an intelligent, successful, healthy doctor who voluntarily and contentedly retired from active practice. I have seen many who tried to, but they were not happy away from their patients. The real doctor just cannot become a cop-out.

13.

Here is your doctor

The patient's welfare and comfort were of great concern to him, his goal was not merely to make a diagnosis but to use his knowledge in a practical way in order to help the patient, in relieving symptoms and prolonging useful and happy life in the best traditions of medicine.

Excerpt from
A TRIBUTE TO
ARTHUR L. BLOOMFIELD,
Professor of Medicine,
Stanford 1926-54.
Stanford Medical Bulletin 1961-2

Given a choice everyone would want an Arthur Bloomfield, M.D., as his doctor. But the sixty-seven subspecialties of medicine in our time cannot separately or in any combination fulfil the doctor image that people visualize and sense and that Doctor Bloomfield personified.

Few citizens on this continent will ever on average be treated by more than one or two doctors and the chances are that eight out of ten M.D.s who do treat them will be subspecialists. Unless the doctors, whether subspecialists or generally qualified physicians, are Good Samaritans in soul and healers in their innermost beings, the unfortunate patients will be destined to physical and mental anguish.

I had intended to define Your Doctor as a recognizable professional person, but the task proved unattainable. It became a matter of providing the wounded ones and their relatives with some reasonable expectations to look for in any doctor with the M.D. on his sign. Having appreciated the present unbalanced state of medicine's personnel, I decided to outline, with everyday examples culled from personal observations, those character and professional marks in doctors of every kind that seekers after health should

211

try to find. It seemed to me that, if the health-seekers would take note of the favourable and the unfavourable features that characterize these doctors, they will not only be better served but they will encourage a new generation of doctors that will derive more satisfaction from caring for their patients. I have exemplified some doctoral characteristics with references to common symptoms and examinations of body parts that require normal experience and skill.

The primary qualification of every M.D. who deals with patients, "who handles human freight" — the mastery of the instruments in the doctor's black bag — should be the hallmark of every real doctor. I believe that any doctor should be capable of removing a foreign body from an eye or of lancing a boil. This approach to medicine will slow the headlong rush into what is becoming the doctorless society, because the doctor who is expert in simple acts can be trusted with greater tasks if he persists.

This example illustrates what a doctor can do even when he is on vacation, away from his office and his hospital, and without even his little black bag:

A young family had come from Detroit to vacation in the Lake Huron home of a grandmother. They had a two-year-old son under the care of an allergist who had hesitated to give his consent to the vacation, and no sooner had the family retired for their first night's sleep than the allergist's apprehensions were justified; the two-year-old began to cough and gasp for breath. In a panic, the father ran next door to ask the neighbours if there was a doctor in the area. By good luck a doctor was vacationing nearby. Hurriedly summoned, he found the boy wheezing, blue, and coughing. The question was, was it asthma or pneumonia? The doctor called for the family's rectal thermometer, put his ear to the child's chest, first on one side, then the other. In the background the grandmother whispered to her daughter, "This man is no specialist, Mary Ellen, he's a real doctor." He read the thermometer and made the pronouncement: "This is an attack of asthma. There is no pneumonia. I think we can get some adrenalin and cortisone." The adrenalin and cortisone did their work and the family was able to spend two happy weeks at the lake. The grandmother was quite right; the doctor was indeed real — he was Dr. Chester Keefer, distinguished professor of medicine at Boston University.

"Dr. Keefer was primarily a teacher, and from personal

experience, I can testify, one of the best this country has ever produced. He enjoyed bedside teaching and warmly supported others in their efforts to learn medicine," wrote McGehee Harvey in the *Johns Hopkins Medical Journal* of June 1975.

A Psychiatrist Doctor

One of our psychiatrists was asked to see a young woman, twenty-three, with bruises over her arms and legs. She was complaining of pain in the left loin which had only been relieved by a hot water bottle, which she had been using for months. After four weeks on the gynecology service she could not empty her bladder normally and had become dependent on a catheter. The skin experts had seen her because of a rash over her face and they had concluded that this was a nervous acne.

The psychiatrist who was called to see this involved patient problem obtained the history that the girl had tried nursing but had developed hepatitis, which kept her off for a year. After she returned she developed back pain, which increased to a point where she could not carry on. During her time in the nursing school she had learned something about drugs and had developed an addiction to talwin, a popular pain-reliever.

Instead of writing a consultation note with suggestions for tranquillizers, this psychiatrist took the challenge presented by this young woman's problem very seriously and spent a great deal of time with her and with her parents, unravelling the complicated story of her life over a series of interviews and examinations that took three months.

The psychiatrist was by every definition a real doctor who did everything possible to start this patient on a straight life-path again. It was found that her bruises and her bleeding from the kidney had resulted from the patient's taking blood-thinner tablets in order to alarm her doctors. She had kept them alarmed with one symptom after another for a total of four months of costly hospital care under a series of subspecialists who had all been interested in their small corners of the problem but had never put the puzzle together in a constructive way, and only made the patient worse after every new examination. Every new specialist found something in his own field that he regarded as serious and in need of his special expertise.

It was the psychiatrist in this situation who enlisted the support of the parents, gradually reassured the patient day after day that her individual symptoms were not serious and not real, and that she had the brains to deal with them herself instead of inventing new symptoms needing the attention of more and more new doctors.

Surgical Doctors

A patient with a bowel weakness was referred by his G.P. to a surgeon because of piles. This busy surgeon examined the rectum carefully and spied two small piles. He might have operated before sending the man back to his G.P., but he was not satisfied that the piles explained this man's trouble. He questioned him about any other complaints and found that he had a painful left arm. He checked the reflexes with his percussion hammer and found they were too brisk to be normal. He sent his report to the G.P. and suggested that the patient be checked by a nerve specialist, who found a tumor pressing on the spinal cord, which explained the pain in the arm, the bowel weakness, and the brisk reflexes. That surgeon could have operated and collected his fee quite ethically but he would not have helped the patient.

A woman, forty-seven, developed a breast tumor. She was referred to a high-ranking surgeon who carried out the radical operation. When the patient came out of the anesthetic she asked the surgeon if she had a malignant tumor. He said brusquely "yes", and this blow was followed without pause by, "and when the wound heals you will be transferred to the tumor division for a course of deep therapy".

Even the most stout-hearted person, when confronted quickly by such fear-inducing news, will likely be headed for a sleepless night. While this woman had managed an active household, and had played bridge and golf regularly, she had always required a sleeping capsule at night, because for twenty years she had had insomnia. The surgeon did not believe in sleeping potions. He was unsympathetic towards any patient who used them, and he refused to order a sleeping capsule for her. While he had conducted himself well with the knife, he had behaved rather badly towards a sensitive patient.

The husband asked for his account, paid it, and then called in a physician. Happily, the eventual outcome was favourable. Nevertheless, the immediate surgical experience was a nightmare. The professional image was tarnished by this surgeon's conduct. He possessed great technical competence but he lacked compassion.

Dr. J. M. T. Finney, whose operation, the Finney Pyloroplasty, is still the most common operation in stomach surgery, wrote in his autobiography, *A Surgeon's Life*, "Every doctor worthy of the name knows that not infrequently the personal relationship existing between the true doctor and his patient is one of the most important features in the entire practice of medicine."

> On Wednesday afternoon March 26, 1974, a Dr. Rundle in an American city was consulted by a woman of fifty-nine who feared that she had found a small lump in her left breast. She was anxious about this because two of her neighbours who were close friends had gone to their doctors with the same story and each had had a radical mastectomy. Dr. Rundle soon found that his patient had made no mistake — she did have a lump. He told her that, while there was nothing serious about its size and while he could feel no gland in her armpit, he was going to have his surgical colleague, a Dr. MacDonald, examine her as early as he could get an appointment. Against his patient's remonstrance he telephoned the surgeon's office and was told that the surgeon was at his desk clearing up correspondence. In a moment the surgeon was on the line. After listening to Dr. Rundle's account he said: "In my experience this is urgent business, could you send her right over?" At five o'clock that afternoon Dr. Rundle's telephone rang and the woman said: "Dr. Rundle, I can never thank you enough. Dr. MacDonald agreed with you. He explained that he was as confident as he could be that it would turn out just like you expected. I have had my chest X-ray and it's clear. I shall have my operation two weeks from tomorrow. I was absolutely terrified when I went to see you today and I did not know how I could face the anguish of waiting for an appointment with the surgeon."

Before Mrs. Betty Ford's and Mrs. Happy Rockefeller's courageous examples, a Chicago study revealed that the average woman who finds a breast lump waits twelve months before she can summon up her courage to see her doctor. Surgeons assure me that women do not go to pieces when they are told they have tumors of the larynx or lung or stomach or bladder or bowel but that if it is the breast they are terrified.

The Physician-Internist

> A woman of forty-nine with an attentive husband and three healthy children was taken to her doctor because of severe cramping pains in

her legs and buttocks of three months' duration which had rendered sleep impossible. She was sent to hospital where she was examined and investigated thoroughly by a team made up of students, interns, residents, and the doctor in command, who was a metabolism specialist to whom she had been referred by her family doctor. The examinations were exhaustive and exhausting. While they were being carried out, the pain was so bad that on some occasions her screaming disturbed the entire ward. It was a very hectic ten days, after which she was discharged with a short letter, which read:

"Dear Mrs. Yorke:

"We find that you have a little diabetes, but you won't have to take insulin. You are sixty pounds overweight and you should get your weight down. You have some gout and for this we are giving you a pill which you will take every morning for the rest of your life. Fortunately, your blood calcium is normal so there is no need to worry about the cramps in your legs. These cramps are just nerves. If they bother you again you could take a tranquillizer tablet to relieve them. We are sending your family doctor a full report and he will explain everything. I have been away and at committee meetings during the last ten days or I would have seen you myself. My team associates have given me all the evidence they obtained about your complaint.

Yours very truly,
S. R. Lavier, M.D."

This woman went home with more pain than she had when she went to hospital. Another doctor was called, and he in turn referred her to another specialist, this time a physician-internist. In his general examination he found that the circulation was normal — no sign of artery or vein trouble to account for the leg pains; the joints were not rheumatic; the muscles were well developed and strong; and the reflexes were all normal.

He was arrested by the constant restless activity of both legs as she lay on the examining table. This woman presented a very marked condition of restless legs or leg jitters. She could not keep them still. He did not repeat the dozens of lab tests that had been done in the hospital — he knew it would have been waste effort, because no queer lab result ever explains the kind of nervousness expressed in these quite uncontrollable leg motions that always bother the patient more by night than by day.

On direct questioning, she said that she had been plagued by these nervous legs for six years on and off but that only in the last three months had the awful pains developed in her legs. The doctor listened to her history and then enlarged on it in a discussion in his consulting room with the patient's husband. Two daughters were going to get married during the coming summer, and the patient would then be left alone. The son? Six years before, her favourite oldest child, the son, had developed leukemia. One day, as the family was getting ready to go on a picnic, the son could not be found. The mother went through the house calling him. She finally went to the cellar and found his crumpled body on the floor. Life had become too hard for him and he had ended it. Beginning on the night of her son's death this mother had experienced the distressing restlessness of her legs.

When she was reminded that her legs first began to twitch and jump after she lost her son six years before and that this jumping was now so constant that it had become painful at the prospect of having her two daughters marry and leave home, she at once realized with relief that this was the root of her trouble. She was relieved to know that it was not cancer. She was a very grateful patient and her gratitude was reflected in her husband, who had been completely bewildered, "when all the tests were normal", and then angered, because he knew his wife was suffering.

The computer could not have helped with this diagnosis. The students who took her history and the interns who check-examined the students' findings were too inexperienced to deal authoritatively with a delicate situation like this. The residents were training to become specialists in metabolic diseases and they were most interested in the blood reports. The team commander handled this disheartened woman by treatment in absentia and it did not work. It never does work if the patient is really sick.

Sickness never affects the patient alone. The family is always very much involved in an illness, especially a serious one. The real doctor, therefore, must always consider the family, even if he becomes the most skilled and the hardest-to-see consultant.

The Urologist

A general physician was called to see an elderly woman at midnight because of pain with voiding and bloody urine. The woman had high blood pressure and a bad heart. After checking her over he felt unsure about the bladder condition and he strongly advised her to go into the hospital under the care of a kidney expert. When she stubbornly refused, in desperation he called the kidney expert and asked if he would come to the house and examine the patient. This expert came promptly and after getting all of the available evidence on the spot he told her that she could be helped but that he would have to do a more thorough examination in hospital. The two doctors together could not change her mind, but the urologist told the G.P. to go home and to leave her in his hands. He patiently waited until she had her bag packed and then he, the busiest urologist in the city, took her to the hospital himself. By this act he proved that he was a real doctor who appreciated the woman's reluctance and the fact that many older patients cannot be rushed into hospital even if the treatment is very necessary. From his broad experience he knew that some patients have to be led to the cure gently or they will not get cured at all.

A Radiologist Doctor

A story illustrating the value of continuing clinical experience is that of Dr. Harvey Cushing's ulcer. Himself one of the most illustrious members of the profession as a brain surgeon, Dr. Cushing was afflicted with a painful stomach complaint in his late years, after he had changed his medical school affiliation from Harvard to Yale. One of his old students, the Yale professor of surgery, Samuel Harvey, examined him, found that he had a large ulcer, and recommended surgical removal. Dr. Harvey, not wanting to operate on his former chief himself, invited another distinguished surgeon, Dr. George Heuer of New York's Cornell, to come to New Haven. Dr. Cushing agreed to having Dr. Heuer but asked that his own personal physician of long standing, Dr. Merrill Sossman, also be invited as a consultant. (Dr. Sossman was the head of the radiology department at Harvard.)

The consultation was held in Dr. Cushing's hospital room on a Sunday morning. Dr. Heuer made his examination, studied the X-rays, and seconded Dr. Samuel Harvey's recommendation of prompt surgery. Dr. Sossman was then asked for his opinion.

"This is a large ulcer," he agreed, "but I am going to suggest that Dr. Cushing stay in bed and be given a strict Sippy diet. I think the ulcer will heal if we give it a chance."

Dr. Heuer, nonplussed by this opinion, asked, "How do you know this ulcer will heal?"

"Clinical experience, Dr. Heuer," said Dr. Sossman. He then

added a prediction: "Under the diet treatment the ulcer will get worse for a week, but in the second week X-rays will show improvement, which will then continue."

Dr. Sossman's advice was taken, the treatment followed, and the course of recovery proved precisely what Dr. Sossman had forecast.

Dr. Harvey and Dr. Heuer were prompt in their congratulations, which were mingled with frankly expressed amazement. Dr. Sossman merely smiled and repeated the phrase he has used before: "Just clinical experience." It was not the first time or the last that this man, a great doctor as well as a great radiologist, had amazed his colleagues by shrewd clinical estimating.

Your doctor is important to you not only in what he says but also in the way he says it. Recently I knew a woman who had been diagnosed as suffering from a bladder tumor. How should this diagnosis have been conveyed to her? One doctor examined her and bluntly said, "You have a cancer of the bladder that is highly malignant." For any patient this would be a crushing statement, leaving no hope. A second consultant was called to see the discouraged woman. When he examined her he said, "Mrs. Johnson, there is a tumor in your bladder but I have seen this tumor respond to treatment. Some people live for many years with this kind of growth. I shall see that you have the best treatment and I am very hopeful." This doctor showed both humility and true concern for his patient. No cancer specialist can pronounce exactly the course any cancer will take. Even more important, no doctor should ever destroy a patient's hope.

A real doctor is capable of explaining cirrhosis of the liver to the man who has it, and to the wife who must transmit the message to the teen-aged children. He must be able to state what can be done about the man's alcoholism at this stage, whether and when he can return to his job. He must if necessary explain the situation to the man's supervisor or the president of his company. Such explanations can only be given by a doctor who knows a lot about liver disease and alcoholics, and who is wise and compassionate. They require far more than the results of liver tests and X-rays and the pronouncing of the hope-destroying word "cirrhosis".

The real doctor can see a patient in the bedroom of a luxury apartment, on an iron bed in a garret, in the out-patient cubicle across a plain oak desk, in the operating room, or on a stretcher in the heavy traffic of the emergency ward of a busy city hospital, examine him, and help him.

A Busy Physician and a Poor Patient

> An Italian fruit vendor was brought to the emergency department at the Massachusetts General Hospital in a state of supposed shock with bubbling respirations. The intern placed him in the head-down position prescribed for some shock victims and he got rapidly worse. Dr. George Minot happened by and paused. He looked at the neck, felt the pulse, and tilted the gasping man into the feet-down position. Within twenty minutes the patient was breathing more comfortably and his chest had stopped bubbling. This patient was not in shock, but in a particular kind of heart failure. He was able to walk out of the hospital the next afternoon, but before leaving he got Dr. Minot's name from one of the nurses "because that man saved my life". Next day he brought a dozen oranges for the doctor. To Dr. Minot those oranges were priceless.

The patient always needs the doctor's instructions about returning to work after a strep throat or an operation for a stomach ulcer or a slight stroke. This is pretty straightforward business, which follows the ordinary rules. But with the diagnosis and treatment settled, the factors outside the body need to be weighed carefully against the body factors. This is where the doctor faces his greatest test. It involves plotting the patient's future life-course, that is, making the prognosis: whether he should continue his business; re-marry or not; have his prostate operated before or after his trip to Switzerland; build a new home; or stand for re-election.

> An industrial executive, sixty-two, was admitted to hospital at the request of his family doctor. The latter still believed that there was some hope for his patient, even though the man had just returned from six weeks of intensive treatment in one of the large clinics where he had been given a very discouraging prognosis. A few examinations coupled with his history and physical examination left the heart specialist in no doubt about the existence of serious heart disease. However, he gave a cautious but favourable prediction and told the patient that he would have to take a month of complete bed rest before a reasonable judgment could be made.
>
> The man co-operated perfectly and conserved his resources. At the end of the month he was so much improved that he broached the question of spending the summer aboard his cabin cruiser. At that point his heart doctor told him that the physical activities and the inevitable decision-making for a skipper on the Great Lakes would

never be wise no matter how much improvement he appeared to show, in view of his heart handicap. He was further advised to put his cruiser up for sale while his health was intact. This he did from his hospital bed and added the $35,000 to his bank account.

Towards the end of the second month, he was continuing to improve and was moving about the hospital ward without any distress, his breathing easier and his dropsy cleared. He was told that he might go home. Before discussing the details of his summer activities, he asked if, in view of the fact that he had been a widower for four years, was lonely, and missed his two children who were married and away, he could marry a woman whom he had come to know and like very much.

The doctor reminded him that he had been through a long and serious illness but that as things were going the outlook could be considered encouraging.

However, he was advised to go at a slow pace and to come back at the end of six months before taking the big marital step. At the end of four months the patient was getting along so well in his home community that he and his bride-to-be, after discussions with the immediate families, decided on a vestry wedding at once, without even conferring with the family doctor. On the morning of the wedding, which was scheduled for three o'clock, the patient died suddenly.

This example illustrates difficulties that may develop in any serious illness. In this man's case, there was no question that he was sick with a bad heart. But there is no test that enables a doctor to say "this man will die within a month". No living doctor can ever say that a patient with a terrible E.C.G. or a bad X-ray will die at any specified time. But the doctor with experience can say that a given patient after a stroke or heart attack will shorten his life if he subjects himself to certain stresses and strains and worries. The heart diagnosis in this man was well established in the first six weeks in the clinic. The first prognosis given him was defeating, and uncertain, and in the following six months of his life it was wrong.

This man's history highlights some of the public's criticisms of the medical profession that are unreasonable. When he left the clinic he and his children were discouraged and dissatisfied. They yearned for a doctor and they were all gladdened when a doctor took command and he recovered from heart failure. However, the doctor can only work within the confines of his profession. He cannot compete with the white steed of passion when a patient gives that white steed the rein at the wrong time.

The doctor confronted with a business tycoon who is losing the power and co-ordination in his legs, as the result of steady indulgence in grain alcohol, can make the exact diagnosis and outline the exact treatment. If the tycoon will not give up the grain alcohol permanently, then even with the best doctor in the world his legs will get wobblier and weaker, and he will court the daily risk of a fall and a broken hip. Eventually the control of his rectum and his bladder may be lost and he will end up spending his days on a commode chair and his nights in a soggy bed. In many ways the alcoholic brain and nerves are more tragic than the alcoholic liver.

Sound medical advice that is disregarded is money wasted.

In spite of the marvels of modern medicine the best doctor will always be the one who can most skilfully use the tools in his black bag. What tools does he have?

1. The stethoscope is the very symbol of doctoring and facilitates the diagnosis of almost every disease of the heart and lungs. It permits the doctor to hear and assess murmurs in the heart, or vital organs or limbs, and to hear the friction rubs of pleurisy and inflammation of the heart-covering (pericarditis). What the doctor sees and feels and then hears with his stethoscope determines his next move. Will it be an E.C.G.? Fluoroscopy by an X-ray specialist? Blood counts and differentials and enzymes and electrolytes? Deciding on the right course with full consideration of the probable benefits to the patient, and always with a view to costs, requires that the doctor's brain connected through his stethoscope to the patient must be well stocked with all of the modern approaches to general medicine and controlled by an enlarging experience.

2. The blood pressure machine has universal importance for measuring the pressure in the arms and in the legs if the patient has arterial disease in one or both of them, with cold or pale or bluish feet.

3. The use of the tape measure is a "must" in following the size of neck enlargements, chest expansion (usually decreased or lost in emphysema), organ measurements at repeated examinations, and leg swelling from day to day in phlebitis.

4. The glove. Reference has been made to the infrequency of the examination of the rectum or the female pelvis by the average doctor. Too many still shrink from these important examinations. Our clinical study group was recently stunned by the attitude of one honour student. He was examining a man of sixty-two who had had a stroke. As we moved down the body in examination we noted that there was only one testicle. The other one had never come down into the scrotum. We wanted to know whether

the one that was visible and that appeared to be enlarged was normal. The student had to feel it. He asked for a glove! This is one place where the glove only makes the examiner's fingers less sensitive.

5. The little box of electric instruments in every doctor's black bag has great importance. The auroscope permits him to decide if an ear drum is inflamed or perforated, or the ear canal is full of wax. The electric torch illuminates the gums, the teeth, the throat, and the sinuses. The laryngoscope permits him to see whether the patient has a smoker's voice box, a paralysed vocal cord to explain hoarseness, or an ulcer or tumor. Examining the eye with the ophthalmoscope, he can detect evidence of brain tumors, hemorrhages, heart conditions, artery and vein diseases, blood diseases, kidney diseases, diabetic complications, and others.

6. Knowledgeable use of the percussion hammer and the tuning fork allow the doctor to localize a tumor, an abscess, an arterial block or rupture, or an inflammation of the brain or spinal cord or nerves. If he is competent in using these two instruments and those in the box, he can reasonably call for more complicated techniques and X-rays for the diagnosis of organic nervous diseases.

7. The hypodermic case should contain the drugs that are required for the treatment of acute emergencies, especially those associated with pain or shock or asthma.

To know how to use all of the instruments in the doctor's bag means knowing a great deal about medicine and the surgical possibilities and needs of patients. The patient is immediately reassured by the doctor who uses his tools skilfully. This makes medicine better for the patient and more satisfying for the doctor. Dr. Douglas Wigle of Toronto has remarked that the practice of medicine is fun when the doctor knows what he is doing.

In addition to a well-used bag of tools, any real doctor will also have a thorough appreciation of common human complaints like dizziness. This is usually diagnosed by history-taking (i.e., asking the right questions and listening carefully to the patient's answers) rather than by examination.

Every fourth reader will experience some dizziness for a few seconds or hours of days within the next twelve months if he is more than forty years of age. Dizziness is always a terrifying symptom and when it is bad it is much worse than pain because there is no treatment that will relieve it quickly. Pills help a few cases but they do not act quickly. Sometimes they protect patients from future attacks. The surest relief is bed rest, and sometimes the patient cannot even turn in bed if the attack is severe.

Dizziness is very rarely an indicator of stroke or brain tumor. It may come if the blood pressure is high (not often) or when it is low, if the patient gets up too quickly. Some patients have trouble in the inner ear and they usually have ringing in the ear. Dizziness is rare with inflammation of the ear and therefore antibiotics do not help. It may be associated with eye conditions and an eye specialist may be needed. In other cases, heart conditions are responsible, while in still others it is a matter of thin blood or too much blood. It is not uncommon in blood vessel disease.

The patient with dizziness could be seen by five or six specialists and one or other of them might make the correct diagnosis. It might be the brain specialist, the eye specialist, the ear specialist, the heart specialist, the blood specialist, or the blood pressure specialist who makes the diagnosis. It would make more sense — would it not? — to have more doctors who were capable of diagnosing such a common complaint. It would be a lot cheaper for the patient and for the medicare system.

Your doctor should also have a developed skill in seeing, touching, and feeling for diagnostic clues in particular parts of the body. One body area where wide clinical experience is necessary is in the examination of the neck. Every neck tells its particular part of the diagnostic story. It may be abnormally fat or scrawny, long or short, smooth or goitrous, straight or curved, quiet or shaking. The neck contains the voice box with its vocal cords, and the windpipe; the gullet along which food and fluid are carried from throat to stomach; the muscles and ligaments that hold the head erect unless they waste away or become paralysed or tremulous; the arteries that carry blood to the brain and may become narrowed by diseases; the veins that bring the blood back from the brain; the nerves that regulate the heart and lung and diaphragm; the spinal cord, with the nerve supplies to the neck and shoulders and arms; the spinal column of the neck, with the discs that are so prone to wear and tear; the skin that covers it; the thyroid and parathyroid glands, which may be affected by tumors and disease; and the lymph glands, which are present on both sides of the neck and which may enlarge on one side with infections or growths in the nose or mouth or tongue or throat, and which will enlarge on both sides with conditions like mononucleosis, leukemia, and sometimes in Hodgkins' disease.

Scarcely one doctor in 100 can go about the examination of the neck and its contents in confidence and with competence. A practising doctor should be capable of handling most patients with troubles in the neck. Every doctor should at least know enough to choose the right subspecialist for the neck area, whose help he may sometimes need. Examples of head and neck diagnostic difficulties confront every doctor in the active practice of medicine, surgery, and cancer and underscore the need for wide experience.

In addition to the skills every patient expects his doctor will possess, there are qualities of character, especially compassion, that are rare and even unfashionable in today's doctors. At the entrance to the School of Medicine of the University of the British West Indies in Jamaica there is a magnificent mural of the Good Samaritan, done by the artist-wife of one of the professors in the hope that medical students will be reminded that if they are to be good doctors they will always act like Good Samaritans.

A physician-internist was called in consultation to a city forty miles from his home on a wet cold Sunday afternoon. Driving through the slum outskirts of his own city he saw a little boy lying on the pavement unconscious. He had been struck by a car as he was crossing the road. One glance showed that he was in severe shock, his eyes were sunken and there was a fracture across the forehead of his skull, which gave the appearance of a cracked egg. As a crowd began to gather at the scene of this accident, the M.D. went to the closest phone booth and called an ambulance. Instead of dispatching the boy to the emergency room and hurrying on to his Sunday afternoon consultation in the next city, he called the chief of the brain surgery service at the hospital and asked him to rush to meet the ambulance at the emergency. He also suggested that the neurosurgeon call the surgical chief to deal with the state of obvious shock. He never saw the little boy again.

He went about his business in consultation with the doctor in the next city and spent an hour discussing a case of liver failure.

Six weeks later he bumped into the neurosurgeon in his own hospital who said: "You know, that little Campbell boy you sent in with the fractured skull turned out to be the most interesting head case I have had in many months. I was able to reduce the skull fracture and there isn't a mark on his head now. Mentally he is bright and we are sure that he is going to be a normal boy mentally. My surgical confrere told me that the boy had a ruptured spleen, but it turned out to be the first one he had ever treated without removing it — he had just read about how some cases with this kind of spleen injury do not have to have the spleen removed. He was very excited about it and delighted."

Neither the brain surgeon nor the general surgeon got a dollar for their Sunday afternoon of work on this little boy. His parents had no money. The father had a little garden in his backyard and the day they took the boy home he brought a prize squash to the hospital for the neurosurgeon and also one for the surgeon who had not removed the spleen. Twenty years later this neurosurgeon had become a great brain surgeon with patients coming to him from all over the world. His fees were unlimited as money was literally pressed into his hand. In a recent conversation he told me that no cheque had ever meant as much to him as the squash from that fellow Campbell.

A school teacher of fifty-nine was driving back to her town on a Sunday afternoon after a weekend in the city. When passing through a village she was apprehended by a motorcycle police officer and given a traffic ticket for a fine of $100 "because of careless driving on the left side of the main street median". On reaching her home, twenty-five miles beyond that village she went directly to the hospital emergency where her G.P. examined her. He found that she could not speak and her right arm was paralysed. Next day he called a neurologist in consultation. This specialist diagnosed a stroke caused by a blockage of a small artery on the left side of the brain. He called the G.P. to give him his diagnosis. But he did not just dictate his report and put on his hat and drive back to the city. He asked about how this teacher was regarded in the community. When he heard about the $100 fine he exclaimed: "That police officer fined your patient while she was developing a stroke. Of course she was not guilty and we must make sure that the fine is revoked. Do send a letter to the head of the Traffic Division with a short description of the incident and enclose a Xerox copy of my report." The fine was cancelled. The neurologist was more interested in the patient than in himself. He had the Good Samaritan mark on his brow.

In observing generation after generation of students I have become impressed with one fact. The student who will become the real doctor prepares himself thoroughly and then gets into his clinical (bedside or patient-side) experience with everything he's got. It is this kind of student with growing clinical power who encourages me most about the future of the profession of medicine. Today's tragedy lies in the fact that so few students build this kind of foundation. In some medical classes not more than 20 per cent of the students display the interest and concern that mark the real doctor in the making.

I have tried to portray the ideal doctor as a blending of the best of those who looked after the patients mentioned in this chapter. When doctors have been well taught, their lives are more likely to have purpose and direction.

The best G.P.s all emulate this doctor type. The best teachers all belong in the real doctor section. The doctors who possess intellect, compassion, and the touch will be real. They are always capable of making reasonable decisions in homes or community hospitals, or in emergencies anywhere.

Patients in need should seek them out!

While most doctors only practise medicine or surgery, some do so along with other work. It is convenient to think of gifted M.D.s as belonging in one or more of the following five categories:

- The one-talent man who devotes his best energy to the practice of medicine alone or one of its branches.
- The two-talent man who practises good medicine and acts as a consultant to other doctors. He often teaches medical students and doctors, because they want to see how he grapples with difficult clinical problems.
- The three-talent man who consults, teaches, and holds an administrative position, whether as dean of a medical school or as an executive of a medical society.
- The four-talent man who consults, teaches, administers, and does original work (research).
- The five-talent man who consults, teaches, administers, does research, and has a political touch that allows him — because of his recognized authoritative position as a "top" doctor — to approach leaders in government on behalf of the medical school he represents.

Ideally, the head of a school of medicine possesses all five talents. Their combination in a keen, energetic, and diplomatic man is ideal. Lacking one or more of these talents, the medical leader will be limited in his administrative potential. Naturally, such highly talented men in medicine, as in business, are the most sought-after members of the profession. The classic example of this kind of man was David Edsall, who moulded the Harvard Medical School in its most remarkable years of development.

It is important to point out that the first talent is the most vital one. All of the others only have relevance in education, in administration, in good original work, or in political contacts *when the man is a good doctor*. Because only then do the students, the faculty, the practising doctors, and the people believe that he knows what he is talking about.

Discovery: Penicillin: Sir Alexander Fleming

To repeat the details of this unequalled discovery in therapeutics would not tell the reader anything he does not already know. However, I think Sir Alexander Fleming should be every medical student's hero, because he possessed attributes they should try to emulate. In this chapter I decided to refer to elements of his character and abilities that would have endeared him to every reader in search of a good doctor.

Undoubtedly, Fleming's greatest power rested in his ability to handle disappointments that would have ground ordinary doctors into dust. Having obtained the fellowship of the Royal College of Surgery, he hoped to qualify for the program at St. Mary's Hospital, but the only vacancy in surgery went to the brilliant Zachary Cope. As a result of this disappointment Fleming had to take a place "in the lab" under Almoth Wright.

During his years in the lab he moved quietly from one experiment to another with the single objective of finding something that would cure the common fatal infections resulting from the pneumococcus, streptococcus, and staphylococcus. He decided to be a bacteriologist when surrounded by soldiers dying with severe infections in World War I in France.

Professor Wright always insisted that his lab men should remain in practice in their private offices outside the hospital so as to "keep their feet on the ground". Fleming made morning rounds with his chief in the hospital of the public ward patients and shared with his associate R. Colebrook an office where he saw his private patients. In diagnosis he was keen and in treatment he was skilled. Having learned a great deal in what he called "this school of life experience" during his four years working as a clerk in London before entering medical school, he was always interested in the personality of the patient and was actually one of the first physicians to realize that psychosomatic medicine is not the answer to every patient's complaints. He derived a tremendous personal satisfaction from making an accurate diagnosis and curing his patients. On one occasion his attention was drawn to a man who had been referred to St. Mary's from another hospital with tuberculosis of the tongue. After examining the man he made a diagnosis of syphilis of the tongue to the astonishment of those around him. With the pathologist's report of tuberculosis on the chart he thoroughly enjoyed curing the patient with one dose of salvarsan, which was then the cure for syphilis. Sir Almoth Wright was the only British physician to obtain a supply of this new drug in 1910 from his friend Paul Ehrlich in Berlin. His student Fleming was the only physician in Britain who possessed the necessary skill to administer this irritating drug by vein with complete accuracy and therefore its use was entrusted to him and his office associate, Colebrook.

Although his greatest work was the discovery of penicillin, this resulted in his worst life disappointments. With his experiments completed, he reported the results to the British Society of Bacteriologists in 1929. Not one word of encouragement or commendation was uttered following his presentation. Five years later, Gerhard Domagk reported the dramatic effects of the sulfa drugs and the headline news of their miraculous effects circled the world many times. This proved to be very disheartening to Fleming, because the sulfas cured several of the diseases he hoped to cure with his penicillin. At this point any ordinary human would have quit his lab experimentation and retired to practice. But not Fleming. He quietly observed that the sulfas did not cure many of the worst bacterial infections and that they had many serious side effects that ruled out their use in patients with severe infections. He continued his work with penicillin and in 1936 reported it again to the British Society of Bacteriologists, with the same chilly reception he had received in 1929. In spite of this second blow, he kept telling his friends that if he could just get a chemist who would purify penicillin for human use he was sure it would have great value. During this black period of discouragement he even predicted that his penicillin would cure syphilis!

When the war clouds loomed in 1939, the medical authorities anticipated severe battle infections and experimentation for agents that might cure infections was encouraged. Quite by accident Dr. Howard Florey, an Australian, and Dr. E. B. Chain of Berlin, began to work together at Oxford on unravelling the chemistry of penicillin. After surmounting many difficulties "this team" succeeded. It is well to recall that Chain wrote, "the work of the team is important for the development of an idea already formulated, but I do not believe that a team has ever produced a new idea".

As has happened so often in science, the men who were immediately responsible for the final stages of a discovery got the headlines. Florey and Chain were the great heroes when the world first heard about penicillin. At this critical point, Sir Almoth Wright wrote a letter to the editor of *The Times* following the appearance of a front-page story about penicillin. This letter by that undisputed authority in bacteriology placed the laurel leaf for all time on the brow of the real discoverer of penicillin, Alexander Fleming. After that, the name of Fleming and penicillin were always associated. Many new antibiotics have since been developed and used in infections that did not respond to penicillin. However, the principle evolved so clearly by Fleming has been the guide to all later antibiotic discoveries. The discovery of the second antibiotic, streptomycin, by Schatz and Waxman resulted in the defeat of tuberculosis.

Alexander Fleming the physician possessed a "second talent" that made him the greatest discoverer of his time. It was natural that he was knighted and later made a Nobel Laureate.

In 1947 my youthful associate, Dr. Montague Thomson, broke local tradition by treating a little boy suffering from an acute mastoid infection with penicillin. His three senior surgical colleagues had all insisted on immediate operation. Recovery was complete with the penicillin treatment. It did away with the need for the long series of painful post-operative dressings that were required for weeks after every mastoid operation.

Thomson wrote a letter of appreciation to the discoverer:

> Dear Sir Alexander:
>
> I don't know if you get many letters from doctors thanking you for penicillin. I want you to know how much it meant to my little patient with mastoiditis and to me personally. The insurance companies should give you a bag of gold for your great discovery.
>
> Yours respectfully,
> Montague Thomson

The reply interested me:

> Dear Doctor Thomson:
>
> Thank you very much for your kind letter and the results of treatment in your little patient with mastoiditis.
>
> To answer your question, very few doctors write to thank me for penicillin.
>
> With regard to your suggestion about life insurance companies, I can assure you that they will never send me a bag of gold because their annuitants now live too long because of penicillin.
>
> Yours sincerely,
> Alexander Fleming

Conclusions

Medicine's greatest obligation is the education of more real doctors. Rational alterations in the teaching program would bring obvious improvements within months, and better doctors for more people within two years.

The motto, "what nature hath denied, this university cannot provide", placed over the entrance to the University of Salamanca should not be forgotten. There are many promising candidates for medicine outside the walls of the ivy-league colleges who by circumstances are denied the privilege of studying to become doctors. Too many never try for medicine because they know they cannot get high enough marks in mathematics. This is unfortunate, for history shows that the best doctors rarely possess outstanding mathematical ability. The mathematics yardstick of eligibility for medical school should be shortened.

From observing medical students who are still floundering in search of their destinies in their final year in medicine, I am sure that more careful searching for the best candidates should begin years before it does now. Moreover, the students in high school and college who are thinking of medicine should do more self-judging based on what is known about the arduous life of the doctor.

Every student who is seriously considering medicine should have the chance of an exploratory interview in his sixteenth or seventeenth year. This should be done by permanent committees sitting in every state and province in North America. The purpose would be to identify candidates with the instinctive desire to doctor. Character traits rather than the amount of stored information would be the qualities considered at that stage. Promising students would be advised about the college work they should stress in preparation for the second interview when they would be trying for entrance to the medical school of their choice at the age of nineteen or twenty. This policy would encourage more suitable candidates to study the most relevant subjects and get the necessary grades for entrance to medicine.

The candidate for medicine should be capable of reading with retention and satisfaction, of writing legibly, and of speaking clearly. While his intelligence quotient is of some interest, his informed common sense coupled with his feeling for people are of much greater importance. He should be people-conscious, interested in and concerned about every face and expression and body on the subway, at the airport, and in the market place. Lacking this human interest, he will be wise to choose some other career.

Candidates undertake an obligation to do their best when they enter medical school. Every action which reduces their maximum effort is wrong, and helps to make them second rate doctors.

The candidate should firmly believe that being a student-doctor is a privilege. There is nothing commonplace about the study of medicine. If a student is not intrigued by the constant variations of disease it means that his dull days come not because the work is dull but because he has failed to select the right career. The wrong career selection inevitably leads to a life of awful boredom in practice, or to the need to seek refuge in one of the non-practice fields after graduation.

None of the methods currently employed for choosing the candidates who will be allowed to become doctors can measure integrity, perseverance, or compassion. When a candidate for medicine is being interviewed, his answers to the standard question: "Why do you want to be a doctor?" should be taped and kept as a permanent part of his curriculum vitae to be used as a future character reference.

Students who are considering medicine should never miss an opportunity of meeting doctors, talking with them, and observing them in action. The student who presents himself to a committee on admissions should have a better answer than "I like people," or "because I want to help people" when the stock question, "Why do you want to become a doctor?" is presented to him. Prospective firemen, policemen, clergy, bus-drivers, teachers, and lawyers could all be expected to give that reply if asked why they wished to enter those particular fields.

The candidate for medicine must want to be a doctor so desperately that he will have considered the hard four years in medical school carefully. He should not be naïve about the following four years of hospital post-graduate work, which will be the most intense and exciting time he will ever spend.

If he has his heart set on being a great physician or surgeon (and I pity the candidate whose teachers have not set him the example of greatness), every puzzling patient will stir his imagination and goad him to get into the books and journals to settle the diagnosis and map out his own treatment before discussing it with his chief. The lazy interns and residents who want to be spoon-fed or taught everything never amount to very much because when they get into their own practices they only do what they have been told to do. The chiefs who are not critical and who just let their interns go along as they wish do not play the teaching game squarely. Their students will not look back on them with admiration, because they have only been taught what to think, not how to think. Teaching "how to think" takes a lot more knowledge and personal interest in the students and interns than teaching "what to think."

Most medical schools have encouraged candidates with degrees in science because they expected that such degrees would increase the likelihood of candidates doing research and making discoveries and bringing renown to their schools. This belief was unsound, because discovery-making is something that cannot be taught. Does a medical student with a degree in computer science, sociology, engineering, biochemistry, genetics, or administration make a better doctor? This is really the question. Medical schools are expected to educate doctors, not train scientists.

A candidate who has devoted two valuable learning years to acquiring a science degree in addition to the two pre-medical years, before doing the four heavy years in medicine has wasted energy and in the process has developed that serious state called "academic fatigue", which goes with the monotonous competitive studying of a subject which bears no relation to medicine. We need well-trained doctors who are qualified to practise before they are old men. To achieve this objective, any educational pattern such as this one should be strongly discouraged: four years for a science degree, followed by four years in medical school, followed by one year of internship (or occasionally two years). This makes a total of nine (or ten) years of study of which only 55 per cent (or 60 per cent) is medical.

Rather than this ten-year program of which only 60 percent is medicine, the doctors, who have so much to learn, should have: two years of pre-medical studies, four years in medical school, and four or more years of post-graduate work in hospital. Eighty per cent of these ten years will be *true* medical years.

Regardless of which course the student chooses, he will be in some debt, will usually be married with a small family, and will be finished and ready to practise as a G.P. or as a well-rounded physician or surgeon nine or ten years after finishing high school.

It is vitally important for prospective students and patients to understand the difference between these two programs. One well-trained doctor with four years of post-graduate work in hospitals can do at least five times the amount of necessary practice that a family medicine doctor can do after one solid year of post-graduate internship. This is because, with his larger experience, he can diagnose and treat the patient's condition quickly and accurately. He will not need the $250,000 of lab tests and subspecialists' opinions that the average family doctor utilizes every year in order to keep his practice running in North America when money is no object. The computers from the medicare system in the Province of Ontario have established that alarming figure as average.

All the important advances that have been made, but are not being adequately used by today's M.D.s, leave too many patients without the treatments and cures they deserve. Their doctors have simply not been taught the right things. This is not only past history but current history and it needs to be thought about.

One reason for it is that the elective time now takes up more than 30 per cent of the students' life, which was previously devoted to class lectures and bedside teaching throughout the four medical school years. The huge blocks of elective time have not only deprived the students of good teaching but have tempted faculty members to abdicate their roles as teachers "because the students were not on hand for them to teach". Like all ordinary humans, the teachers willingly yield to temptation. Teachers who do less teaching not only become less effective as teachers but in the process they actually become lazy and disinterested. They should provide the students with leadership in clinical and possibly research projects in the elective time. However, having abdicated as lecturers they have also reneged on the teacher-student role at the bedside and in the laboratories.

The single most flagrant example of inadequate teaching concerns cancer. Not one graduating M.D. in ten is capable of examining the female breast and the organs of the body to which that particular cancer may spread. In many schools the subject of cancer, its diagnosis and treatment, and the kindly and skilled management required during the patient's life after all the modern treatment has been used, may not add up to two weeks out of the four years in medical school. In some medical schools no time whatever is given to cancer treatment and cancer management. The complete inadequacy in the teaching of this subject and its extensions is underlined by two facts. Forty-eight million North Americans now living will die of cancer. Of almost equal significance is the fact that 100 million will die of some other disease accompanied by cancer. While the cancer will not cause death in those 100 million people, it will be present in them and will frequently require its own particular treatments by the doctor.

Certainly, the frequency of cancer is proof positive that the students of medicine cannot afford to waste 30 per cent of their four years in electives that rarely relate to medical and surgical practice, if we take cancer as just one of many examples.

The net cost of educating the doctor who doctors is very high. It seems unbelievable, in a time of so much knowledge, that no dean can give a clear answer to the fundamental question of what kind of doctor his medical school intends to produce. No dean of any medical school can put a figure on the net cost to society of graduating an M.D. from his school.

We may assume that, with a graduating class of 100, a medical school of good standing has an annual budget of $20 million and is therefore spending roughly $200,000 dollars per graduate.

When the cost of the one to five years of post-graduate training is added to the cost of producing the M.D., society will have invested more than $250,000 for a doctor by the time he is ready to hang out his shingle. Since the cost of an M.Sc. or Ph.D. science graduate is more than $75,000, it is clear that when a science graduate is accepted for medical school the total investment by the time the M.D. is granted and before any post-graduate training has been taken is nearly $300,000. Permitting these science M.D. graduates to do general practice is extravagance in the extreme.

Most North American medical schools are financed by the states or provinces, and by the governments of Washington or Ottawa. The public pays dearly for the education of doctors. In this time of economic depression, people are going to insist on knowing what kind of doctor they are getting for their money. How long will the people be satisfied if their $200,000 doctors just pick up their degrees and then proceed to psychiatry or administration or research or drug houses or public health or life insurance?

When pricing any commodity, the items that are normally costed are raw material, labour, and overhead. In medical schools, these three items are represented by the students (who come free); the faculty (the most costly item, varying with the size of the teaching staff and the emphasis the school places on research); and the buildings, special laboratories and supplies, non-professional help, travel accounts, management, and expensive laboratory equipment that rapidly becomes obsolete (the thousands of tons of obsolete equipment in North American medical schools alone represents billions of spent dollars).

It should be possible for governments to estimate the cost of producing a doctor. At first glance, this could be determined by the kind of teaching that he is given and the grandeur of the medical school. This does not take the waste factor into consideration. If 100 students begin, they will expect to finish in four years, or $20 million later. Should only ninety of the 100 beginners graduate, there will be empty seats and the actual per-graduate cost will be approximately $220,000 instead of $200,000.

No studies have ever been made of the adjusted price society pays for educating the M.D.s who do not practise throughout their lifetimes as doctors in medicine or surgery or obstetrics.

Retracing the chapters of this book will throw some light on the importance of the waste factor. The people who pay the taxes assume that, for $200,000 per M.D., they will be guaranteed a flow of doctors who will attend them, should they fall sick with cancer, pleurisy, phlebitis, jaundice, heart pain, or any of the diseases mentioned.

This is not what the people always get for their money. Out of 350,000 certified M.D.s in North America we find that more than 100,000 work in the grey zones that have been referred to as "non-doctoring". These 100,000 "doctors" never touch living patients. They have no more experience in judging between the quick and the dead than sensible lay onlookers. More than 80 per cent of the 350,000 North American M.D.s are specialists of one kind or other. While some of the grey doctors think of themselves as specialists in their fields, it must be noted that they are never held in the same respect as neurologists, cardiologists, endocrinologists, and all the other doctors in medicine and surgery.

When the run-offs to the non-doctoring and many of the highly specialized groups in the profession are subtracted from the 350,000 M.D.s, there are not 50,000 doctors left who can be called and who answer their calls and who will have acceptable diagnostic and treatment skills for looking after the patients who call them.

Therefore the waste factor, added to the cost factor of the doctor product, will increase the cost to the taxpayer substantially.

It will never be possible to provide good doctoring if the medical schools just churn out more M.D.s.

I believe that by choosing students for medicine differently, educating them better, cutting down and then cutting out the soft non-doctoring jobs, and reducing the numbers of specialists it will be possible to provide a steadier and more lasting supply of what the patients think of as dedicated doctors.

Extending the costing factor to the doctors who doctor introduces other considerations. Governments do not commission students to study medicine. Students choose medicine and ruthlessly try to get into medical school by fair means or foul. The monetary consideration does operate beyond the "wanting to help people" motif for too many. Remember the student who said: "I knew that if I blew that biochemistry exam I was kissing that hundred thou per year job good-bye." The four out of five subspecialists in the total M.D. population who can tidily make $100,000 a year doing a forty-hour work week give a poor image to the public and set a poor example to incoming students.

> *I only quarrel with the man who, resting satisfied with what he holds to be his high commission, is not eager to match it with a high character.*
>
> PHILLIP BROOKS

The candidate who succeeds in entering medical school should realize that he has not been admitted to a sinecure for life but he is obligated to repay, to the best of his ability, the high investment society has made in him.

Acknowledgments

I wish to acknowledge my teachers at medical school, in my post-graduate years at hospitals, and my teaching associates at Victoria Hospital, London, Ontario, where I have practised and taught. To all of them I owe a debt which cannot be repaid. I also wish to thank the many medical educators and physicians and surgeons whom I have visited in their teaching and non-teaching hospitals in Europe and North America. The consultants who have counselled me on difficult problems, and my research colleagues over many years, I rank with my teachers.

Maude Abbott, Montreal
Howard Alexander, Tillsonburg, Ontario
Gerard Allison, Winnipeg
W. Ferguson Anderson, Glasgow
Edward Archibald, Montreal
John Armour, Montreal
Mario Austoni, Padua
Charles Austrian, Baltimore
Lewellys F. Barker, Baltimore
Bruce Barton, London, Ontario
Edward Bartram, London, Ontario
William Bigelow, Toronto
Thomas Boggs, Baltimore

238

William Boyd, Toronto
Francis Brien, London, Ontario
Lord Brock, London
Ray Brow, Montreal
Alan Brown, Toronto
Thomas Brown, Baltimore
H. H. Bullard, London, Ontario
Howard Burchell, Rochester
Alan Burton, London, Ontario
Eldon Busby, London, Ontario
Gordon Byers, Montreal
Roderick Byers, Montreal
F. J. H. Campbell, London, Ontario
Maurice Campbell, London
William Castle, Boston
John Caughey, Cleveland
A. J. Cawley, Guelph, Ontario
Roy Childs, London, Ontario
Henry Christian, Boston
B. Cinader, Toronto
Howard Clarke, Chicago
F. R. Clegg, London, Ontario
William Cone, Montreal
James Wellington Crane, London, Ontario
Thomas Cullen, Baltimore
H. B. Cushing, Montreal
Harvey Cushing, Boston
William Dameshek, New York
Walter Dandy, Baltimore
James Dauphinee, Toronto
Russell DeJong, Ann Arbor
Norman Delarue, Toronto
K. W. Donald, Edinburgh
Lester Dragstedt, Gainsville, Florida
Charles Drake, London, Ontario
William Drucker, Toronto
A. S. Duncan, Edinburgh
Lawrie Dunn, Vancouver
Robert Ebert, Boston
John Evans, Toronto
Ray Farquharson, Toronto
Warfield Firor, Baltimore
John Fisher, London, Ontario
Reginald Fitz, Boston
M. C. G. Fletcher, Exeter, Ontario
Frank Ford, Baltimore

Wallace Foulds, Glasgow
Thomas Futcher, Baltimore
W. T. Gemmell, Stratford, Ontario
John Girvin, London, Ontario
Frank Glenn, New York
Louis Goodman, Salt Lake City
Archie Grace, London, Ontario
Duncan Graham, Toronto
Roscoe Graham, Toronto
Ramsay Gunton, London, Ontario
Sir Alexander Haddow, London
George Hale, London, Ontario
J. G. Hall, Canberra
G. A. Hallenbeck, Rochester
Louis Hamman, Baltimore
Fred Heagy, London, Ontario
Ray Heimbecker, London, Ontario
John Heller, Ridgefield, Connecticut
William Holden, Cleveland
Frank Horsfall, New York
Charles Huggins, Chicago
Roger Inch, London, Ontario
Joseph Janes, Rochester
Chester Keefer, Boston
Frank Kennedy, London, Ontario
John C. Kennedy, London, Ontario
Harold Kenner, Stratford, Ontario
John Knowles, New York
Samuel L. Kountz, San Francisco
John Laidlaw, Hamilton
Lucien Leger, Paris
Dean Lewis, Baltimore
John Lewis, London, Ontario
Warfield Longcope, Baltimore
Frederick T. Lord, Boston
Jere Lord, New York
M. D. W. Low, Edinburgh
Ian MacDonald, Toronto
John A. Macgregor, London, Ontario
David MacKenzie, Toronto
Charles Macklin, London, Ontario
Madge Thurlow Macklin, London, Ontario
Edward MacMahon, Boston
R. M. Marquis, Edinburgh
E. H. Mason, Montreal
John McCredie, London

Edward McGirr, Glasgow
Douglas McGregor, Saranac, New York
Kenneth G. McKenzie, Toronto
Paul McKibben, London, Ontario
Charles McPeak, New York
Jonathan Meakins, Montreal
James Means, Boston
Adolf Meyer, Baltimore
G. L. Montgomery, Edinburgh
Francis Moore, Boston
Russell Morgan, Baltimore
D. A. Morrison, Brantford
Gordon Murray, Toronto
Joseph Murray, Boston
L. H. Newburgh, Ann Arbor
Gustav Nylen, Stockholm
Horst Oertel, Montreal
Trevor Owen, Toronto
Sir John Parkinson, London
James Paterson, London, Ontario
Wilder Penfield, Montreal
J. A. Phillips, Brantford
Sir George Pickering, Oxford
John W. Pierson, Baltimore
E. D. Robertson, Toronto, Ontario
Lorne Robertson, Stratford, Ontario
Beverley Robinson, London, Ontario
T. Ferguson Rodger, Glasgow
Norman Roome, Toronto
Graham Ross, Montreal
Leonard Rowntree, Philadelphia
Colin Russell, Montreal
S. T. Rutherford, Stratford, Ontario
E. Samuel, Edinburgh
John Scott, Edmonton
F. A. C. Scrimgeour, Montreal
Jessie Boyd Scriver, Montreal
Walter de M. Scriver, Montreal
Reginald Secord, Brantford
Arthur Shipley, Baltimore
Harris Shumacker, Jr., Indianapolis
Evan Shute, London, Ontario
Murray Simpson, London, Ontario
David Smith, Stratford, Ontario
William Spaulding, Hamilton
Arthur Squires, Toronto

David State, New York
Thomas Starzl, Denver
Harvey Stone, Baltimore
Somers Sturgis, Boston
Emerick Szilagy, Detroit
Helen Taussig, Baltimore
W. S. Thayer, Baltimore
Montague Thomson, London, Ontario
George Thorn, Boston
Frank Walsh, Baltimore
Harold Warwick, London, Ontario
T. A. Watson, London, Ontario
J. A. Watt, Edinburgh
L. G. Whitby, Edinburgh
Paul White, Boston
George Whitfield, Birmingham
Kager Wightman, Toronto
Paul Wood, London
Barnes Woodhall, Durham, North Carolina
Sir Michael Woodruff, Edinburgh
George Young, Toronto
Hugh Young, Baltimore
Robert Zollinger, Columbus.

Index

Dr. L. DeWitt Wilcox is a physician-internist living in London, Ontario. He grew up in Stratford and was educated at the University of Western Ontario. He did his hospital work at the Stratford General Hospital, the Brantford General Hospital, the Royal Victoria Hospital (McGill) and the Johns Hopkins in Baltimore. He has taught for many years at the University of Western Ontario Medical School. For 16 years he was visiting examiner in medicine at the University of Toronto. He is actively engaged in research with publications in *American Journal of Surgery, Journal of Surgical Research* and *Cancer*. Throughout his career Dr. Wilcox has regularly visited professors and teachers and made hospital rounds at the leading medical centres of Britain, Europe, and North America. He maintains a full-time practice, as well as a regular teaching clinic.

During his practice, lifetime clinical problems have intrigued Dr. Wilcox and have often pushed him into the investigative laboratories to try for answers. From 1932 to 1977 he presented scientific papers in general medicine and sub-specialties before the following societies, The Canadian Medical Association, The Montreal Medical-Chirurgical Society, The Royal College of Physicians and Surgeons of Canada, The Western Hemisphere Heart Congress and the World Heart Congress.